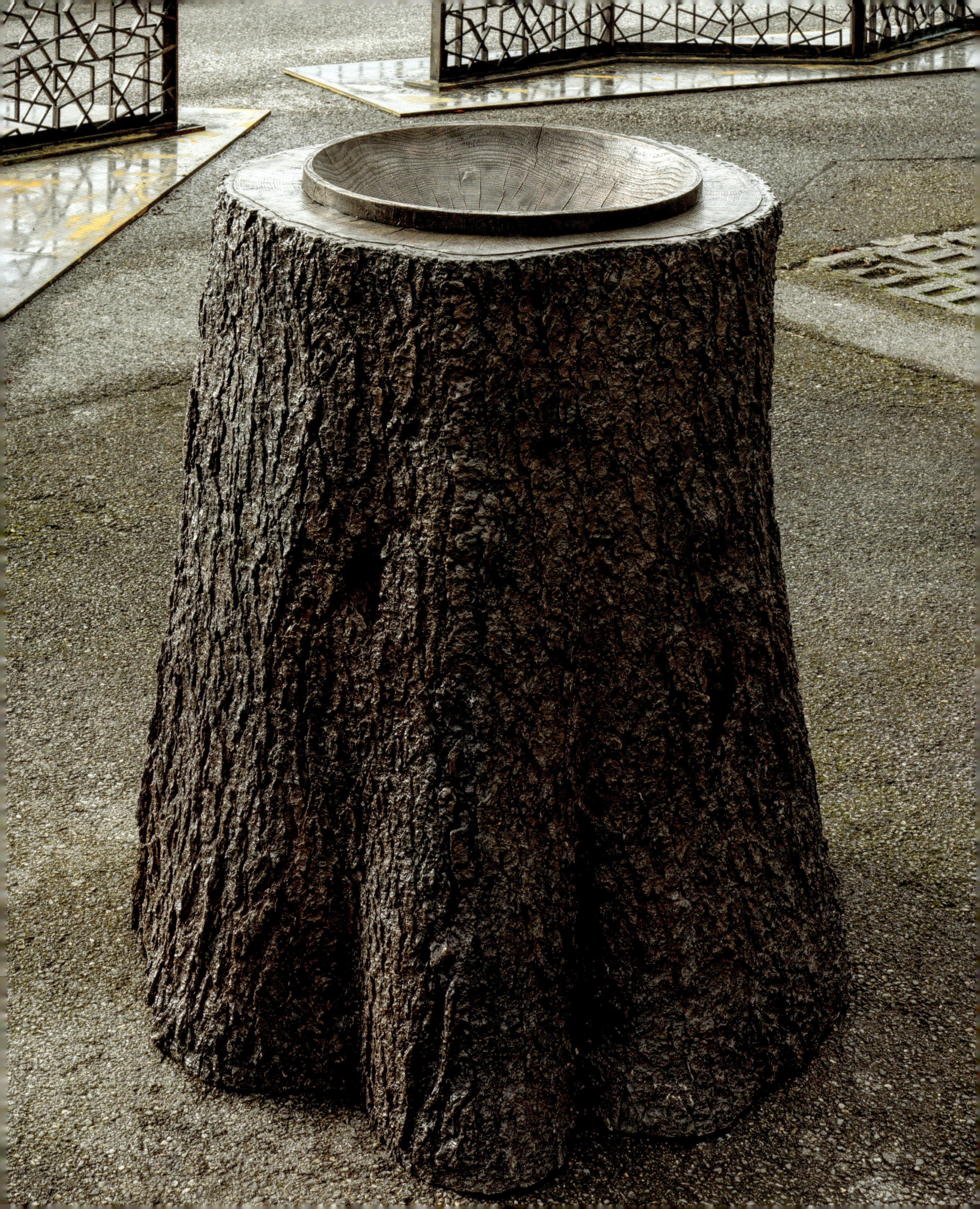

MIRKO BASELGIA

Der Baum von Valbella
The Tree of Valbella

Herausgegeben von / Edited by
Christoph Eggenberger
Laura Giudici
Jérôme Neutres

SilvanaEditoriale

APRICUM
CIRCLE

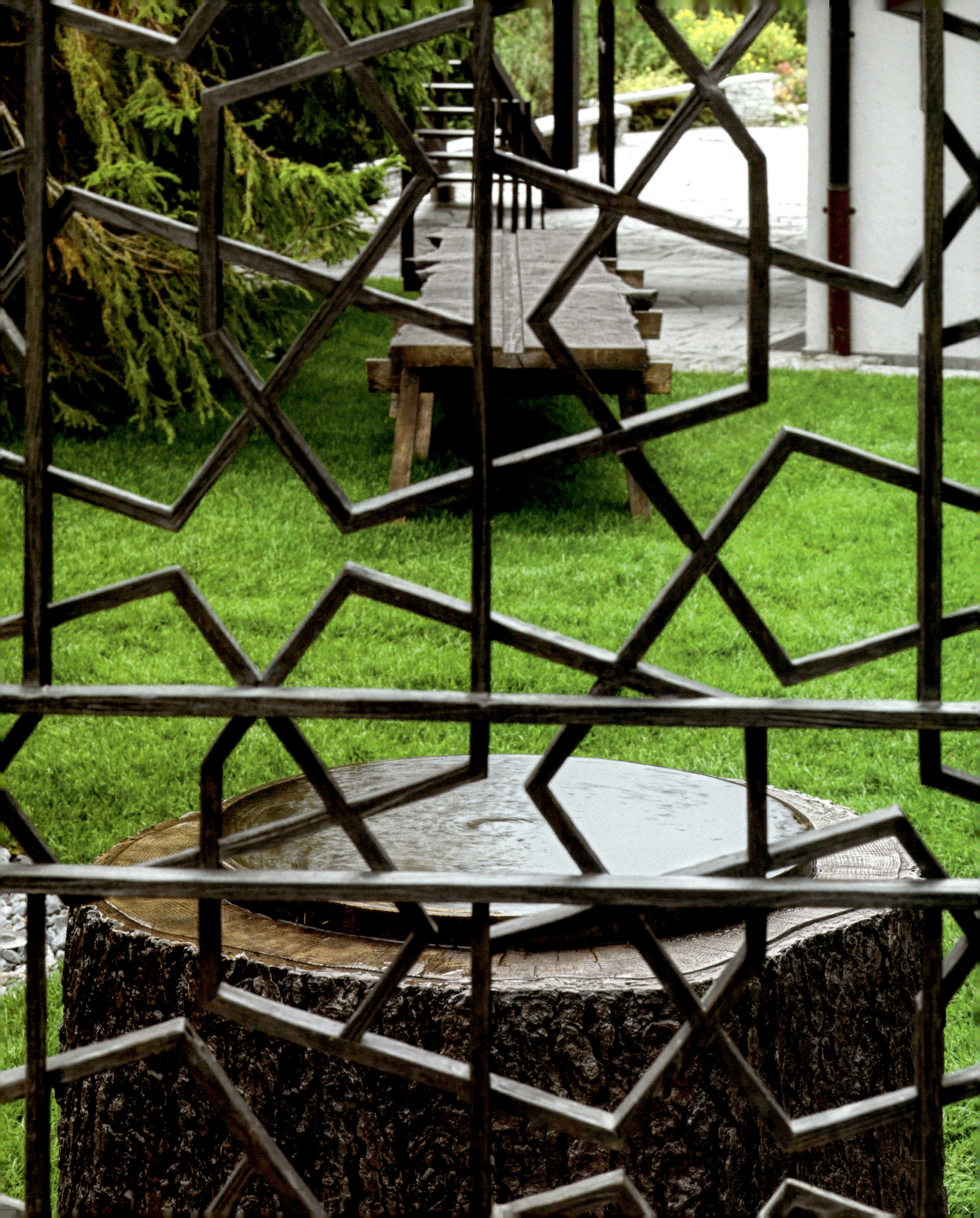

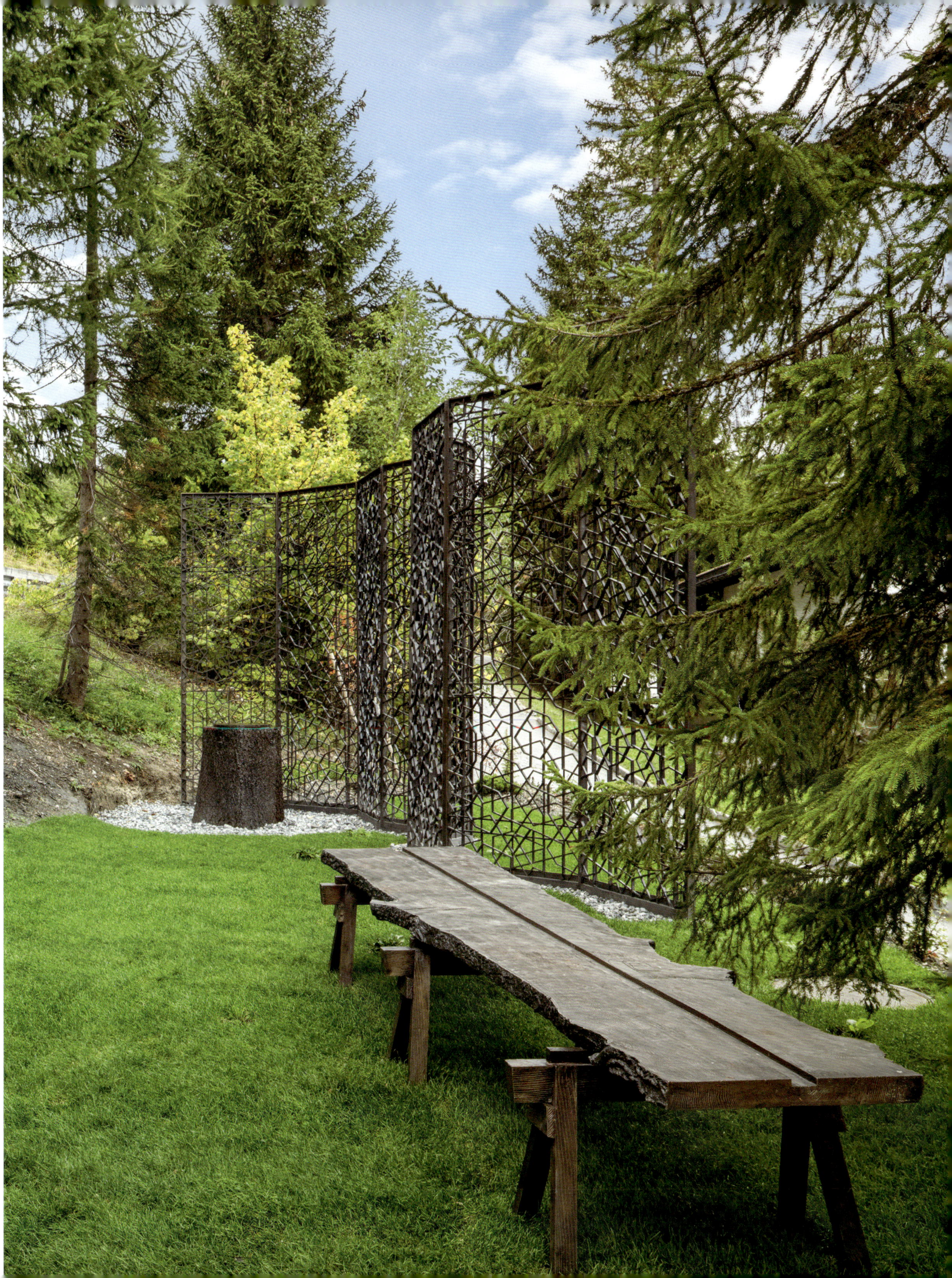

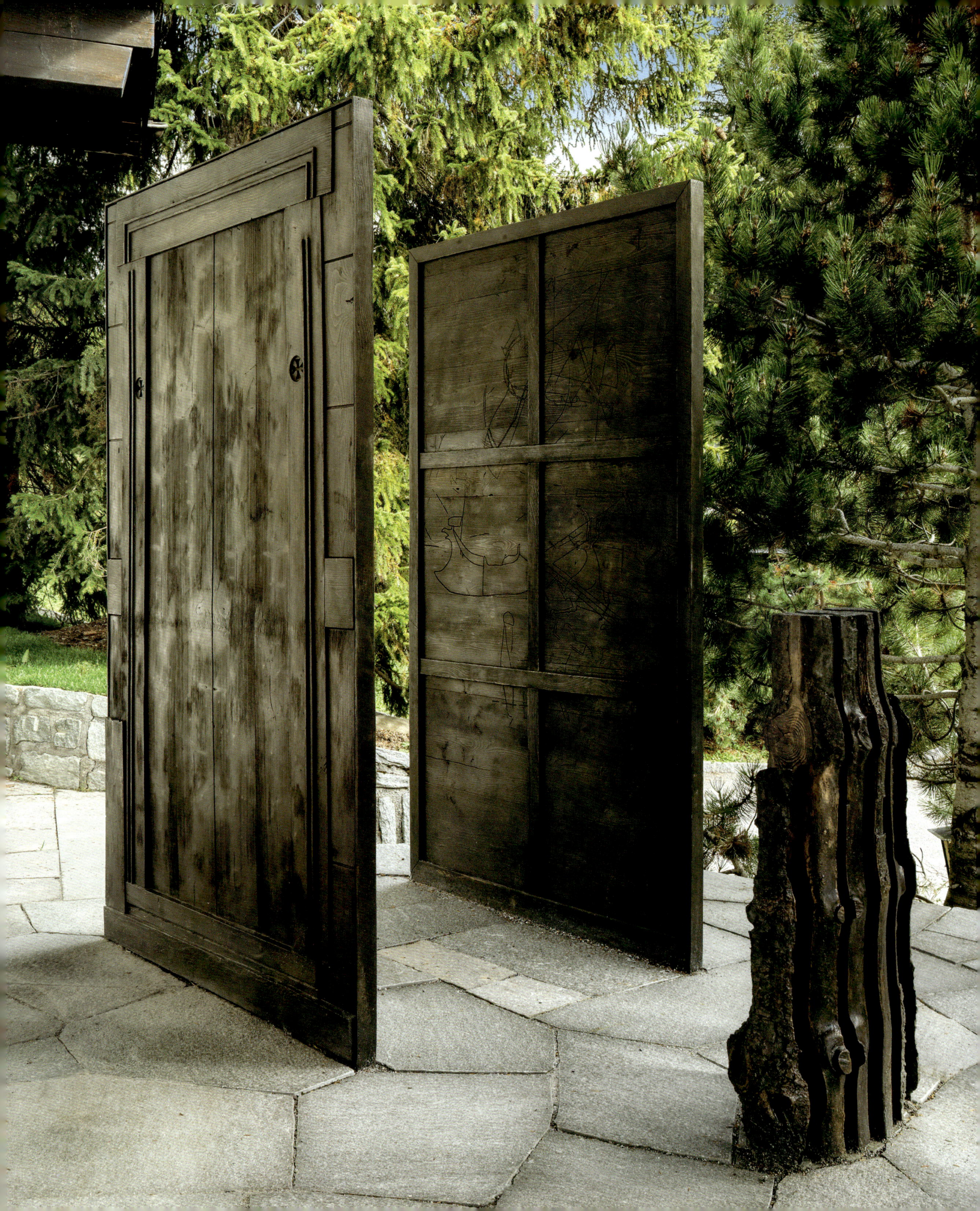

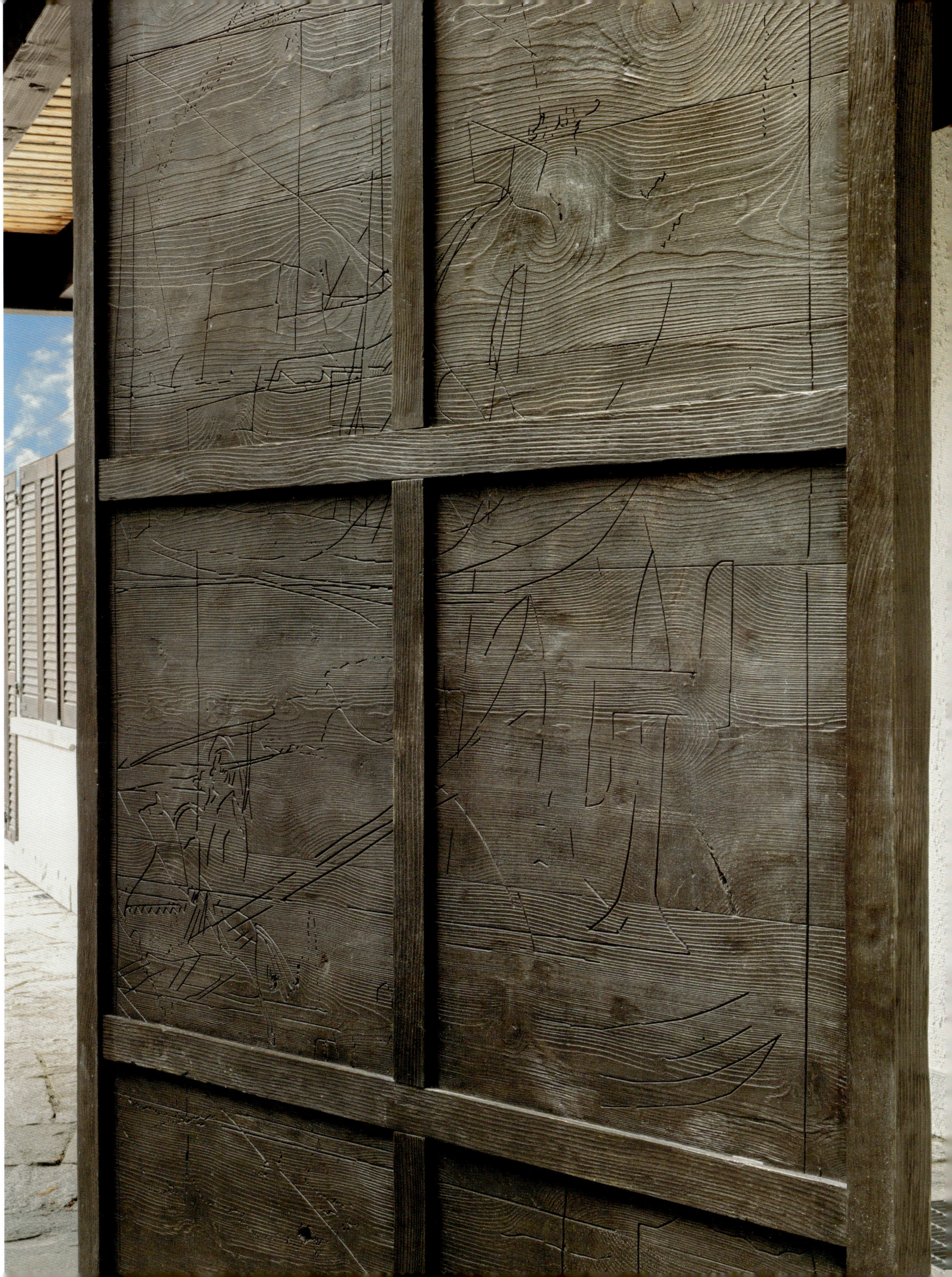

VORWORT
DIE KUNST IST DAS LEBEN

THOMAS ABEGG

Die Kunst ist Sinngebung des Lebens, zum einen als noble, oft auch verstörende Ausdrucksweise und zum anderen als tiefes Erinnern und kreatives Vorausschauen. Meine Kunstsammlung ist aus dieser Überzeugung entstanden, aber auch aus meiner Leidenschaft für die Persönlichkeit der Künstler. Sie sind die grossen Visionäre, die Erfinder von Form und Sprache, die wahrhaften Pioniere der Gesellschaft.

Seit Jahren bemühe ich mich, Werke zu vereinen, die Zeugnis ablegen von dieser innovativen Dimension der künstlerischen Kreativität und von deren Fähigkeit, die Energie der Schöpfung sichtbar zu machen.

Ich bin stolz, die Produktion der Werke einiger Künstler begleiten zu dürfen und die Entstehung ambitionierter Projekte zu ermöglichen, und die Künstler unterstützen zu können, ihre künstlerische Sprache weiterzuentwickeln.

So ist es auch mit dem einzigartigen und spannenden Abenteuer mit *The Tree of Valbella*.

Die Kunst kennt keine Grenzen, die Künstler sind Bürger und Bürgerinnen dieser Welt, doch sie sehen mehr und anders. Deshalb habe ich Werke von Künstlern von überall her gesammelt, von Europa bis China, von Indien bis Afrika.

In meiner Nähe jedoch, in Graubünden in der Schweiz, arbeitet Mirko Baselgia. Seit den Anfängen seines Kunstschaffens öffnet er uns die Augen und den Geist, die Natur auch aus metaphysischer Sicht zu sehen. Er nahm und nimmt die Debatte der Gesellschaft über das Klima und die Umwelt voraus und vertieft sie.

Die Künstler haben sich immer wieder durch die Natur inspirieren lassen und in ihr Vorbilder für ihr Werk gefunden. Aber Mirko Baselgia nimmt die Natur nicht nur als Vorbild, sondern verarbeitet sie auch zu Kunst, ja er nutzt die Natur als sein künstlerisches Medium.

The Tree of Valbella steht heute als Kunstwerk in meinem Garten als Metamorphose des Baumes, der seit mehr als hundert Jahren dort stand. Mirko schuf das Werk als Erinnerung an den Baum, und ermöglicht ihm sein zweites Leben. Die Kunst ist das Leben.

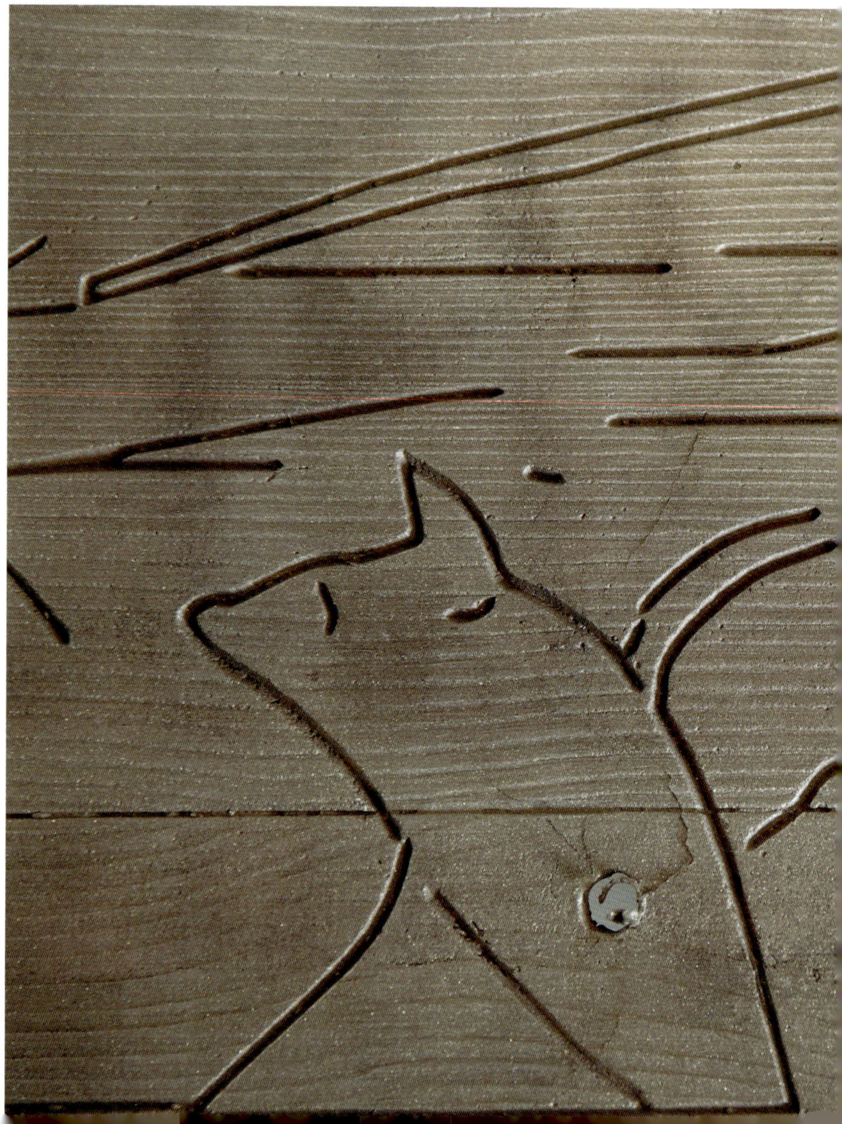

Mirko Baselgia, *The Tree of Valbella*, 2014-2019, Bronze, Detail: Porträt des Auftraggebers Thomas Abegg als Reiter auf einem Pferd auf einer der Türen / Portrait of the patron Thomas Abegg as a rider riding a horse on one of the doors

FOREWORD
ART IS LIFE

Art is the meaning of life; on the one hand, as an ennobled, often disturbing mode of expression and, on the other, as profound remembrance and creative foresight.

My art collection grew out of this conviction, but also out of my passion for the persona of the artists. They are the great visionaries, inventors of form and language, the true pioneers of society.

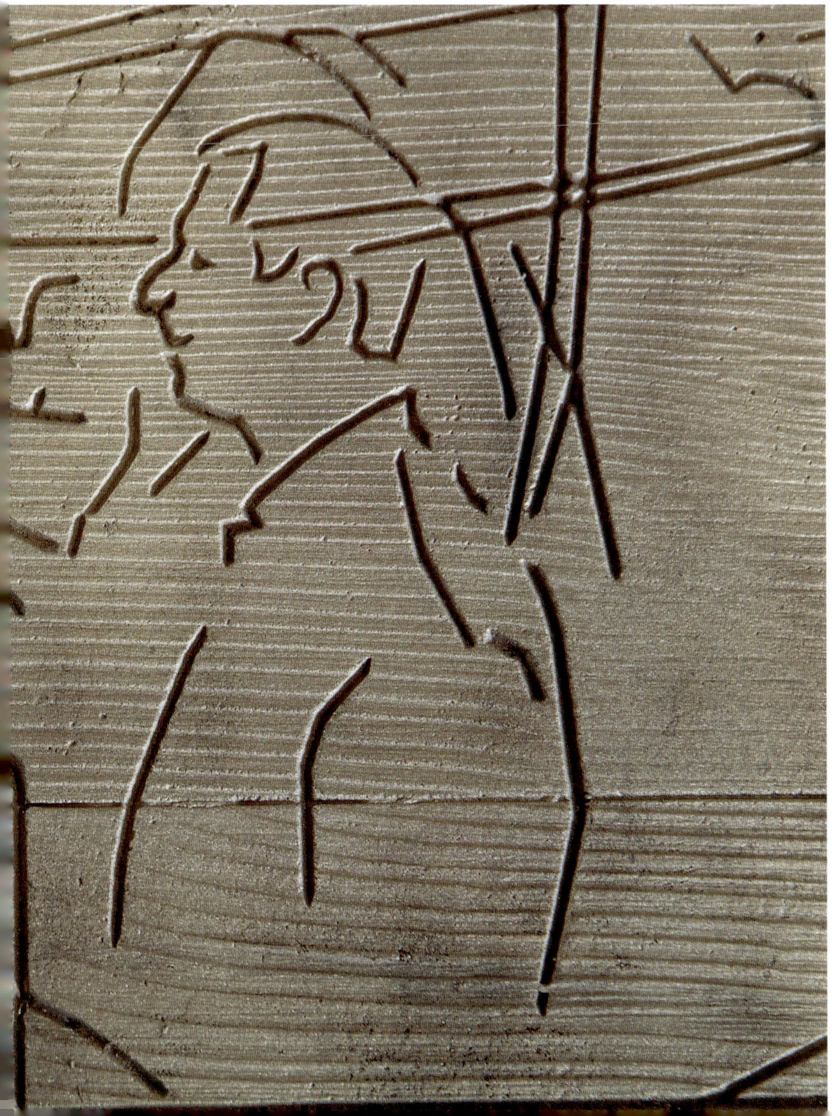

For years, I have endeavoured to combine works that bear witness to this innovative dimension of artistic creativity and its ability to make the energy released through creation visible.

I am proud to be able to accompany the production of the works of some artists, and to enable the creation of ambitious projects, as well as being able to support the artists in developing their artistic language further.

This is the mechanism underpinning the unique and exciting adventure experienced with *The Tree of Valbella*.

Art knows no borders; artists are citizens of this world, but they see more and differently. This is the reason I have collected works by artists from all over the world, from Europe to China, from India to Africa.

However, Mirko Baselgia works near my holiday house, in Graubünden, Switzerland. Since the beginnings of his artistic, creative endeavours, he has opened our eyes and minds to see nature from a metaphysical standpoint. He anticipated and uses the societal debate on climate and the environment and has amplified it.

Artists have always been inspired by nature and found in it models for their work. But Mirko Baselgia not only takes nature as a model, he also processes it into art, moreover, using nature as his artistic medium.

The Tree of Valbella stands today as a work of art in my garden, as a metamorphosis of the tree that stood there for more than a hundred years. Mirko created the work as a memory of the tree, enabling it to have a second life. Art is life.

EINLEITUNG

CHRISTOPH EGGENBERGER

Wer sich selbst und andere kennt,
Wird auch hier erkennen:
Orient und Okzident
Sind nicht mehr zu trennen.

Johann Wolfgang von Goethe
aus dem *West-Östlichen Divan*

Der Künstler und sein Oeuvre, der Auftraggeber. Das skulpturale Ensemble *The Tree of Valbella*

Die Fichte nahe des Igl Lai, des Heidsees von Valbella in Graubünden, 1484 Meter ü.M., bildet das Rückgrat des skulpturalen Ensembles von Mirko Baselgia. Er schuf es im Auftrag von Thomas Abegg. Von 1892 bis 2016 stand die Fichte in dessen Garten und musste gefällt werden, um ihrer Nachbarin mehr Platz zu verschaffen. Der Künstler formte aus dem Holz der gefällten Fichte ein Kunstwerk, das er in Bronze giessen liess und 2019 fertiggestellte: *The Tree of Valbella.*

Den Baum bindet Mirko Baselgia in weit verzweigte Zusammenhänge ein wie in ein Spinnennetz, das sich vom Heidsee bis nach Athen und weiter in den Orient, nach Persien erstreckt. Er verbindet sein Netzwerk mit demjenigen des Auftraggebers. Die Verbindung von Künstler und Auftraggeber spielt, seit es Kunst gibt, eine zentrale Rolle. Kunst im eigentlichen Sinn entsteht erst, wenn der Macher sich als Künstler fühlt und sich so bezeichnet, und der Auftraggeber den Künstler als solchen respektiert. Erst im Spätmittelalter und in der frühen Neuzeit bildet sich dieses subtile Verhältnis aus; subtil deshalb, weil der Auftraggeber seine Vorstellungen hat, während der Künstler seine eigene Sprache entwickelt.

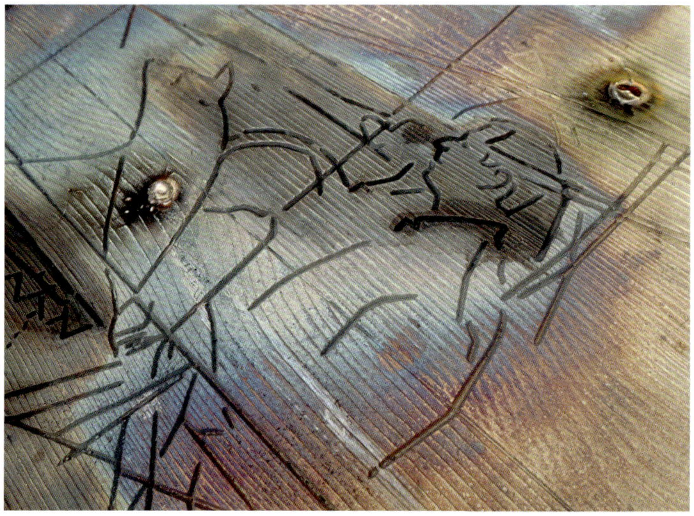

Mirko Baselgia, *The Tree of Valbella*, 2014-2019, Bronze, Detail: Porträt des Auftraggebers Thomas Abegg als Reiter auf einem Pferd auf einer der Türen / Portrait of the patron Thomas Abegg as a rider riding a horse on one of the doors

Hugo von Tschudi (1851-1911), zunächst Direktor der Nationalgalerie Berlin, dann der Staatlichen Galerien München, schrieb: „Gewiss war es kein Zufall, dass gerade Raffael und Michelangelo von Julius II. und Leo X. mit den grossen Aufgaben betraut wurden oder dass gerade Holbein von Heinrich VIII. oder Velasquez von Philipp IV. beschäftigt wurden.“ Wolfgang Ullrich stellt fest, gute Kunst entstehe im Tandem von genialem Künstler und anspruchsvollem Auftraggeber; Michelangelo und der Papst schufen noch gemeinsam Schönes. Giorgio Vasari (1511-1574) berichtete vom Briefwechsel zwischen Michelangelo und Papst Julius II., wo das meist schwierige Verhältnis zwischen dem unberechenbaren Künstler und seinem herrischen Auftraggeber deutlich wird, aber auch, wie befruchtend eine lange Unterredung über einen Auftrag wirken konnte. Bei einer Diskussion über die Kuppel des Petersdoms hätten Michelangelo und der Papst, so sagt es zumindest

INTRODUCTION

He who knows himself and others
Will also recognise here:
Orient and Occident
Can no longer be separated.

Johann Wolfgang von Goethe
from the *West-Eastern Divan*

The artist and his oeuvre and the patron.
***The Tree of Valbella* sculptural ensemble**

The spruce near the Igl Lai, the Heidsee of Valbella in Graubünden, 1484 meters above sea level, forms the backbone of the sculptural ensemble by Mirko Baselgia. He created it after receiving a commission from Thomas Abegg. From 1892 to 2016, the spruce stood in his garden and had to be felled to make more space for its neighbour. The artist carved a work of art out of the felled spruce, which he had cast in bronze, and completed it in 2019: *The Tree of Valbella.*

Mirko Baselgia ties the tree to broadly ramified connections like a spider web that stretches from the Heidsee to Athens and further afield into Orient, to Persia. He connects his network with that of the patron. The connection between artist and patron has played a key role since art has existed. Art, in the real sense of the word, only comes about when the creator feels and describes himself as an artist, and the patron respects the artist as such. Only in the late Middle Ages and early modern times did this subtle relationship develop; subtle because the patron has his own ideas, while the artist develops his own language.

Hugo von Tschudi (1851-1911), first director of the National Gallery in Berlin, then of the State Galleries in Munich, wrote: "It was certainly no coincidence that Raphael and Michelangelo were entrusted with major commissions by Julius II and Leo X, or that Holbein was employed by Henry VIII or Velázquez by Philip IV." Wolfgang Ullrich states, good art is created in tandem between a brilliant artist and a demanding patron; Michelangelo and the Pope created beautiful things together. Giorgio Vasari (1511-1574) reported on the exchange of missives between Michelangelo and Pope Julius II, where the usually difficult relationship between the unpredictable artist and his bossy patron becomes clear, but they also show how fruitful a long conversation about a commission could be. In a discussion about the dome of the Basilica of San Pietro, Michelangelo and the Pope – at least based on Vasari's words – together "endowed the building with almost all of its current beauty."[1]

Mirko Baselgia and Thomas Abegg also had long conversations, and in an interview with Jérôme Neutres, Mirko Baselgia tells of a decisive youthful experience when his grandmother gave him Irving Stone's book on Michelangelo to read. While reading it, Mirko realised that he would be a sculptor; this foundation has shaped him: "Yes, sculpture was dead." Sculpture in Florence lay fallow after the deaths of Donatello, Pollaiuolo, Verrocchio and della Robbia. Niccolò Pisano (1210/20-1278/87) was the first true sculptor since Phidias completed his work on the Parthenon in the 5th Century B.C. This is what Michelangelo exclaimed about the sculpture: "(...) but all sincere efforts to recreate what God has created (...) is a form of worship (...)" and "(...) reflects a love for God's world. What else should the artist be struggling for? (...) I have always loved God."[2] These are potent words – the love for God's world and its nature –, this could also be the message of *The Tree of Valbella.*

As a donor portrait in the medieval sense, the artist carves the portrait of the patron in the wood of the spruce and has it cast in bronze.

Vasari, gemeinsam „dem Bau nahezu seine gesamte gegenwärtige Schönheit verliehen."[1]

Auch Mirko Baselgia und Thomas Abegg führten lange Gespräche. Und im Interview mit Jérôme Neutres erzählt Mirko Baselgia von einem entscheidenden Jugenderlebnis, als seine Grossmutter ihm das Michelangelo-Buch von Irving Stone zu lesen gab. Bei der Lektüre wurde Mirko klar, dass er Bildhauer werden wird; es sind diese Formulierungen, die ihn geprägt haben: „Ja, die Bildhauerei war tot." Die Bildhauerei in Florenz lag brach nach dem Tod von Donatello, Pollaiuolo, Verrocchio und della Robbia. Niccolò Pisano (1210/20-1278/87), war der erste wahre Bildhauer, seit Phidias sein Werk am Parthenon im 5. Jahrhundert v.Chr. beendete. Dies lässt Michelangelo über die Skulptur ausrufen: „(...) aber alle ehrliche Mühe, das, was Gott geschaffen hat, neu zu schaffen, nachzuschaffen (...) ist eine Form der Anbetung (...)" und „(...) trägt eine Liebe in sich zu Gottes Welt. Wozu sonst sollte sich der Künstler plagen? (...) Ich habe Gott immer geliebt."[2] Das sind starke Worte, die Liebe zu Gottes Welt und ihrer Natur, das könnte auch die Botschaft des Baumes von Valbella sein.

Gleichsam als Stifterbild im mittelalterlichen Sinn ritzt der Künstler das Portrait des Auftraggebers in das Holz der Fichte und lässt es in Bronze giessen.

Kunst ist stets in Bewegung und schaut immer nach vorne. Andrej Tarkowsky sagt in *Die versiegelte Zeit. Gedanken zur Kunst, zur Ästhetik und Poetik des Films* von 1985: „(...) Die Gesellschaft strebt nach Stabilität, der Künstler dagegen nach Unendlichkeit. Ihn beschäftigt die absolute Wahrheit, weshalb er auch nach vorne schaut und so früher als andere etwas erblickt." Die Definition jeder guten Kunst, ist der Blick nach vorne, unabhängig davon, wie der Blick des Künstlers auch in die Geschichte zurück gerichtet ist. Mirko Baselgia blickt auch zurück und vor allem dahinter, spürt die Bahnen auf, die das Universum zusammenhalten, und setzt sie im skulpturalen Ensemble künstlerisch um. Der Auftraggeber beeinflusst den Stil nicht, er befördert aber mit dem Auftrag die Sprache des Künstlers und die Verfeinerung seines Stils.

The Tree of Valbella entspringt einer besonderen, heute hochaktuellen Konstellation. Die Geschichte des Projektes kam im Juli 2019 nach einer langen Ideen- und Produktionsphase zum Abschluss mit dem Aufbau des Ensembles in Valbella. Eine Fichte im Garten des Auftraggebers musste im Jahr 2016 gefällt werden, ein wunderbarer, 124 Jahre alter Baum, ein kostbarer Teil der Schöpfung. Die Fichte steht im Zentrum des Kunstwerks von Mirko Baselgia. Das skulpturale Ensemble verewigt den Werdegang des Baumes und sein Schicksal; aus seinem Holz sind die Teile geschnitten, die der Fonderia Nolana Del Giudice in Neapel für den Bronzeguss als Formen dienten. Einen Baum fällen ist in Zeiten des Klimawandels problematisch. Künstler und Auftraggeber setzten ihm mit dem Ensemble ein Denkmal, nein, sie lassen der Fichte neues Leben einhauchen.

Das Ensemble besteht aus fünf Teilen von der Quelle, zum Paravent, den liegenden Reliefs und den Toren bis zum „Schlussstein", der kein echter Schlussstein ist, vielmehr sechs schmale Elemente, zwei Säulen wie Speerspitzen und vier Stelen: die Spitze der Fichte.[3] Laura Giudici spürt den Bedeutungsebenen dieser Elemente nach. Die „porta clausa", das geschlossene Tor weist in der Kunst oft auf die Vision des Propheten Ezechiel (44,2) hin: „Da sprach der Herr zu mir: Dieses Tor bleibt geschlossen, es wird nicht geöffnet, und niemand wird hier hineingehen, denn hier ist der Herr, der Gott Israels, eingezogen, und es wird geschlossen bleiben." Es wird am Jüngsten Tag geöffnet werden: *The Tree of Valbella* lenkt den Blick und die Gedanken des Betrachters von der Gegenwart aus in die Vergangenheit, in die Zukunft und in die Ewigkeit.

Die Herkunft des Künstlers, sein Werdegang, seine Ideen, seine Arbeitsweise

Der Künstler ist fest verwurzelt mit seiner Herkunftsregion und gleichzeitig offen für die Einflüsse aus der ganzen Welt. Die Enge der Schweiz und die Weltläufigkeit der Schweizer sind immer wieder ein Thema, neuerdings auch als Zufluchtsort in der globalisierten Welt.[4] In der

Art is constantly in motion and always looking ahead. Andrej Tarkowsky states in *Die versiegelte Zeit. Gedanken zur Kunst, zur Aesthetik und Poetik des Films* (*Sculpting in Time. Reflections on the Cinema*) published in 1985: "(...) Society seeks stability, the artist – infinity. The artist is concerned with absolute truth, and therefore gazes ahead and sees things sooner than other people." The definition of all good art is looking ahead, regardless of how the artist might direct his eye back over history. Mirko Baselgia also looks back and, above all, behind, tracking down the paths that hold the universe together, and transposing them artistically in the sculptural ensemble. The patron has no influence over the style, but with his commission he promotes the language of the artist and the refinement of his style.

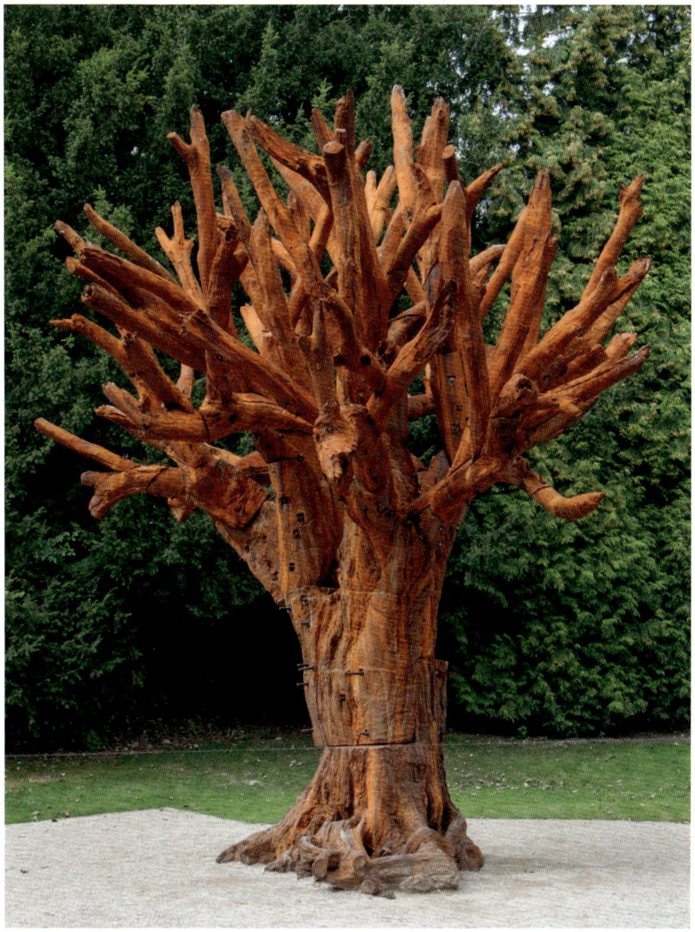

Ai Weiwei, *Iron Tree*, 2013, Gusseisen / Cast iron, 680 x 650 x 650 cm, Yorkshire Sculpture Park, Wakefield

The Tree of Valbella arises out of a special, highly topical constellation in current times. The story behind the project culminated in July 2019 after a long conceptual and production process, resulting in the construction of the ensemble in Valbella. A spruce in the patron's garden had to be felled in 2016, a wonderful 124-year-old tree, a precious part of creation. The spruce takes centre stage in Mirko Baselgia's work of art. The sculptural ensemble perpetuates the growth of the tree and its destiny; the parts that were used by the Fonderia Nolana Del Giudice in Naples as moulds for bronze casting were cut from its wood. Felling a tree is problematic in times of climate change. Did the artist and patron create a monument to it with the ensemble? No, rather, they breathed new life into the spruce.

The ensemble consists of five parts from the spring, the screen, the horizontal reliefs and the doors to the final stone, which is not a real final stone, but rather six narrow elements, two columns like spearheads and four steles: the top of the spruce.[3] Laura Giudici traces the semantic levels of these elements. The "porta clausa", the closed door, often indicates in art the vision of the prophet Ezekiel (44.2): "Then said the Lord unto me; This gate shall be shut, it shall not be opened, and no man shall enter in by it; because the Lord, the God of Israel, hath entered in by it, therefore it shall be shut." It will be opened on the Day of Judgement: *The Tree of Valbella* directs the observer's eye and reflections from the present to the past, to the future and into eternity.

The artist's origins, his career, his ideas, his working mode

The artist is firmly rooted in his region of origin, while, at the same time, open to influences from all around the world. The narrowness of Switzerland and the cosmopolitan outlook of the Swiss are always an issue, recently also as a place of refuge in the globalised world.[4] In the small-scale development on the banks of the Heidsee in Valbella (Valbella-Lenzerheide), the large-scale installation creates its space with allure and precious details. The term "installation" falls short and the term introduced

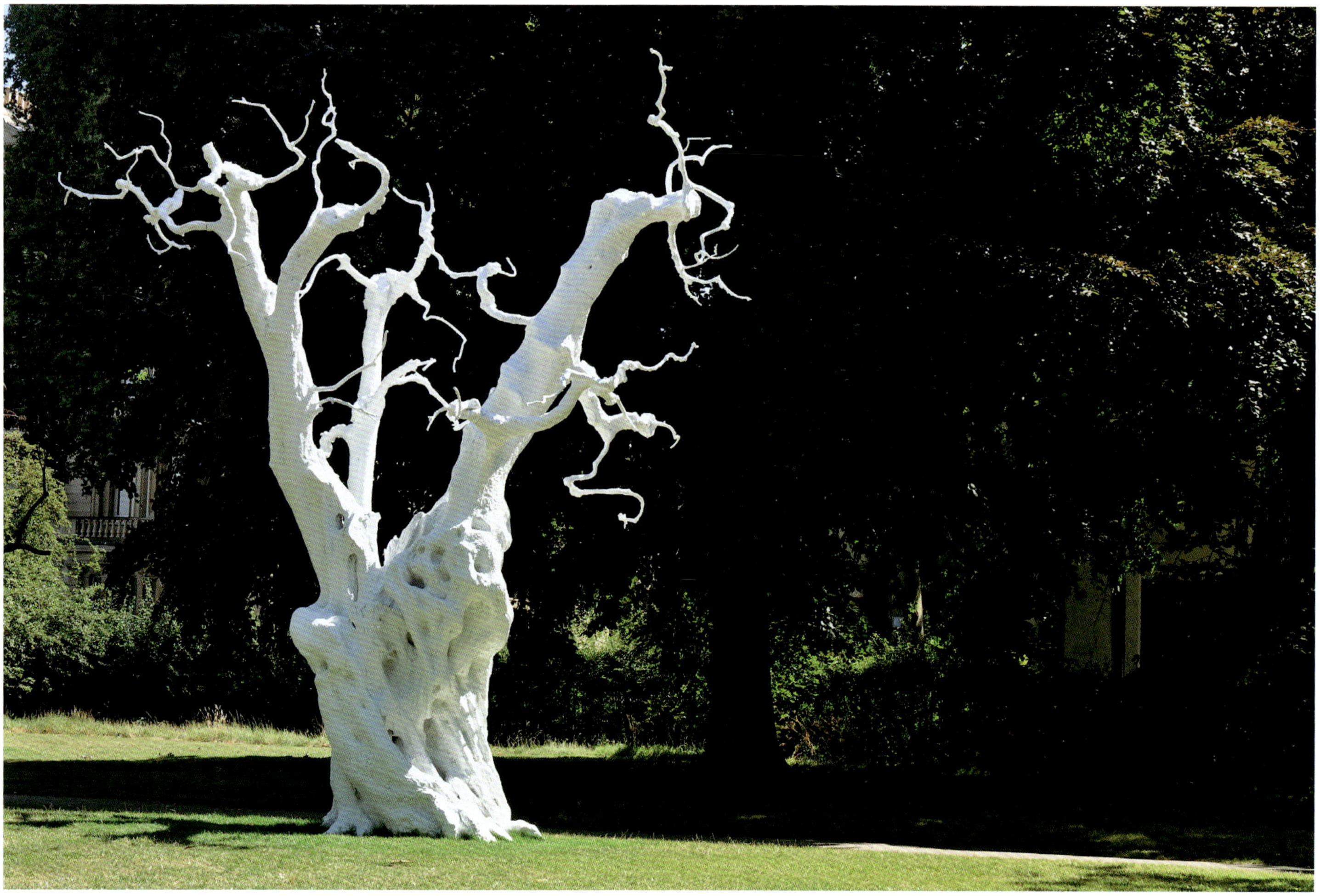

Ugo Rondinone, *Summer Moon*, 2011, Ausstellungsansicht / Exhibition view *Frieze Sculpture* 2017, English Gardens of The Regent's Park, London, Aluminiumguss, weißes Email / Cast aluminium, white enamel, 550 x 600 x 550 cm

kleinteiligen Überbauung am Ufer des Heidsees in Valbella (Valbella-Lenzerheide) schafft sich die grosszügige Installation mit Allüre und feinen Details ihren Raum. Der Begriff „Installation" greift zu kurz, der von Jérôme Neutres hier eingeführte Bezeichnung als „ensemble sculptural" trifft weit besser auf Mirko Baselgias Kunstwerk zu. Diese Konstellation birgt aufregende Aspekte, die das Ensemble wie seine Umgebung aufwerten, sensibilisieren und auch in Frage stellen, Kontrapunkte schaffen; der Künstler liess sich von der Idee herausfordern, die Fichte zu neuem, künstlerischem Leben zu erwecken.

Das Ensemble erzählt nicht nur die Geschichte des Baums, sie nimmt auch Elemente aus dem Leben des Auftraggebers und des Künstlers auf. Mirko Baselgia nahm seit seinen frühesten Werken seine unmittelbare Umgebung und die Natur tiefgründig war; er setzt seine Erfahrungen mit Feinsinn künstlerisch um. Er schafft Werke der Kunst aus der Betrachtung und dem Studium der Natur, seien es Bienenwaben, Murmeltierhöhlen, Pflanzen, Früchte, Tannzapfen, Schildkröten... Baselgia hat auch ein Gespür für Sprache; er spricht die Sprache der kleinsten Minderheit der Schweiz, das Rätoromanische, das von Tal zu Tal in unterschiedlichen Idiomen gesprochen wird; das grosse Ganze und die Kleinteiligkeit der Sprache, prägt auch die Werke des Künstlers. Sie tragen manchmal rätoromanische Titel, die in den Ohren von anderssprachigen Menschen einen archaischen Wohlklang erzeugen. Genannt seien bloss *Igl*

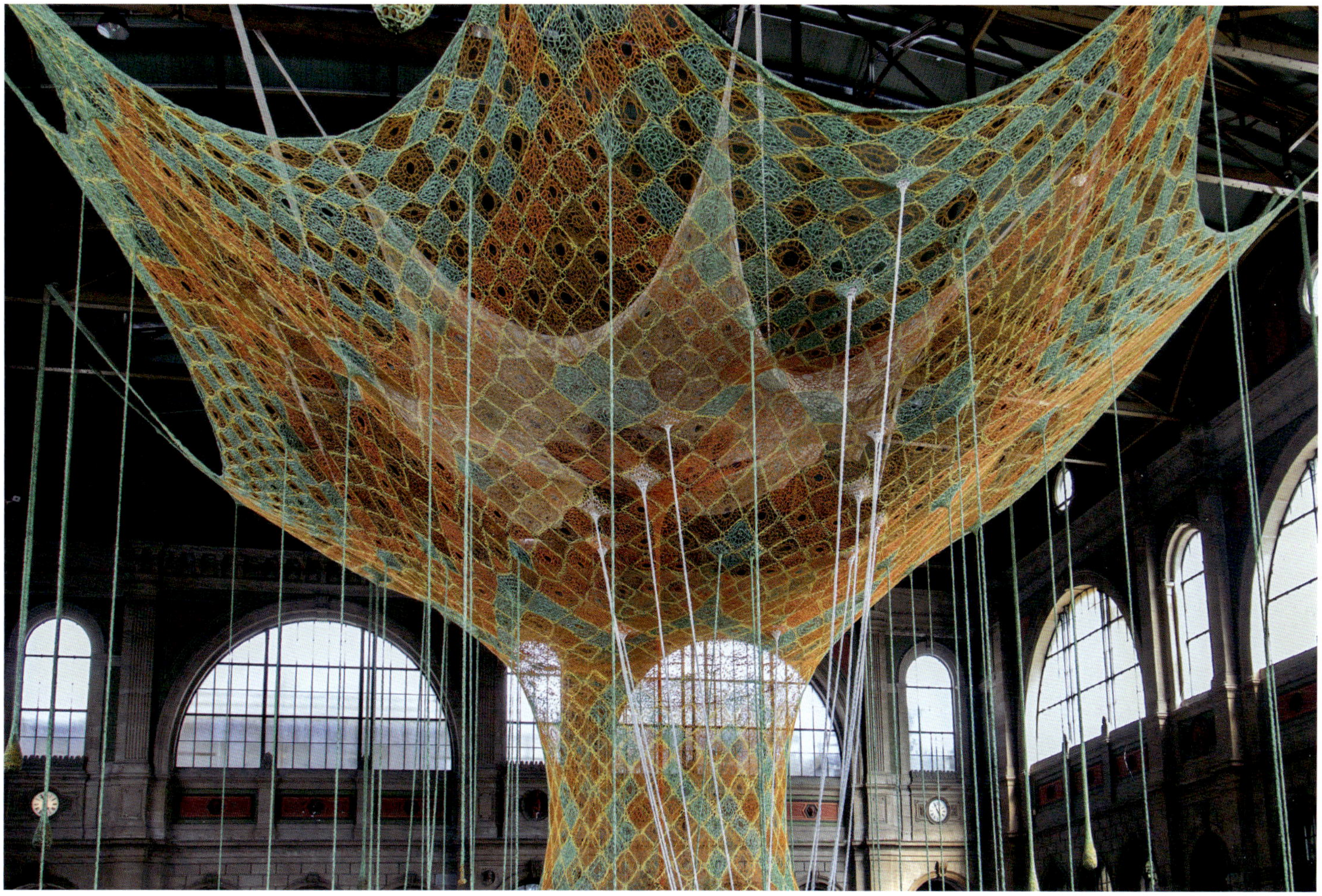

Ernesto Neto, *GaiaMotherTree*, 2018, Installationsansicht im Zürich Hauptbahnhof / Installation view at Zurich Main station, handgeknüpfte Baumwollstreifen / hand-knotted cotton strips

here by Jérôme Neutres as "ensemble sculptural" fits Mirko Baselgia's work of art far better. This constellation contains exciting aspects that enhance and raise awareness, as well as questioning the ensemble and its surroundings, creating counterpoints; the artist was challenged by the idea of awakening the spruce to a new, artistic life.

The ensemble not only tells the story of the tree, it also incorporates elements from the life of the patron and the artist. From his earliest works, Mirko Baselgia's perception of his immediate surroundings and nature was profound; he translates his experiences with subtlety artistically. He creates works of art from the contemplation and study of nature, be it honeycombs, marmot burrows, plants, fruit, pine cones, turtle ... Baselgia also has a feel for language; he is a native speaker of the smallest linguistic minority in Switzerland, Romansh, which is spoken in different dialectal variants from valley to valley; the big picture and the detailed nature of language also shape the artist's works. Sometimes, they have Romansh names that create an archaic echo in the ears of people who speak other languages. Suffice to recall: *Igl secret da David*, *Structura digl gôt*, *Tartaruga*, *Transmutaziun* or *Midada da structura* and *La mort digl paeis purpurign*.

Likewise, for the name of the ensemble in Valbella, Baselgia also thought of the metamorphoses of a tree, the spruce, which in the bronze ensemble, with the surface shaped by wood, tells its own story next to other ones.

secret da David, *Structura digl gôt*, *Tartaruga*, *Transmutaziun* oder *Midada da structura* und *La mort digl paeis purpurign*.

Als Titel für das Ensemble in Valbella dachte Baselgia auch an die Metamorphosen eines Baumes, der Fichte, die in dem bronzenen Ensemble mit der vom Holz geprägten Oberfläche neben anderen auch ihre eigene Geschichte erzählt.

Das Ensemble *The Tree of Valbella* im Umfeld der Kunst heute, die Stellung des Oeuvres in der Kunstgeschichte

The Tree of Valbella reiht sich in die Tradition der Kunstinstallationen, die so erst seit den 1970er Jahren bezeichnet werden, und auch der Land Art. Baselgia greift auf Projekte früherer Künstler zurück, bewusst oder unbewusst; oder wie Hans Belting sagt, jeder hat seine Erinnerungen gespeichert, nicht alle aber nutzen sie.[5] Erst durch die Interpretation von Jérôme Neutres (in diesem Buch) wird das Werk zum „ensemble sculptural", dem skulpturalen Ensemble im Sinne von Constantin Brâncuși (1876 -1957) und seinem Werk in Targû Jiu.[6]

Wie der rumänische Bildhauer, der zum Klassiker der Moderne wurde, sich in die Erinnerungen des Krieges vertiefte, fühlt sich Mirko Baselgia in die Seele der gefällten Fichte ein, um ihre Geschichte zu schreiben, mehr noch, sie weiterzuschreiben; oder wie Neutres treffend sagt, der Betrachter muss in diesem künstlerischen Palimpsest blättern.[7]

Als Mediävisten gefällt mir der Begriff des Palimpsests, der auch immer etwas Geheimnisvolles an sich hat, da es nur selten gelingt, alle Textschichten genau zu lesen. Bei Mirko bleibt stets auch der Freiraum für die Betrachter, sich selbst in seinen Werken zu spiegeln. Neutres spricht von der Metanatur der Kunst; die Kunst verschmilzt hier in einzigartiger Weise mit der Natur, mit der Schöpfung Gottes, es ist auch ein Werk mit religiöser Dimension. Die verschiedenen Schichten des Ensembles gilt es meditativ abzuschreiten, sich darin zu vertiefen, es mit dem Auge und der Seele aufzunehmen, zu hinterfragen, zu entziffern und in die Sprache des Betrachters zu übersetzen. Es ist ein mehrdimensionales Kunstwerk in Raum – zwischen West und Ost – und Zeit, mit Blick nach vorne bis in die Unendlichkeit und zurück in die Vergangenheit. Die Qualität des Blicks auf das Ensemble ist entscheidend, es erschliesst sich erst in der Meditation, zu der das persische Ornament und die hellenistischen Windgötter anregen. Der Blickwechsel hin zum Osten inspirierte den Künstler und zeigte sich als ein gemeinsames Interesse mit demjenigen des Auftraggebers.[8]

Bäume faszinieren die Künstler seit eh und je – seit den zahlreichen Darstellungen der Schöpfung, des Sündenfalls und der Vertreibung aus dem Paradies. Eva pflückt verbotenerweise den Apfel vom Baum der Erkenntnis und reicht ihn Adam. Der Baum Jesse und der Lebensbaum sind aus der symbiotischen Verbindung mit der Natur nicht aus der Kunst wegzudenken.[9] Nur auf wenige zeitgenössische Beispiele sei hingewiesen: auf die Olivenbäume von Ugo Rondinone, auf die Bäume von Ai Weiwei und der *GaiaMotherTree* (2018) von Ernesto Neto.

Der Vergleich mit Brâncuși stellt einen hohen Anspruch an *The Tree of Valbella*. Baselgia geht von der lokalen Gegebenheit und der Fichte aus und greift von da weit aus, so wie die Äste der Fichte weit hinausgreifen. In der Kunstgeschichte versucht man ein neues Fach zu etablieren, die „Global Art History", deren Definition bisher unscharfe Grenzen aufweist. Der rätoromanische Künstler spricht nicht davon, er realisiert globale Kunst. Er verbindet das perspektivlose Ornament des persischen Mausoleums mit der Anordnung der einzelnen Elemente des Ensembles; die Fluchtlinie, die sich in der langgezogenen Anlage des Gartens in Valbella ergibt, eröffnet einen perspektivischen Blick von der Quelle bis zum Schlussstein. Gelebte „Global Art" entsteht. Ohne die Perspektive des Werkes ins Auge zu fassen, erschliesst sich das Ensemble nicht. Der Sog der – westlichen – Perspektive steht im Widerspruch zur Statik des – orientalischen – Ornaments, möchte man meinen; aber Mirko

The Tree of Valbella ensemble in the context of art today, the position of the oeuvre in art history

The Tree of Valbella joins the tradition of art installations – which have only taken this name since the 1970s – and Land Art, too. Baselgia draws on projects by earlier artists, consciously or unconsciously – or, as Hans Belting puts it: everyone has stored their memories, but not all use them.[5] Only through the interpretation of Jérôme Neutres (in this book) does the work become "ensemble sculptural", the sculptural ensemble in the sense of Constantin Brâncuşi (1876-1957) and his work in Targû Jiu.[6]

Just as the Romanian sculptor, who became a classic interpreter of Modernism, immersed himself in the memories of the war, Mirko Baselgia empathises with the soul of the felled spruce to write its history, and even more so, to continue writing it; or, as Neutres aptly states, the observer has to leaf through this artistic palimpsest.[7]

As a medievalist, I like the term *palimpsest*, which has something mysterious about it, since it is seldom possible to read all the layers of the text carefully. With Mirko, the observer always has the freedom to mirror himself in his works. Neutres talks of the metanature of art: art merges here in a unique way with nature, with God's creation; it is also a work with a religious dimension. The different layers of the ensemble have to be taken in meditatively, immerging oneself in them, absorbing them through the eye and the soul, questioning, deciphering and translating them into the language of the observer. It is a multi-dimensional work of art in space – between West and East – and time, with a perspective looking forward to infinity and back to the past. The quality of the perspective of the ensemble is decisive; it is only revealed in meditation, prompted by the Persian ornament and the Hellenistic wind gods. The change of perspective moving to the East inspired the artist and was revealed as a common interest shared with the patron.[8]

Trees have always fascinated artists since the numerous depictions of creation, the fall of man and

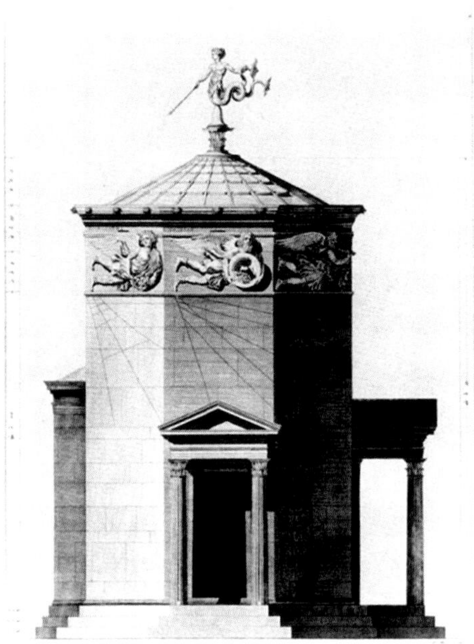

Reconstruction: Stuart and Revett, pl. II, in: Joseph V. Noble, Derek J. de Solla Price, "The Water Clock in the Tower of the Winds", *American Journal of Archeology*, Vol. 72, No. 4 (Okt. / Oct., 1968), Tafel / Plate 112

expulsion from paradise. Eve, although forbidden, plucks the apple from the tree of knowledge and hands it to Adam. The tree of Jesse and the tree of life are indispensable in art because of the symbiotic connection with nature.[9] Reference is made only to a few contemporary examples: the olive trees by Ugo Rondinone, the trees by Ai Weiwei and the *Gaia Mother Tree* (2018) by Ernesto Neto.

The comparison with Brâncuşi places high demands on the Valbella tree. Baselgia takes local conditions just as the branches of the spruce stretch beyond. In art history, one tries to establish a new subject area, the "Global Art History", the definition of which has hitherto remained blurred. The Romansh artist does not talk about it, he creates global art. He combines the perspective-free ornament of the Persian mausoleum with the arrangement of the individual elements of the ensemble; the alignment that emerges in the elongated layout of the garden in Valbella opens up a perspective view from the spring to the final stone. Lived "Global Art" is created. Without looking at the perspective of the work, the ensemble is not accessible. The pull of the – western – perspective is in opposition to the static equilibrium of the – oriental – ornament, one might think; but Mirko Baselgia allows both elements to merge, he

Baselgia lässt beide Elemente miteinander verschmelzen, er bringt Bewegung in das Ornament, eine neue, eigenartige Dynamik entsteht.

Die oberen Teile des Paravents werden durchbrochen durch die Figuren der Windgötter. Sie blasen gleichsam in das an sich statische Geflecht des persischen Ornaments und bringen es in Bewegung. Dazu liess sich Baselgia vom Turm der Winde aus späthellenistischer Zeit in Athen inspirieren.[10]

Das Oktogon übersetzt er in die acht Flügel des Paravents; die Achtzahl ist das Symbol der höchsten Vollendung; man denke nur an den Felsendom in Jerusalem, an San Vitale in Ravenna oder an die Pfalzkapelle in Aachen oder an das Baptisterium San Giovanni in Florenz. Die vorwärtsstürmende Bewegung der Winde und die von ihnen ausgehenden Linien der Sonnenuhr am Turm nimmt der Künstler auf. Er übersetzt sie in das verspielte persische Ornament. Es entsteht ein interessanter Gegensatz zwischen den Winden und dem Ornament, der das ganze Ensemble in eine elektrisierende Spannung bringt. Ost und West berühren sich und verschmelzen mit der Natur, der Fichte von Valbella und mit der das Ensemble umgebenden Vegetation.

Nimmt man Hans Beltings Beobachtung des Blickwechsels auf, ist es hier ein mehrschichtiger Wechsel des Blicks; nicht nur der von West nach Ost und von Ost nach West, es fügt sich auch der Blick aus und in die Berglandschaft an, die Verwandlung der Fichte in die bronzenen Elemente des skulpturalen Ensembles.

1 Wolfgang Ullrich in *Die Zeit* vom 13. August 2015.

2 Irving Stone, *Michelangelo. Inferno und Ekstase. Biographischer Roman*, Berlin: Deutsche Buch-Gemeinschaft, 1961, S. 38f., 43 und 52f. Originalausgabe: *The Agony and the Ecstasy.The biographical novel of Michelangelo*, New York: Doubleday, 1961.

3 Oder wie Mirko sich im Interview mit Jérôme Neutres ausdrückt: „Es gibt eine Quelle, einen Paravent, zwei liegende Reliefs, zwei Tore und einen Schlussstein."

4 Auch der Schriftsteller Arno Camenisch aus dem kleinen Dorf Tavanasa (Brigels) ist weltweit unterwegs. „Beim Schreiben denke ich an die Capuns [ein traditionelles bündnerisches Gericht] meiner Grossmutter", sagte Camenisch in einem Interview. Thomas Hürlimann betont das Partikular-Seltsame seines Landes: „Ja, mit der Literatur gelingt die Heimkehr immer, die Rückkehr in die Wirklichkeit. Weltliteratur – der Begriff ist von Goethe – schafft tatsächlich Welten. (…) Die Hoffnung, dass wir die Heimkehr, die Rückkehr in die Wirklichkeit schaffen: dank und mit der Literatur. Sie schafft Welt, also Heimat." (Thomas Hürlimann, „Über das Unheimliche, das aus der Heimat kommt", Dankrede am 3. Juni 1977 in Weimar aus Anlass des Literaturpreises der Konrad-Adenauer-Stiftung, in: Thomas Hürlimann, *Himmelsöhi hilf! Über die Schweiz und andere Nester*, Zürich: Ammann Verlag, 2002, S. 23–34).

5 Hans Belting, *Das unsichtbare Meisterwerk. Die modernen Mythen der Kunst*, München: C.H.Beck, 1998.

6 Das Denkmal wurde von der National League of Gorj Women in Auftrag gegeben zu Ehren der Soldaten, die 1916 Tâgu Jiu verteidigten. Constantin Brâncuși (1876–1957) lebte damals in Paris; er war dankbar für den Auftrag, in seiner Heimat das grosse Werk zu schaffen. Er nahm 1935 den Auftrag an und lehnte ein Honorar ab (frei nach Wikipedia).

7 Palimpsest [Maskulinum, auch Neutrum, von lateinisch *palimpsestus*, aus altgriechisch πάλιν *palin* „wieder" und ψάειν *psaein* „reiben, (ab-) schaben"] bezeichnet eine Manuskriptseite oder -rolle, die beschrieben, durch Schaben oder Waschen gereinigt und danach neu beschrieben wurde (lat. *codex rescriptus*) (frei nach Wikipedia). Die Seele des Baumes: „Dwelling in the Fuchun Mountains" von Chun Jiang Shui Nuan, China, 2019; als Schweizer Première am Zürcher Filmfestival 2019 gezeigt.

8 Zum Blickwechsel: siehe Hans Belting, *Florenz und Bagdad: Eine westöstliche Geschichte des Blicks*, München: C.H.Beck, 2009, S. 20 und passim.

9 Lebensbäume finden sich auch in den „Indiennes", den Baumwollstoffen, die das Landesmuseum 2019 in Zürich ausstellte (*Indiennes. Stoff für tausend Geschichten*, 30.08.2019-19.01.2020). Ugo Rondinones Gruppe von fünf Abgüssen von tausendjährigen Olivenbäumen, *Notti d'argento* (2016), ausgestellt auf den Mercati di Traiano in Rom (10.06.-01.09.2016). Ausstellung *Freiheit und Baum* von Latifa Echkach in der Kunsthalle Mainz (12.07.-10.11.2019).

10 Hermann J. Kienast, *Der Turm der Winde in Athen*, Wiesbaden: Reichert Verlag, 2014.

brings movement to the ornament and a new, special dynamic emerges.

The upper parts of the screen are broken up by the figures of the wind gods. They blow, as it were, into the intrinsically static network of Persian ornament and set it in motion. Baselgia was inspired by the Tower of the Winds from the late Hellenistic period in Athens.[10]

He translates the octagon into the eight wings of the screen; the number eight is the symbol of highest perfection – just think of the Dome of the Rock in Jerusalem, San Vitale in Ravenna, the Palatine Chapel in Aachen or the Baptistery of San Giovanni in Florence. The artist incorporates the forward movement of the winds and the lines of the sundial on the tower emanating from them. He translates them into the playful Persian ornament. The outcome is an interesting contrast between the winds and the ornament, which brings the whole ensemble into an electrifying tension. East and West touch and merge with nature, the Valbella spruce and the surrounding vegetation.

If one takes Hans Belting's observation of the change of perspective, here, it is a multilayered change of perspective: not only from West to East and East to West, but also embracing the panorama from and to the mountain landscape, completing the transformation of the spruce into the bronze elements of the sculptural ensemble.

1 Wolfgang Ullrich in *Die Zeit*, published 13 August 2015.

2 Irving Stone, Michelangelo. Inferno und Ekstase. *Biographischer Roman*, Berlin: Deutsche Buch-Gemeinschaft, 1961, p. 38 et seq, 43 and 52 et seq. Original edition: *The Agony and the Ecstasy. The biographical novel of Michelangelo*, New York: Doubleday, 1961.

3 Or, as Mirko put it in the interview with Jérôme Neutres: "There is a spring, a screen, two horizontal reliefs, two doors and a final stone."

4 The writer Arno Camenisch from the small village of Tavanasa (Brigels) is also travelling around the world. "When I write, I think of my grandmother's Capuns [a traditional Canton of Graubünden' dish]" said Camenisch in an interview. Thomas Hürlimann emphasises the particular and singular of his home region: "Yes, with literature you always come home, a return to reality. World literature – the term comes from Goethe – actually creates worlds. (...) The hope that we can make it home, the return to reality: thanks to and with literature. It creates the world and also 'Heimat' (place of origin – father's home)" (Thomas Hürlimann, "On the uncanny that comes out of the Heimat", acceptance speech on 3 June 1977 in Weimar at the Konrad Adenauer Foundation's literary prize event, in: Thomas Hürlimann, *Himmelsöhi hilf! Über die Schweiz und andere Neste*, Zurich: Ammann Verlag, 2002, pp. 23-34).

5 Hans Belting, *Das unsichtbare Meisterwerk. Die modernen Mythen der Kunst*, Munich: CH Beck, 1998.

6 The monument was commissioned by the National League of Gorj Women in honor of the soldiers who defended Tâgu Jiu in 1916. Constantin Brâncuși (1876–1957) lived in Paris at the time; he was grateful for the commission to create the large work in his "Heimat" - home country. He accepted the commission in 1935 and refused a fee (source Wikipedia).

7 Palimpsest (from Latin palimpsestus, from ancient Greek πάλιν palin "again" and ψάειν psaein "rub, [scrape] off") denotes a manuscript page or scroll that is marked by cleaning through scraping or washing, so that the page may then be used for another document (lat. codex rescriptus) (source: Wikipedia). The soul of the tree: "Dwelling in the Fuchun Mountains" by Chun Jiang Shui Nuan, China, 2019; with Swiss première at the Zurich Film Festival 2019.

8 On the change in perspective: see Hans Belting, *Florenz und Bagdad: Eine westöstliche Geschichte des Blicks*, Munich: CH Beck, 2009, p. 20 and passim.

9 Trees of life can also be found in the "indiennes", the cotton fabrics that the Landesmuseum exhibited in Zurich in 2019 (*Indiennes. Material for a thousand stories*, 30.08.2019-19.01.2020). Ugo Rondinone's group of five casts from millennial olive trees *Notti d'argento* (2016), exhibited at the Mercati di Traiano in Rome (10.06.-01.09.2016). *Liberty and Tree* exhibition by Latifa Echakhch at the Mainz Kunsthalle (12.07-10.11.2019).

10 Hermann J. Kienast, *Der Turm der Winde in Athen*, Wiesbaden: Reichert Verlag, 2014.

DIE FICHTE ALS HAUPTFIGUR DES SKULPTURALEN ENSEMBLES

CHRISTOPH EGGENBERGER

Geschichte der Fichte

Der Künstler nimmt die Lebensgeschichte der Fichte auf, verwebt sie mit den späthellenistischen und den persischen Elementen. Die Jahrringe bilden das Leben eines Baumes ab; alle 124 Jahrringe von 1892 bis 2016 konnte der Dendrochronologe nachweisen, also von der Entstehung der Fichte bis zum Fälljahr.[1]

Nimmt man das Geburtsjahr der Fichte unter die Lupe, ergibt sich eine erstaunliche Zeitgeschichte. Am 27. Februar 1892 meldet Rudolf Diesel das Patent für den neuen Treibstoff an; der Diesel ist erst in jüngster Zeit in Verruf geraten. Am 9. August erhielt Thomas Edison das Patent für den Telegraphen; am 17. Dezember 1892 erschien die erste Ausgabe von *Vogue*; die Modezeitschrift erscheint noch heute in einer Auflage von 90'000 Exemplaren. Das Ballett *Der Nussknacker – Щелкунчик, Schtschelkuntschik* - von Pyotr Ilyich Tchaikovsky erlebte am 18. Dezember im Mariinsky Theater in St. Petersburg seine Uraufführung. Zu Beginn des Jahres, am 29. Januar 1892 wurde Ernst Lubitsch in Berlin geboren, unvergesslich mit seinen Filmen wie *Ninotchka* (1939), *Sein oder Nichtsein* (1942) oder *Ein himmlischer Sünder* (1943). 1892 malte Paul Gauguin auf Tahiti sein weltumspannendes Meisterwerk *Ta matete* (Der Markt), heute im Kunstmuseum Basel.

Der Wuchsverlauf bis in die 1970er Jahre zeigt keine Auffälligkeit. Mit Ausnahme des Jahres 1897 liegen die Breitenwerte immer über 1 mm. Das Jahr 1975 fällt durch den gegenüber den vorherigen und folgenden Jahren deutlich geringeren Zuwachs auf. Ab 1976 ist die Stärke der Breitenzunahme nicht zu übersehen. Sie könnte damit zusammenhängen, dass durch Auflichtungen in der Umgebung des Standortes für den Baum bessere Wuchsbedingungen geschaffen worden waren, möglicherweise bedingt durch die baulichen Eingriffe in den 1970er Jahren.

Auffällig sind die wellenförmigen Verläufe der Jahrringe vor allem im jüngeren Teil des Stammes. Diese Unregelmässigkeiten und Ausbuchtungen der Jahrringe werden als Haselwuchs bezeichnet. Sie sind genetischen Ursprungs, jedoch wohl auch durch Umweltfaktoren beeinflusst (z.B. starkem Wind), dies ist allerdings eher Spekulation. Bei Fichten ist Haselwuchs hoch gefragt und für den Musikinstrumentenbau besonders gut geeignet, denn es verleiht dem Holz ein sehr ausgewogenes und reiches Klangspektrum. Eine weitere Dimension tut sich auf: der wohltönende Klang!

1 Siehe die Berichte von Mathias Seifert, Chur, und Holger Gärtner, Birmensdorf ZH, im Anhang.

THE SPRUCE AS THE MAIN FIGURE OF THE SCULPTURAL ENSEMBLE

History of the spruce

The artist takes up the life story of the spruce and interweaves it with late Hellenistic and Persian elements. The growth rings show the life of a tree; the dendrochronologist was able to record all 124 rings from 1892 to 2016, i.e. from the genesis of the spruce to the year it was felled.[1]

If you take a close look at the year the spruce took seed, you will discover an astonishing contemporary history. On 27 February 1892, Rudolf Diesel applied for the patent for the new fuel; the diesel had only recently fallen into disrepute. On 9 August, Thomas Edison obtained the patent for the telegraph; on 17 December 1892, the first edition of *Vogue* appeared; the fashion magazine is still published today with a print run of 90,000 copies. The ballet *The Nutcracker Suite – Щелкунчик, Schtschelkuntschik* – by Pyotr Ilyich Tchaikovsky had its world premiere on 18 December at the Mariinsky Theatre in St Petersburg. At the beginning of the year, on 29 January 1892, Ernst Lubitsch was born in Berlin, not to be forgotten for his feature films, such as *Ninotchka* (1939), *To be or not to be* (1942) or *Heaven can wait* (1943). In 1892 Paul Gauguin painted his world-embracing masterpiece *Ta matete* (The Market) in Tahiti, now in the Kunstmuseum Basel.

The growth process up to the 1970s shows no abnormality. With the exception of 1897, width values were always over 1 mm. 1975 stands out because of significantly lower growth compared to the previous and following years. From 1976 on, the robustness of the width increase cannot be overlooked. It could be related to the better growing conditions created for the tree through clearing the area in its vicinity, possibly due to building work in the 1970s.

The undulating patterns of the tree rings are particularly noticeable in the younger part of the trunk. These irregularities and bulges in the growth rings are known as hazel growth. They are of genetic origin, but are also probably influenced by environmental factors (e.g. strong wind), however this is speculation. Hazel growth is in high demand for spruce and it is particularly well suited for making musical instruments, as it gives the wood a very balanced and rich sound spectrum. Another dimension is opened up: a mellifluous sound!

Das Fichtenholz und seine Jahresringe bei der dendrochronologischen Analyse / The spruce wood and its annual rings during the dendrochronological analysis

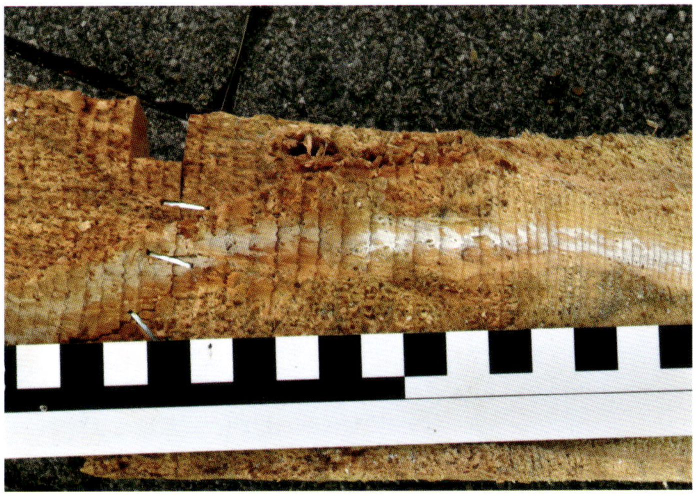

1 See the reports by Mathias Seifert, Chur, and Holger Gärtner, Birmensdorf ZH, in the appendix.

Rechts: Die Fichte im Garten von Thomas Abegg in Valbella / Right: The spruce tree in Thomas Abegg's garden in Valbella / Unten: Das Fällen der Fichtenkrone / Below: The felling of the spruce tree canopy

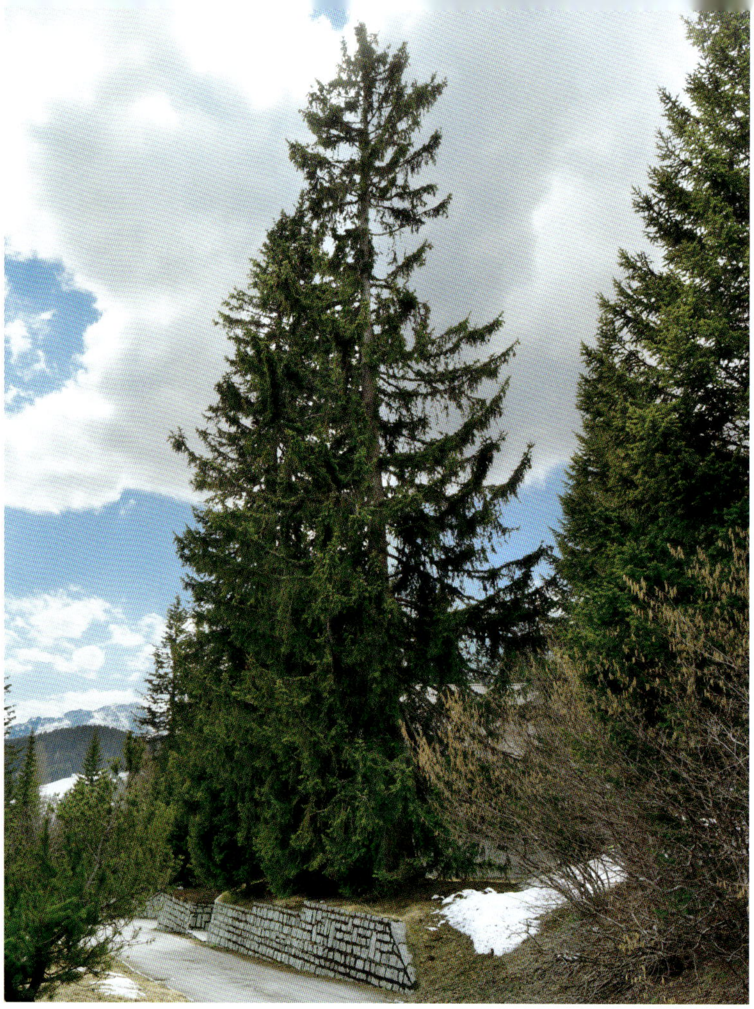

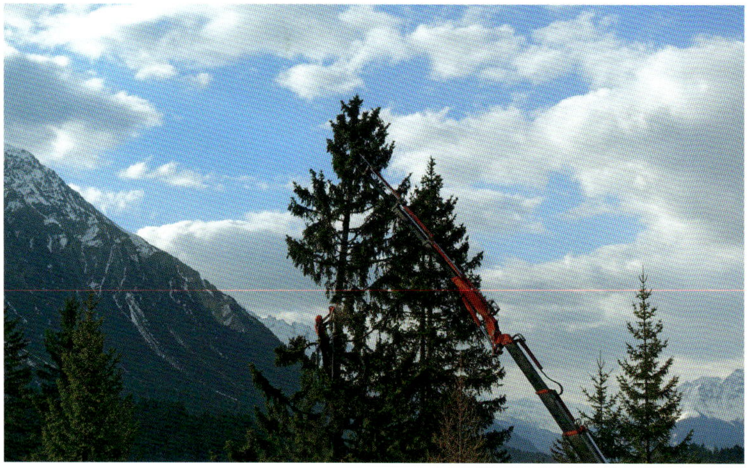

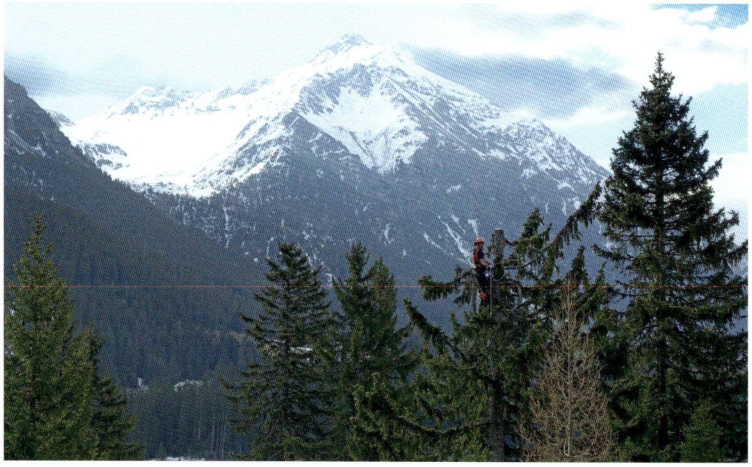

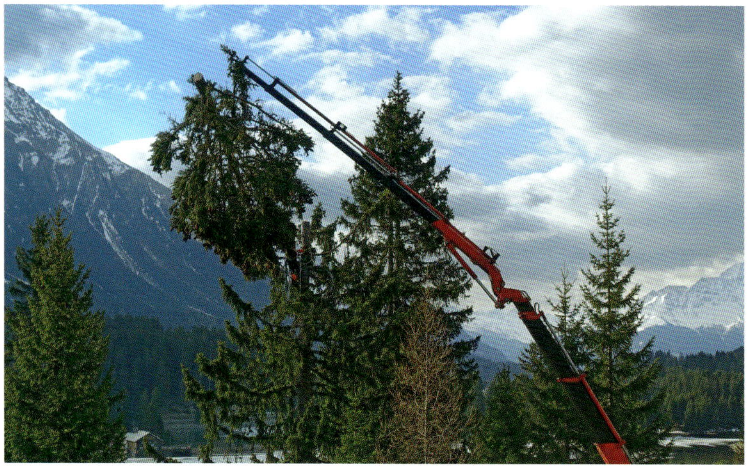

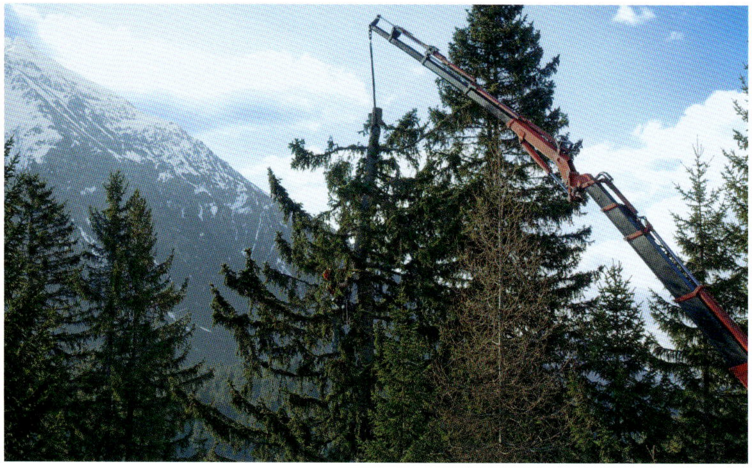

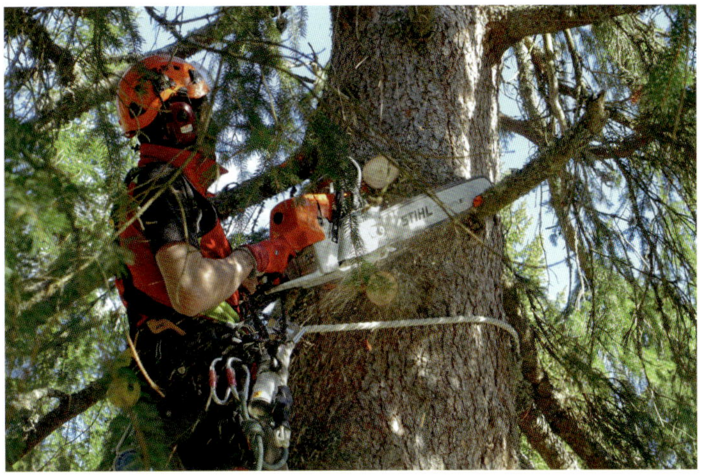

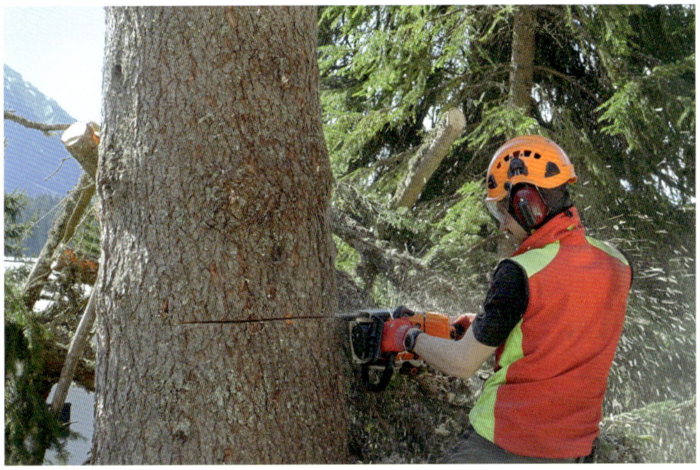

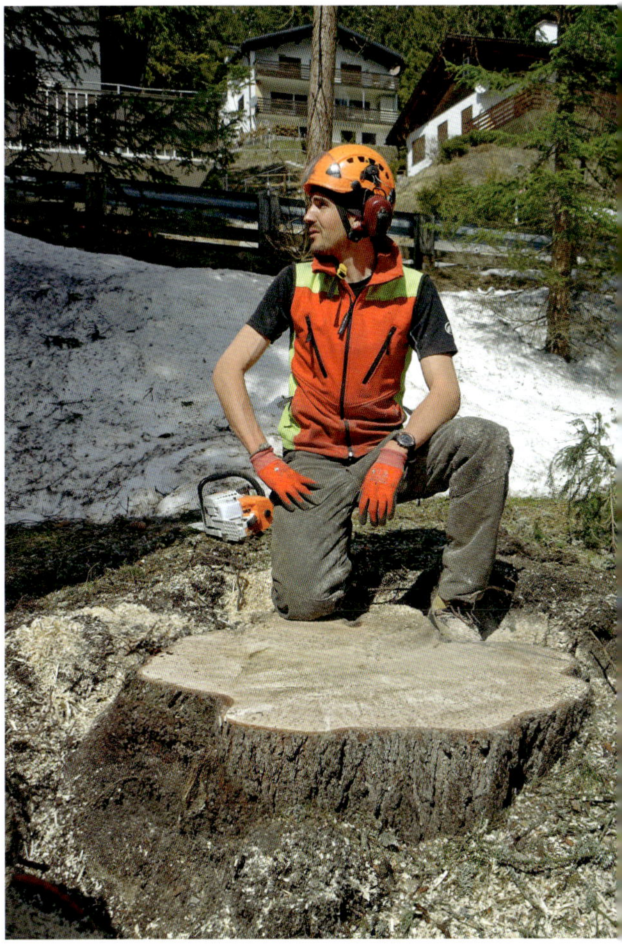

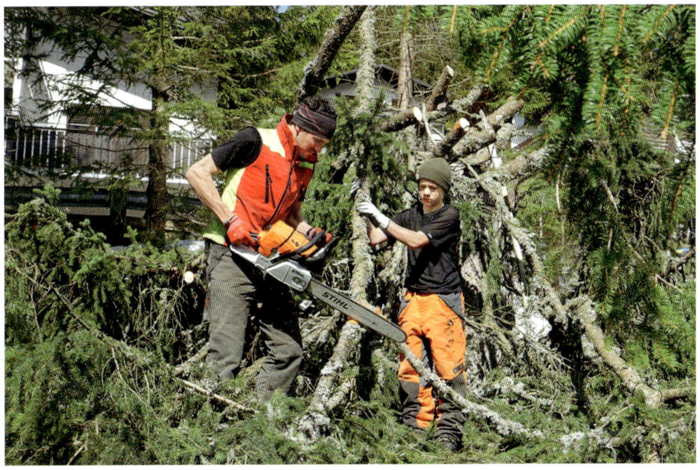

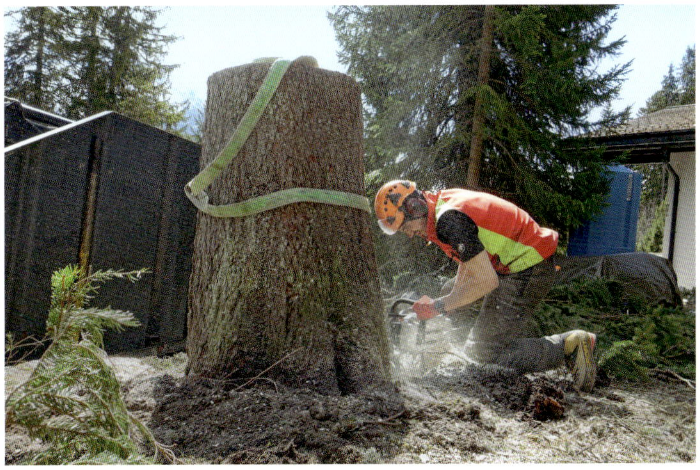

Links: Das Fällen des unteren Teils der Fichte / Left: The felling of the lower part of the spruce tree / Rechts: Curdin Gregori, der zuständige Forstwart für das Fällen der Fichte / Right: Curdin Gregori, the feller responsible for cutting the spruce

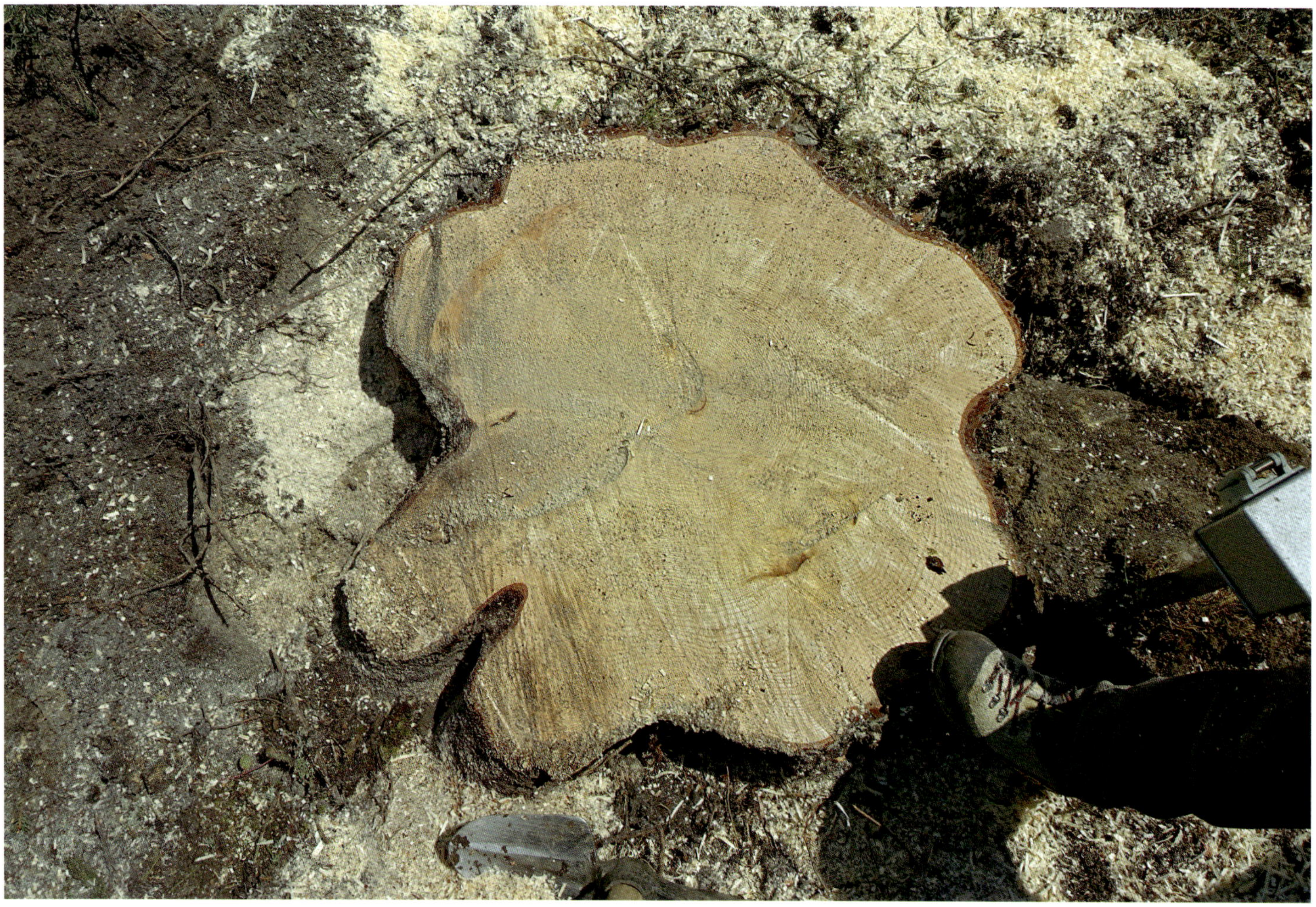

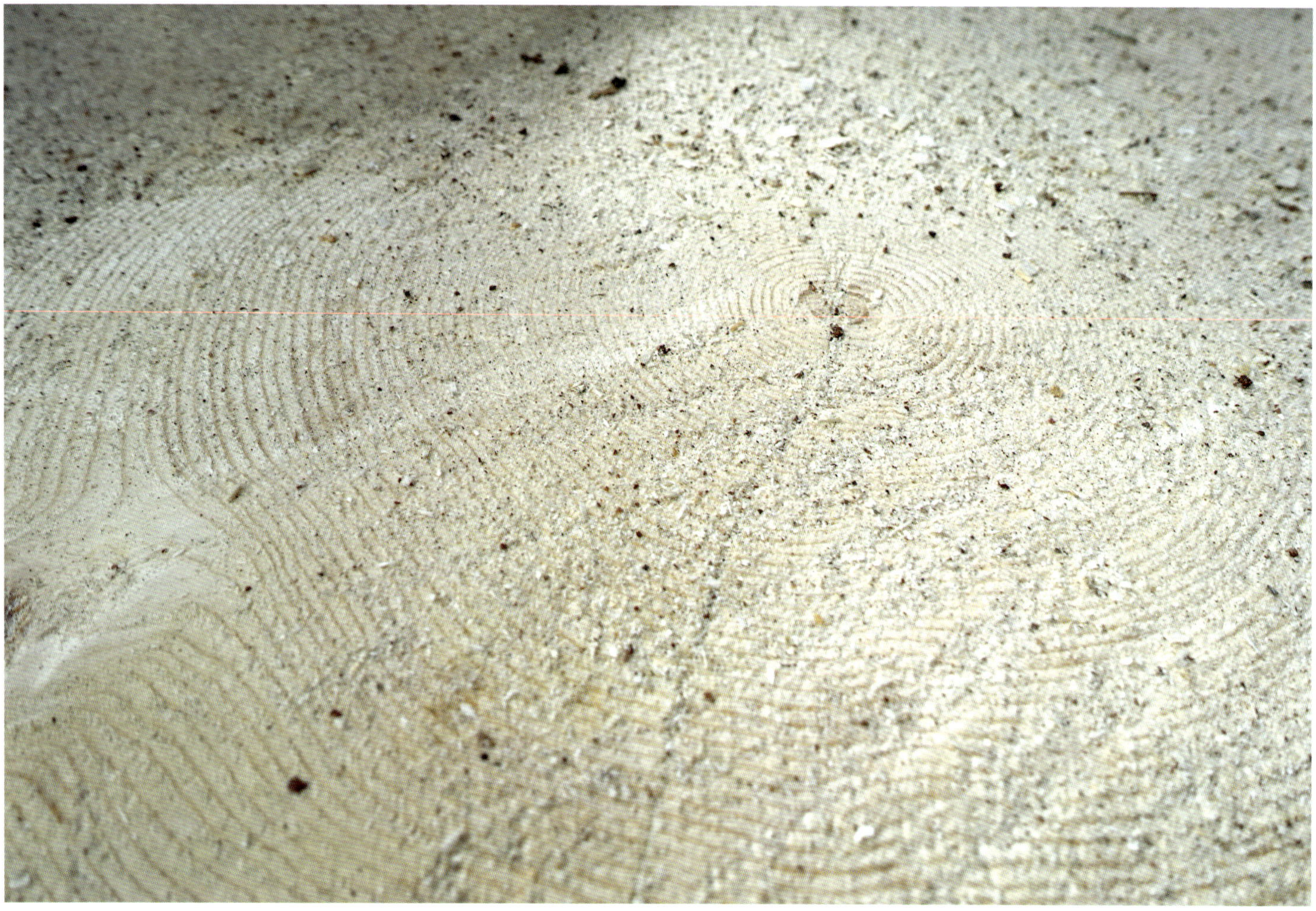

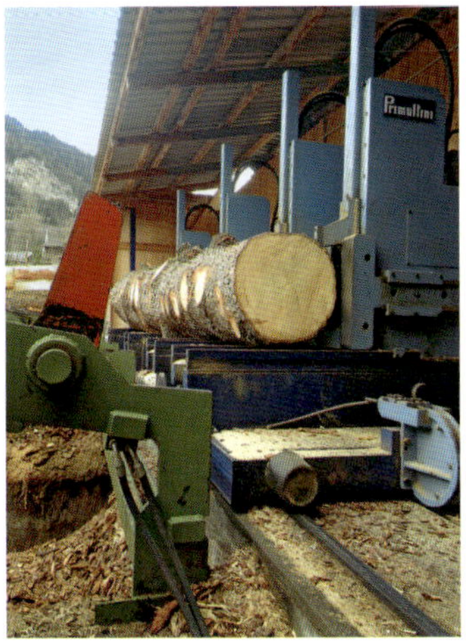

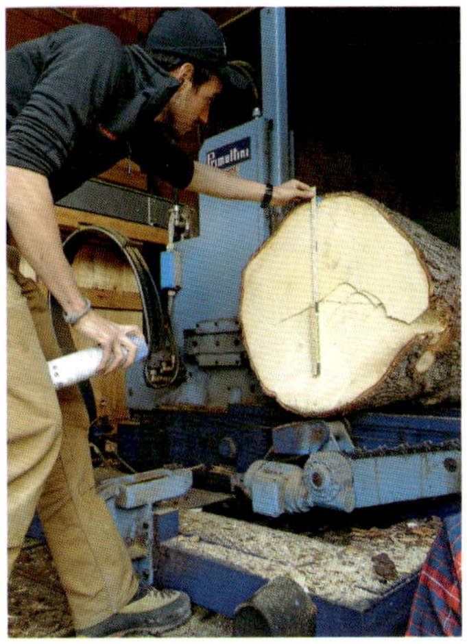

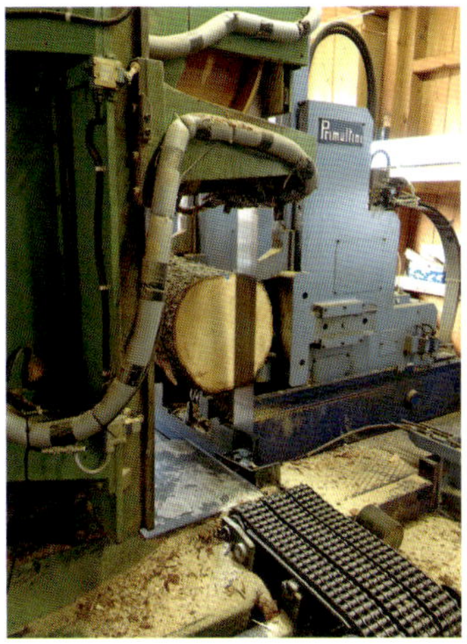

Links: Der Baumstumpf und seine Jahrringe / Left: The tree stump and its annual rings / Auf dieser Seite: Aufschneiden des Stamms in der Sägerei Florinett AG in Bergün, Graubünden / On this page: The lengthwise cutting of the tree trunk at the sawmill Florinett AG in Bergün, Graubünden

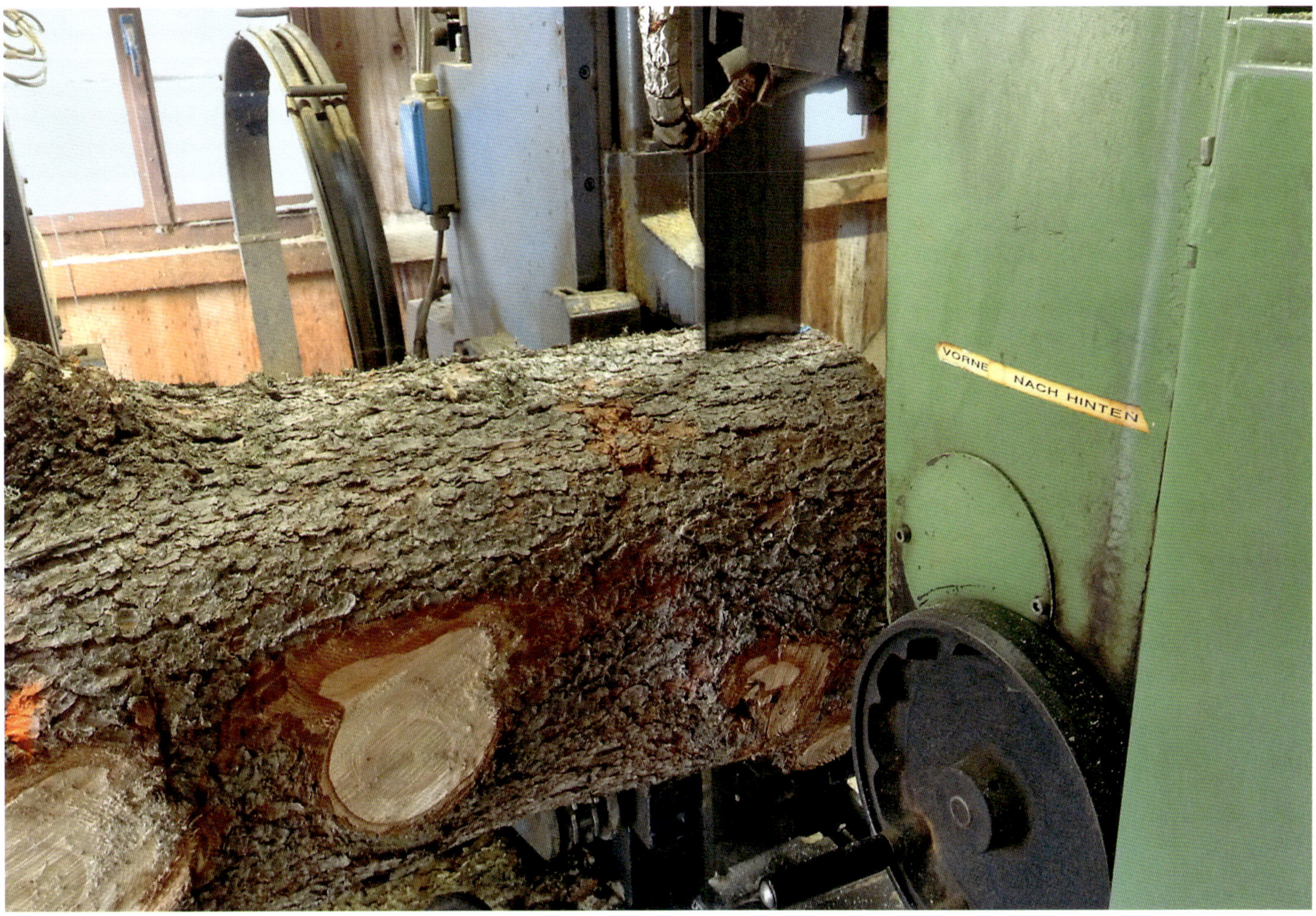

Auf dieser Seite: Detail der von den Jahrringen erzeugten Muster / On this page: Detail of the patterns created by the annual rings / Rechts: Die Platten für die Realisierung der liegenden Reliefs in der Werkstatt des Schreiners Daniel Margreth (hier mit seinem Sohn Linard) und in der Werkstatt der Fonderia Nolana Del Giudice / Right: The boards for the realization of the horizontal reliefs in the workshop of the carpenter Daniel Margreth (here with his son Linard) and in the workshop of the Fonderia Nolana Del Giudice / Nächste Doppelseite / Next double page: Installationsansicht des skulpturalen Ensembles / Installation view of the sculptural ensemble *The Tree of Valbella* für / for *artgèneve / sculptures 2019*, Promenade de la Treille, Genf / Geneva

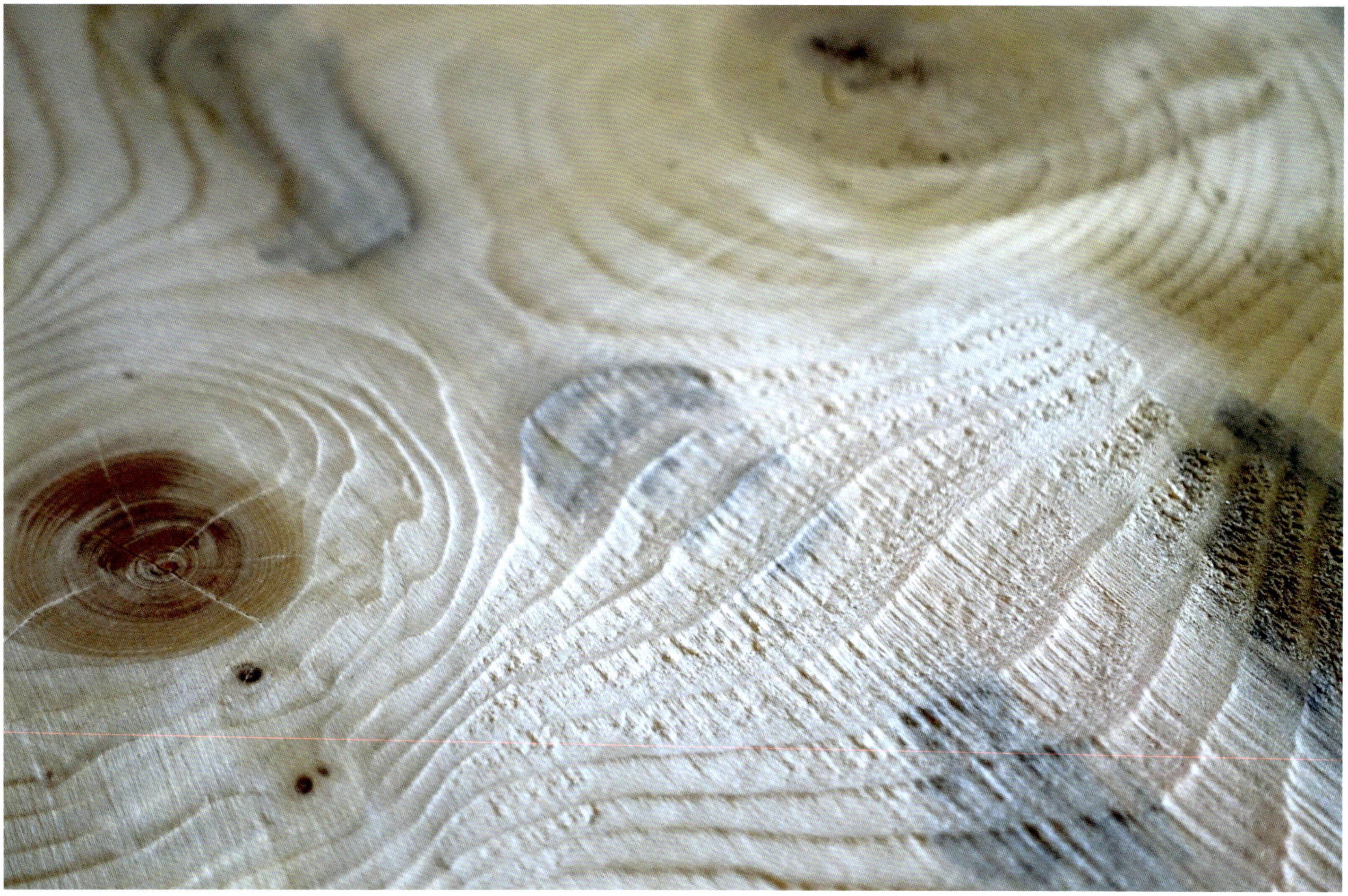

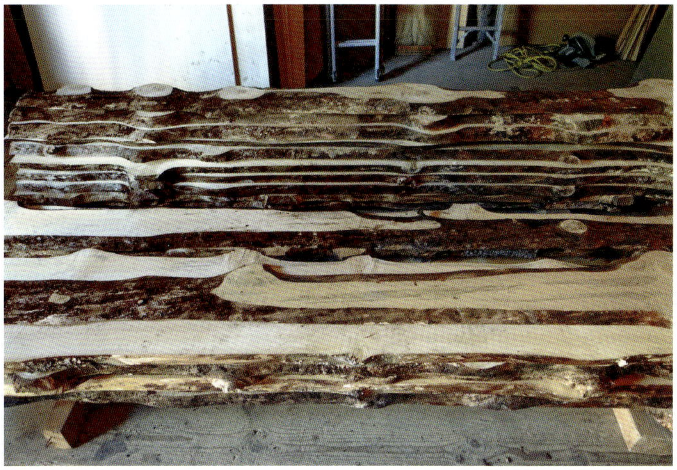

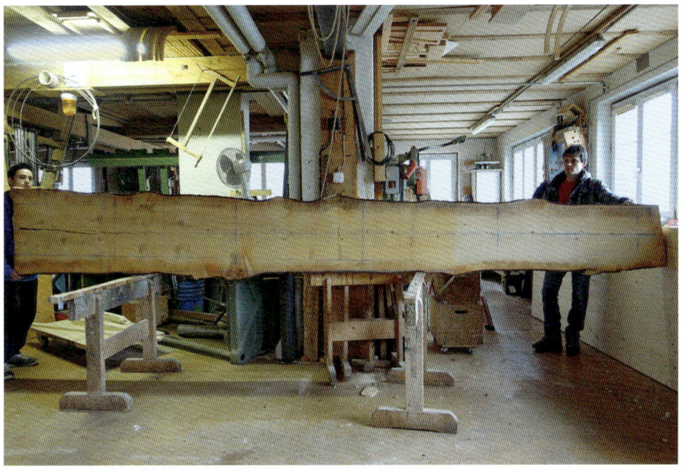

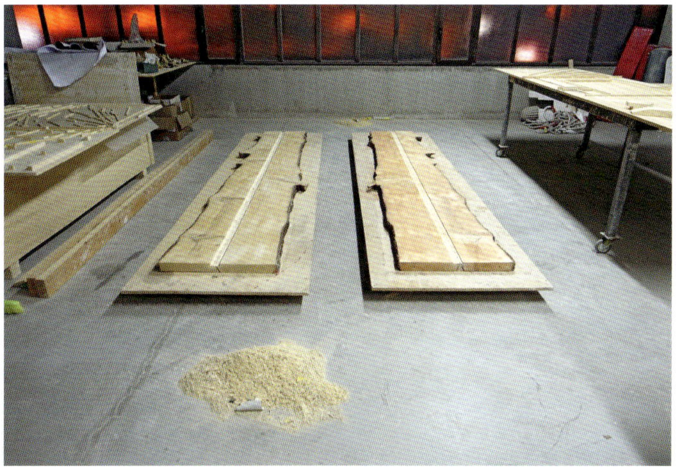

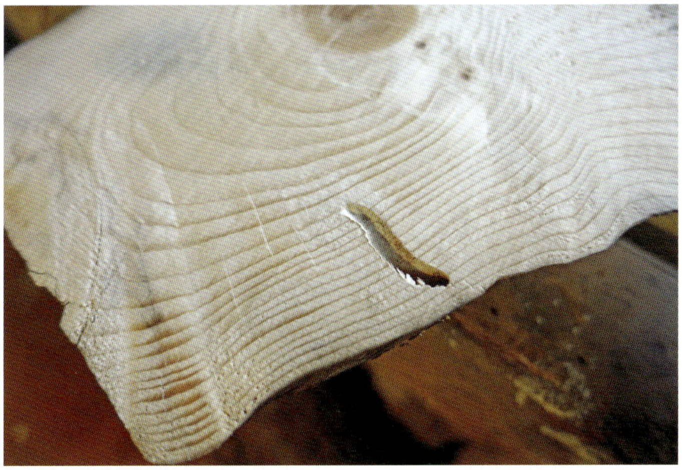

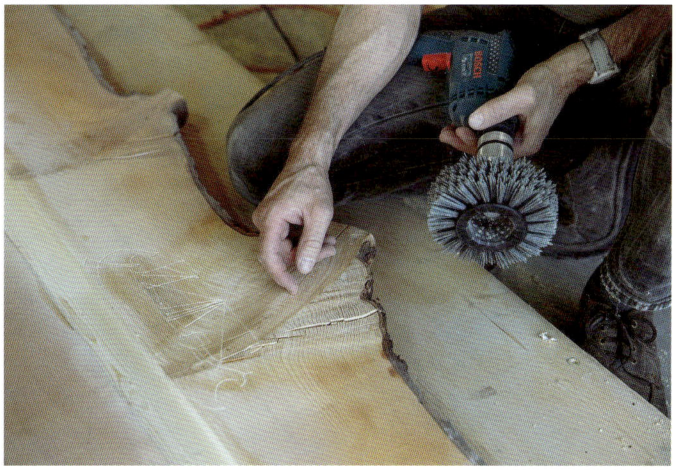

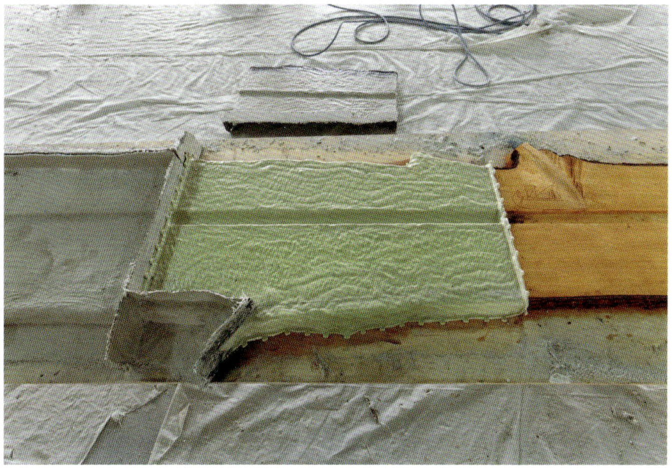

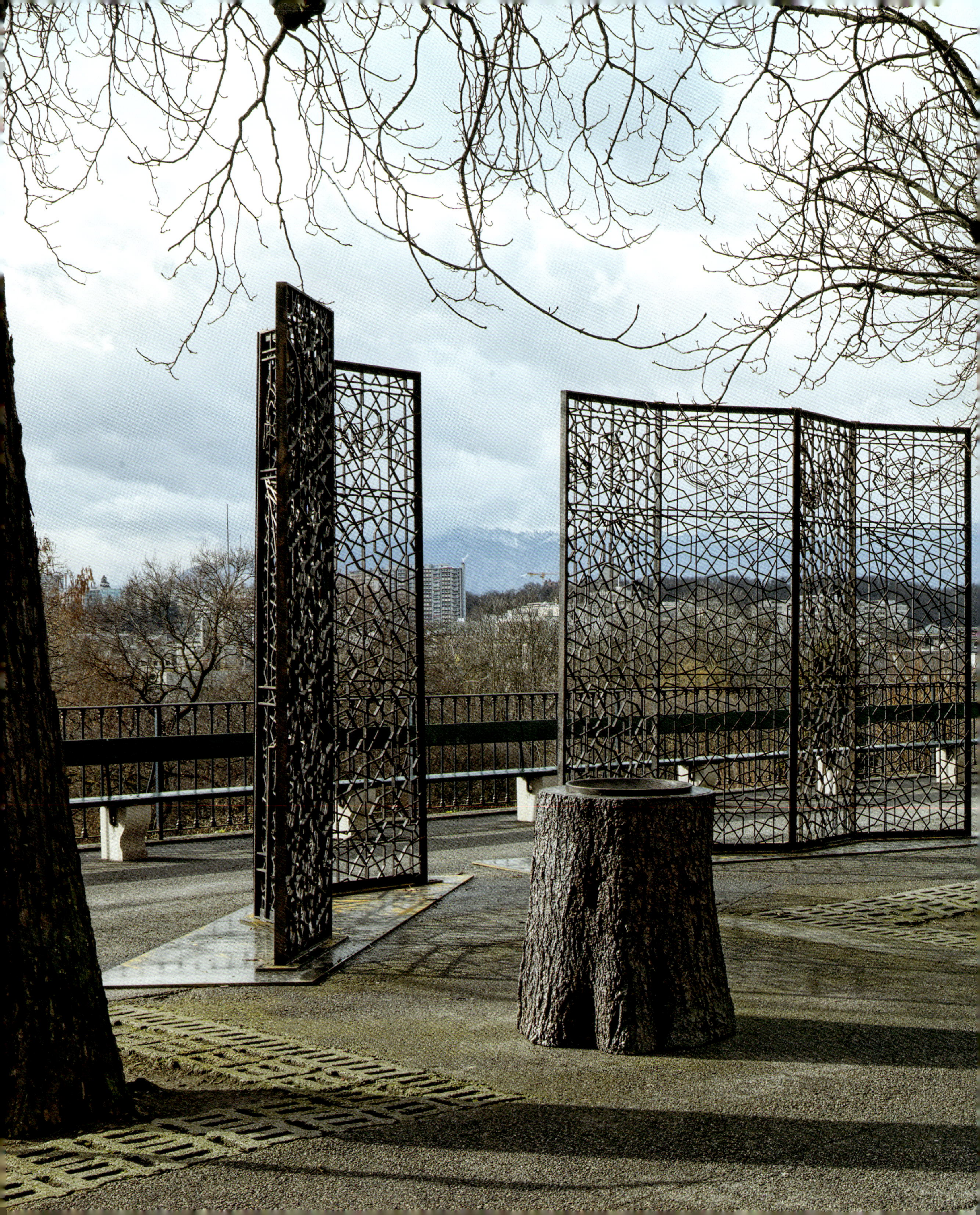

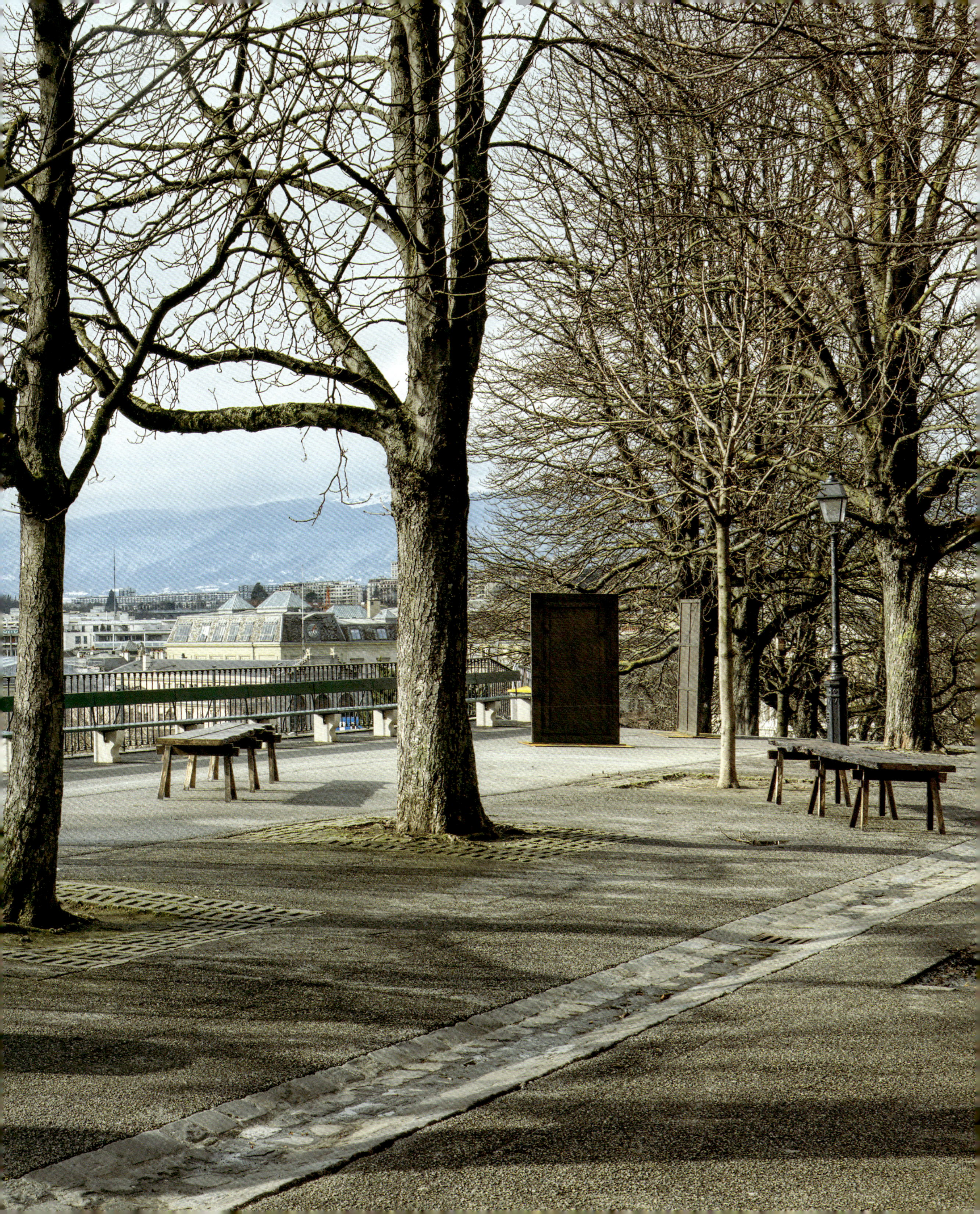

DIE ERZÄHLUNG EINER METAMORPHOSE

LAURA GIUDICI

Glück ist oft Zufall. Thomas Abegg und Mirko Baselgia tauschten sich bereits seit geraumer Zeit über ein Projekt für Abeggs Garten in Valbella aus. Als Baselgia von seinem Auftraggeber darüber informiert wurde, dass ein alter Baum gefällt werden müsse, sah der Künstler das Projekt gleich vor Augen. Die 124 Jahre alte Fichte wurde für ihn zu einer Person, zu einem Individuum mit einem eigenen Leben und einer eigenen Geschichte. Er wollte ihr Tribut zollen und ausgehend von ihr eine allgemeine Reflexion über das Leben anregen. *The Tree of Valbella* ist demnach als Lebensbühne konzipiert, als eine Reise, welche die Themen Leben, Tod und das Leben nach dem Tod miteinander verknüpft. Baselgias Intention ist es, die Biografie des Baums durch seine Gestalt und Materialität zum Ausdruck zu bringen, und eine Verbindung zu unserem eigenen Leben herzustellen.

Da der Wind in Abeggs Garten oft ziemlich stark weht, kam Baselgia die Idee, einen Paravent zu realisieren und sich hierzu auf historische Referenzen zu beziehen, die mit der Wahrnehmung des Windes in Zusammenhang stehen. So entdeckte er den Turm der Winde in Athen, einen etwa 14 m hohen achteckigen Marmorbau, der um 100-50 v. Chr. errichtet wurde und noch immer an seinem ursprünglichen Standort steht. Seine Form und Dekoration dienten als eine der Inspirationsquellen für Baselgias skulpturales Ensemble.[1] Der Turm der Winde, der dem Architekten und Astronomen Andronikos von Kyrrhos zugeschrieben wird, gilt als die weltweit erste Wetterstation. Darüber hinaus nutzten die Händler den Turm – sogar bei Dunkelheit – um sich über die Uhrzeit zu informieren. Seine genaue Funktion bleibt aber weiterhin im Unklaren. Der Turm befindet sich am Rand der römischen Agora – dem Marktplatz – da es für die Händler von großer Bedeutung war, das Wetter abzulesen und die Uhrzeit ihrer Warenlieferungen mitzuteilen. Alle acht Gebäudeseiten sind daher auf einen Punkt des Kompasses ausgerichtet und mit einem Fries mit Relieffiguren versehen, die die Anemoi – die Götter des Windes in der griechischen Mythologie – darstellen. Unter ihnen verlaufen auf den der Sonne zugewandten Seiten die Linien der Sonnenuhr. Ein großes Rätsel gibt es auf, wie die Zeit nachts gemessen wurde. Nach gängiger Meinung versorgte ein hydraulischer Mechanismus eine Wasseruhr mit Wasser aus dem Fluss, der den Akropolis-Hügel durchzieht.

In Baselgias Arbeit wurde aus der Wasseruhr eine Quelle, die den unteren, und ältesten, Abschnitt des Baums darstellt. Form und Rinde sind unbearbeitet, während aus dem oberen Teil ein kleines Wasserbecken gewonnen wurde. Dieser Teil des Baums verkörpert zusammen mit der Vorstellung von Quelle den Auftakt, und markiert den Ausgangspunkt für unsere imaginäre Reise durch das Leben. Wenn man durch das Wasser im Becken blickt, sieht man die Jahresringe des Baums. Sie legen sein Alter offen, und auch die Ereignisse, die sich in Valbella während seines Lebens zugetragen haben. Jedes Jahr fügt dem Baum im Laufe seines Wachstums einen Ring im Stamm hinzu; während des Frühlings und Frühsommers, wenn er schneller wächst, einen hellen Ring und einen dünneren, dunklen Ring im Herbst und Winter, wenn sich sein Wachstum verlangsamt. Die Dendrochronologie, die wissenschaftliche Baumringdatierung, kann das Alter des Baums bestimmen. Sie zeigt auch auf, wie er auf das sich ständig wandelnde Klima reagiert.

Während der Jahre, in denen Temperatur und Regenfall ideal für eine Baumspezies sind, wachsen die Bäume schneller und ihre Ringe sind breiter. In den Jahren, in denen es zu warm, zu kalt, zu nass

TALE OF A METAMORPHOSIS

Good things often happen almost by chance. Thomas Abegg and Mirko Baselgia had already been communicating for a while on a project for his garden in Valbella, when the commissioner informed him that an old tree had to be cut down. It suddenly became clear for the artist what he wanted to do. He saw the 124 year old spruce tree as a person, an individual with its own life and story, and he wanted to pay homage to it, as well as using it as a starting point to reflect on life in general. *The Tree of Valbella* is therefore projected as a journey where the themes of life, death, and afterlife overlap. For Baselgia the key point is to show the tree's biography through its structure, and material essence, and to suggest a connection between the tree's life and our own lives.

As there is often a strong wind in the garden, the artist's first inspiration was to create a screen, so he searched for historical references related to the perception of the wind, which is how he discovered the Tower of the Winds in Athens, an octagonal marble building nearly 14 metres high erected between 100-50 BC and still standing: its structure and decorations were part of the inspiration for the sculptural ensemble[1]. Credited to the architect and astronomer Andronikos of Cyrrhus, the Tower of the Winds is said to be the world's first weather station, and to have been used by merchants to tell the time – even in darkness –, but its exact function remains mysterious. The tower is located in the Roman Agora – market place – as it was of great value for the merchants to read the weather and also calculate the time that their goods could be expected. Each of the building's eight sides faces a point of the compass, and is decorated with a frieze of relief figures representing the Anemoi – the wind gods of Greek mythology –. Beneath them, on the sides facing the sun, are the lines of a sundial. The greatest mystery is how time was measured at night. According to the most prominent theory, a hydraulic mechanism powered a water clock device with water flowing from a stream on the Acropolis hill.

In Baselgia's work the water clock was transformed into a spring reproducing the lower - and oldest - part of the tree. The shape and bark are left rough, and only the upper part is carved to create a little basin for water. Both this part of tree, and the idea of spring symbolize the beginning, the starting point, and mark the entrance to our imaginary journey through life. Looking through the water in the basin, we can see the tree's annual growth rings, which reveal its age, as well as the events that have occurred in Valbella during its lifetime. Each year, as a tree grows, it adds a light ring of new growth to its trunk during the spring and early summer, when growing quickly, and a thinner, dark ring in the fall, when growth is slower. Because climate affects the amount a tree grows and the thickness of the rings, dendrochronology – the science of tree rings – allow us to learn about its age, as well as the climate during its lifespan. During years when the temperature and rainfall are ideal for a species of tree, the trees grow faster and their rings are wider. Other years, when it is too hot or cold or too wet or dry, the trees grow more slowly and their rings are closer together. Furthermore insect plagues and disease epidemics, injuries, thinning, and air pollution also leave their mark on the tree growth rings. The dendrochronological report (see Appendix) points out that our spruce tree had a harmonious growth.

The artist has always been fascinated by the idea that growth rings are tangible signs witnessing the passage of time, and environmental conditions characterizing that time. Tree rings are like wrinkles on the human body, especially the face, and it's clearly

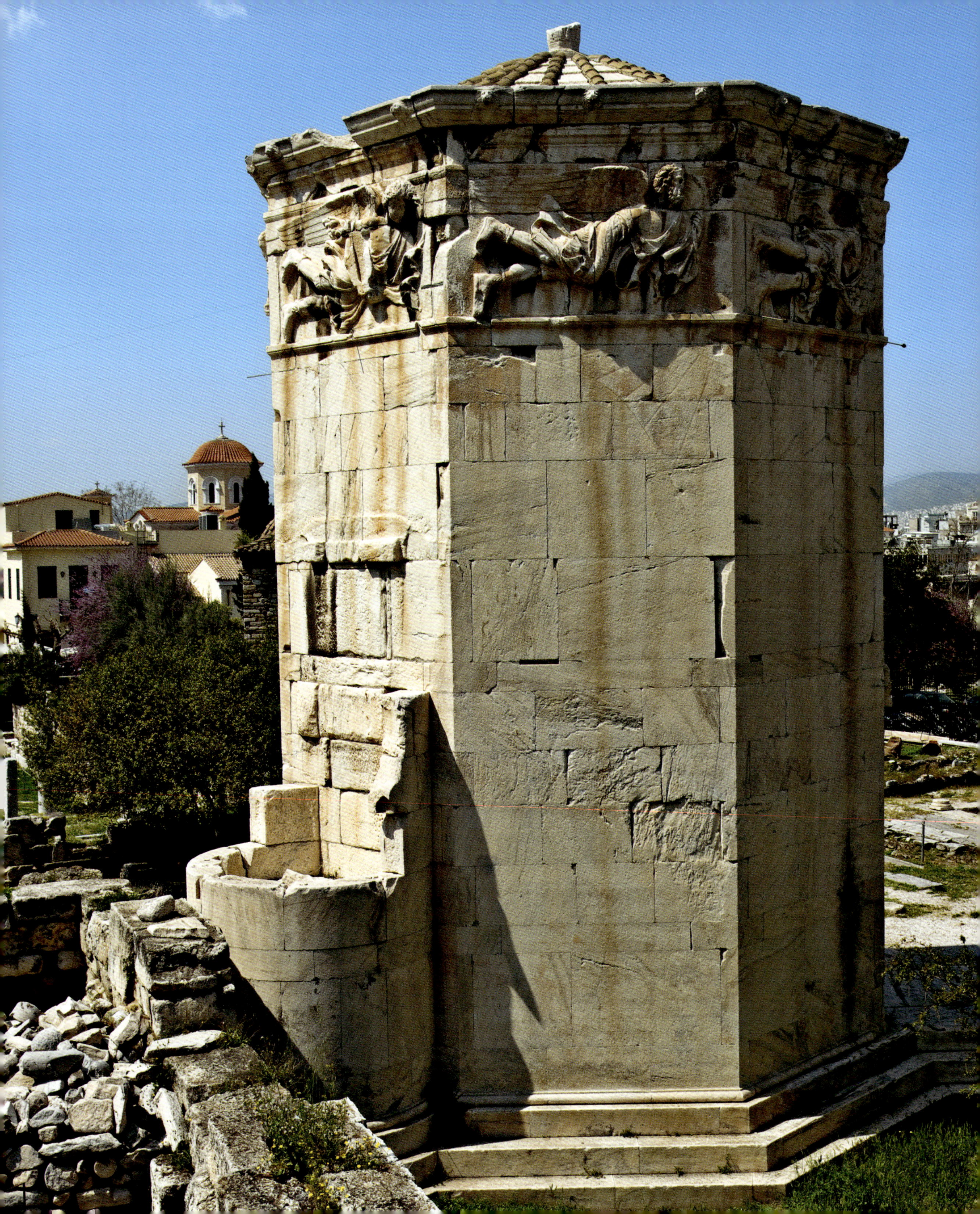

no coincidence if the water in the basin carved in the cross section of the tree reflects our own face when we look at it. Our features dissolve and merge with the tree rings. Our own life mingles with the tree life.

As to the octagonal shell of the Tower of the Winds, the artist reinterpreted it as a screen with eight panels that create an architectural structure which generates an opening movement with respect to the closed form of the Tower of the Winds allowing a sort of explosion of energy. On one side, the panels are decorated with simplified reliefs of the original figures representing the different winds, and of the sundials drawn on the sides facing the sun. The panels of the screen look like large drawings that evolve three-dimensionally in space. If in ancient times knowing the different winds was a precious help for sailing, this elaboration of the tower represents a metaphor of how to sail through life. It becomes a compass, which raises questions such as: where do we go as people? How do we choose the direction we take in our lives?

The other side of thc screen depicts a geometric pattern coming from Gondab-e Qabud, a tomb tower constructed in 1196-97 in Maragha in western Iran. Gondab-e Qabud is decagonal in plan, rising as a ten-sided prism with a round engaged column at each exterior angle. Except for the entry façade, each rectangular face encloses a rectangular niche comprising a panel articulated in an angular polygonal net outlined by ribs in high relief and a curvilinear interlacing in lower relief. This broad band of ornament wraps around nine faces of the building, including all ten engaged columns. The pattern used for the screen comes from the ornamental pattern that surrounds the lower exterior reaches of the building, which has achieved widespread attention because of the mathematical implications of its visual complexity that resides in combinations of five-fold and ten-fold symmetries. As Carol Bier has pointed out[2], these ornamental patterns follow a long line of experimentation with geometric expressions that characterize many pre-Mongol buildings and represent the efforts of local endeavours that engaged both mathematics and the craft of building. In fact, within the development of pre-Mongol brick, glazed ceramic, and stucco decoration, there seems to be a close approximation of patterns that offer visual solutions to geometric problems relating to numbers, shape, and the nature of space among new advances in algebra and geometry. Bier links for the first time the unique combination of architectural form and patterns of Gondab-e Qabud to the local context of an actively engaged mathematical community seeking to explore visual aspects of theoretical understanding with practical applications. She discovers that the practical articulation of problems set forth in texts

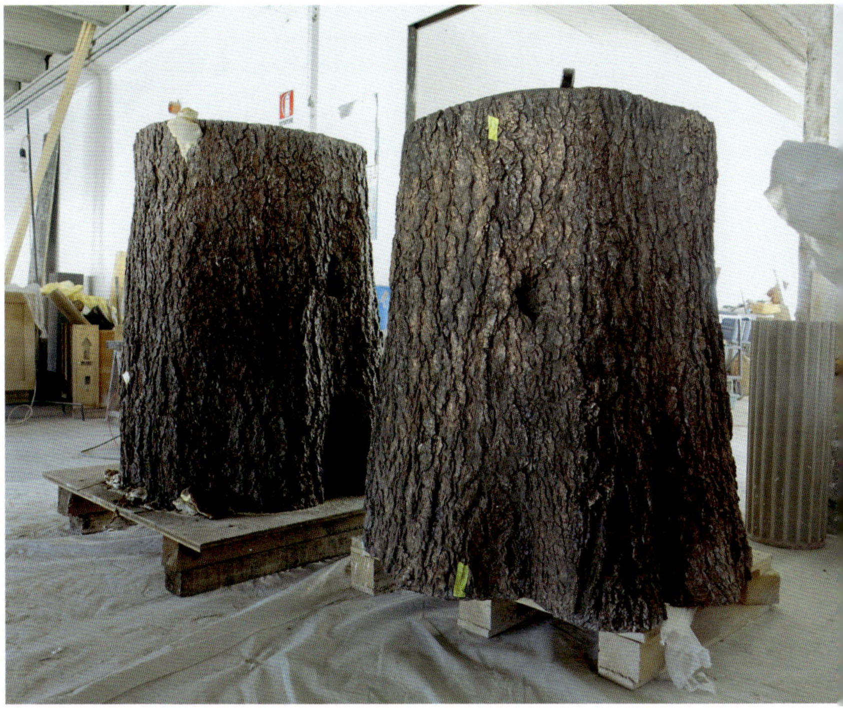

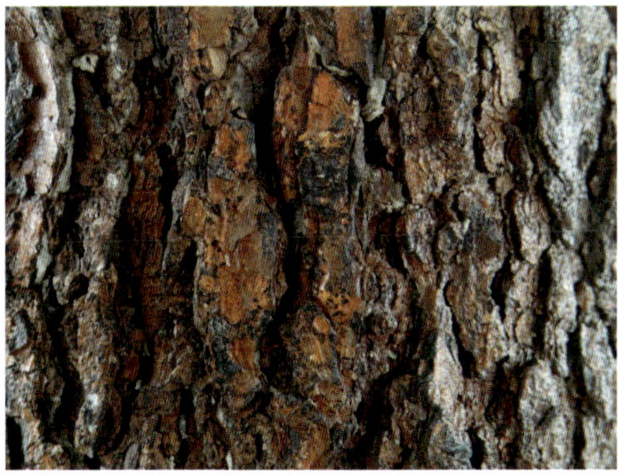

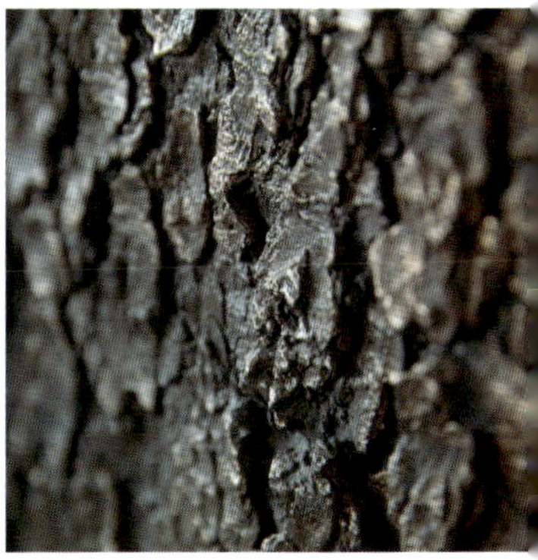

Links: Der Turm der Winde in Athen (um 100-50 v. Chr.) / Left: The Tower of the Winds in Athens (about 100-50 B.C.) / Auf dieser Seite: Baumstrump aus Holz und Bronze nebeneinander / Tree stump in wood and bronze next to each other

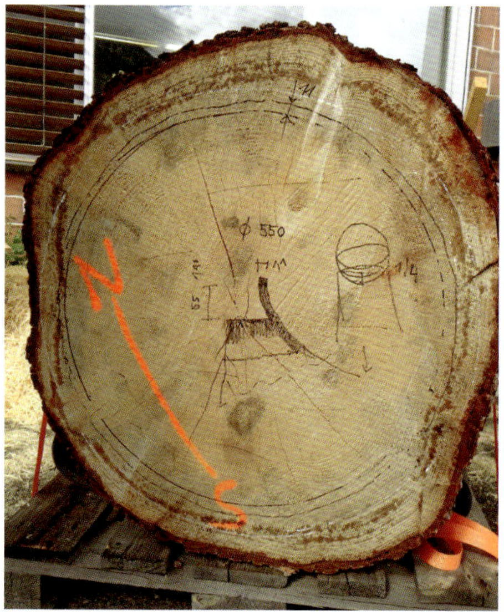

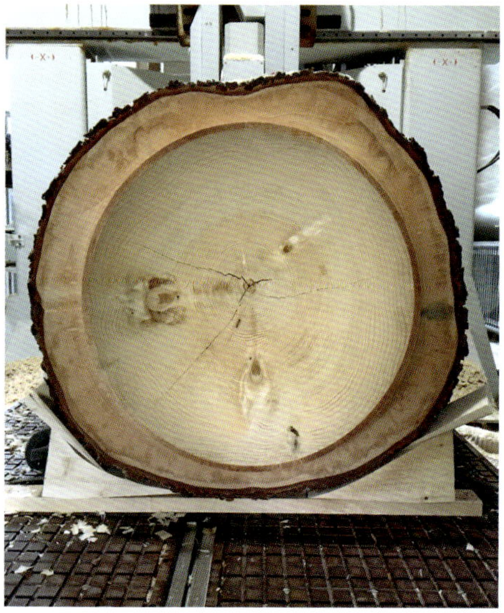

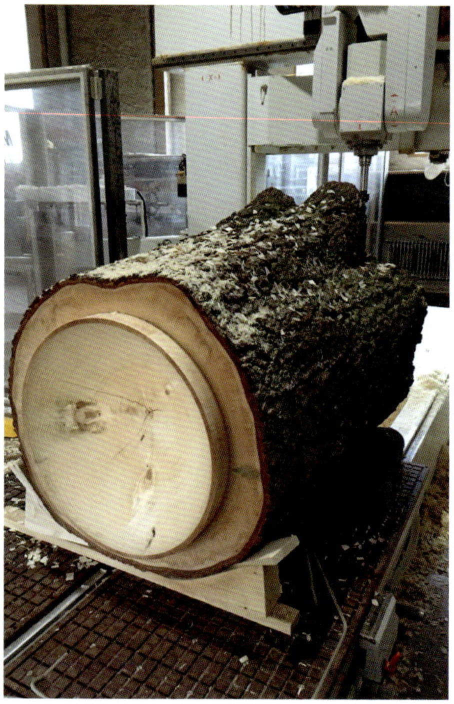

Vorbereitung des Holzmodells für die Quelle / Preparation of the wooden model for the spring

oder zu trocken ist, wachsen die Bäume langsamer, und die Ringe sind dünner. Zudem beeinflussen Insektenplagen und Epidemien, Verletzungen, Durchforstung und Luftverschmutzung das Wachstum der Baumringe. Der dendrochronologische Bericht (s. Anhang) lässt auf ein harmonisches Wachstum unserer Fichte schliessen.

Baselgia fasziniert seit jeher die Vorstellung, dass die Wachstumsringe sichtbare Zeichen sind, die das Verstreichen der Zeit bezeugen, sowie die Umweltbedingungen, die diese Periode prägen. Die Baumringe ähneln den Falten, die sich in den menschlichen Körper einschreiben, insbesondere in das Gesicht, und es ist kein Zufall, dass das Wasser in dem in den Baumquerschnitt eingekerbten Becken unser Gesicht widerspiegelt. Unsere Gesichtszüge beginnen sich aufzulösen und mit den Baumringen zu verschmelzen. Unser Leben verknüpft sich mit dem des Baums.

Der achteckige Turm der Winde wird bei Balsegia zu einem Paravent, der sich aus acht Flügeln zusammensetzt. Diese bilden eine architektonische Struktur, die sich im Gegensatz zur geschlossenen Form des Turms der Winde öffnet und Energie freisetzt. Die Figuren der Winde und die Sonnenuhr vom Athener Turm sind subtil in das Ornament verwebt. Die einzelnen Teile des Paravents ähneln großformatigen Zeichnungen, die eine dreidimensionale Wirkung entfalten. Wenn es früher zum Segeln sehr hilfreich war, die verschiedenen Winde zu kennen, wird der Turm in Baselgias Arbeit zur Metapher für unsere Segelfahrt durch das Leben. Der Paravent gleicht folglich einem Kompass, der Fragen aufwirft: Wohin gehen wir als Menschen? Wie wählen wir die Richtung, die wir in unserem Leben einschlagen?

Das geometrische Muster geht auf das Mausoleum Gonbad-e Qabud zurück, einen Grabturm, der zwischen 1196-1197 in Maragha im westlichen Iran errichtet wurde. Der Zehneck des Gonbad-e Qabud wird an jeder Ecke mit einer runden Blendsäule geziert. Die Felder zwischen den Säulen und die Säulen werden von einem ornamentalen Geflecht überzogen. Dieses umfasst

of contemporary mathematics is evident in this and other monuments of the region. But how should we interpret these mathematically elaborated geometric patterns? In this respect, Bier remarks that André Grabar correctly noted that geometry in the arts is expressive rather than representational and that this is an essential distinction to understanding the significance of pattern in Arab art. In this respect, some chapters of Hans Belting's *Florence and Baghdad: Renaissance Art and Arab Science*[3] have helped Baselgia to a deeper insight into the meaning of geometric ornamentations in Arab art and architecture. Here the German art historian points out that Eastern and Western art expressions result from distinctive ways of viewing the world and, using the metaphor of the mutual gaze, he narrates the historical encounter between science and art, between Arab Baghdad and Renaissance Florence. During the Middle Ages, Arabian mathematics gave rise to a theory of perspective that, later in the West, was transformed into art when European painters adopted the human gaze as their focal point during the Renaissance. Fascinated by this idea of encounter, or, in Belting's words, "exchange of glances", Baselgia decided to merge into the screen figurative elements of the Greek Tower of the Winds with a geometric pattern coming from the Iranian Gondab-e Qabud. All related to some scientific knowledge, but these visual elements are nonetheless the result of two distinct concepts of image. In Arab culture the

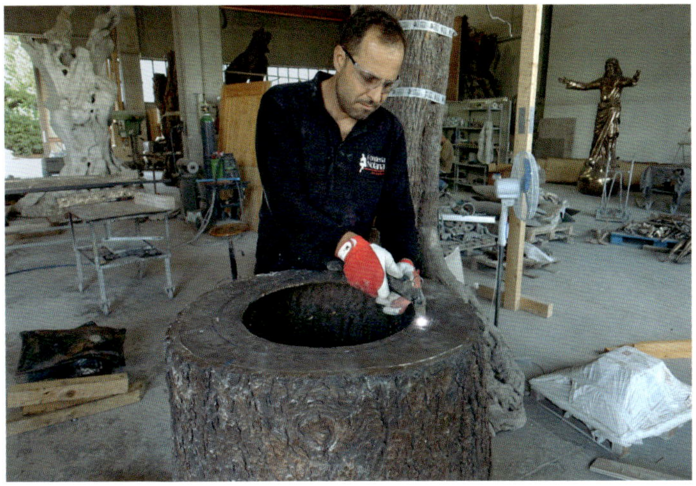

image is conceived as something purely mental, it is not representational like in Western antiquity, but expressive. The mathematically elaborated geometric patterns of Gondab-e Qabud are therefore the expression of cosmic laws, ornaments with semantic significance, and not the mere decorations of Greek antiquity. Arab geometric patterns have a spiritual, metaphysical meaning and their abstract quality is the expression of something bigger. Combining Eastern and Western visual elements, the screen becomes a physical metaphor of the enrichment produced by a trans-cultural encounter.

The journey continues with two vertical sections of the tree, the horizontal reliefs that are laid on trestles creating a sort of bench. In the

Bronzegussausführung der Quelle / Finishing of the bronze casting of the spring

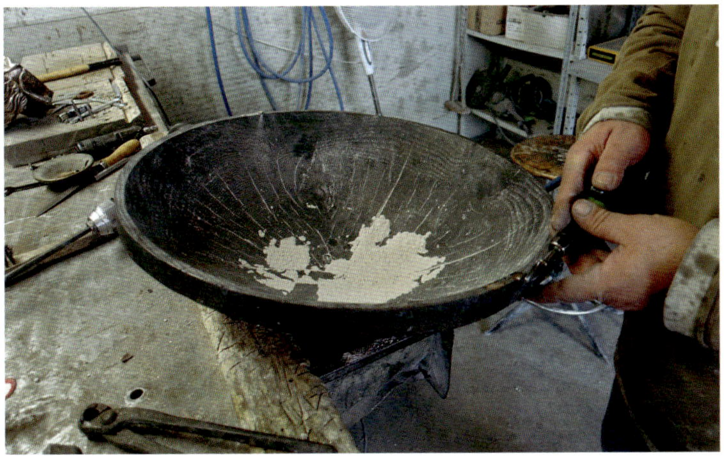

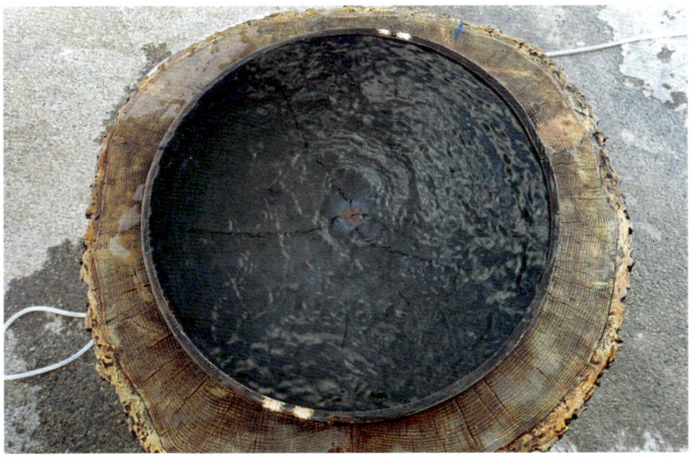

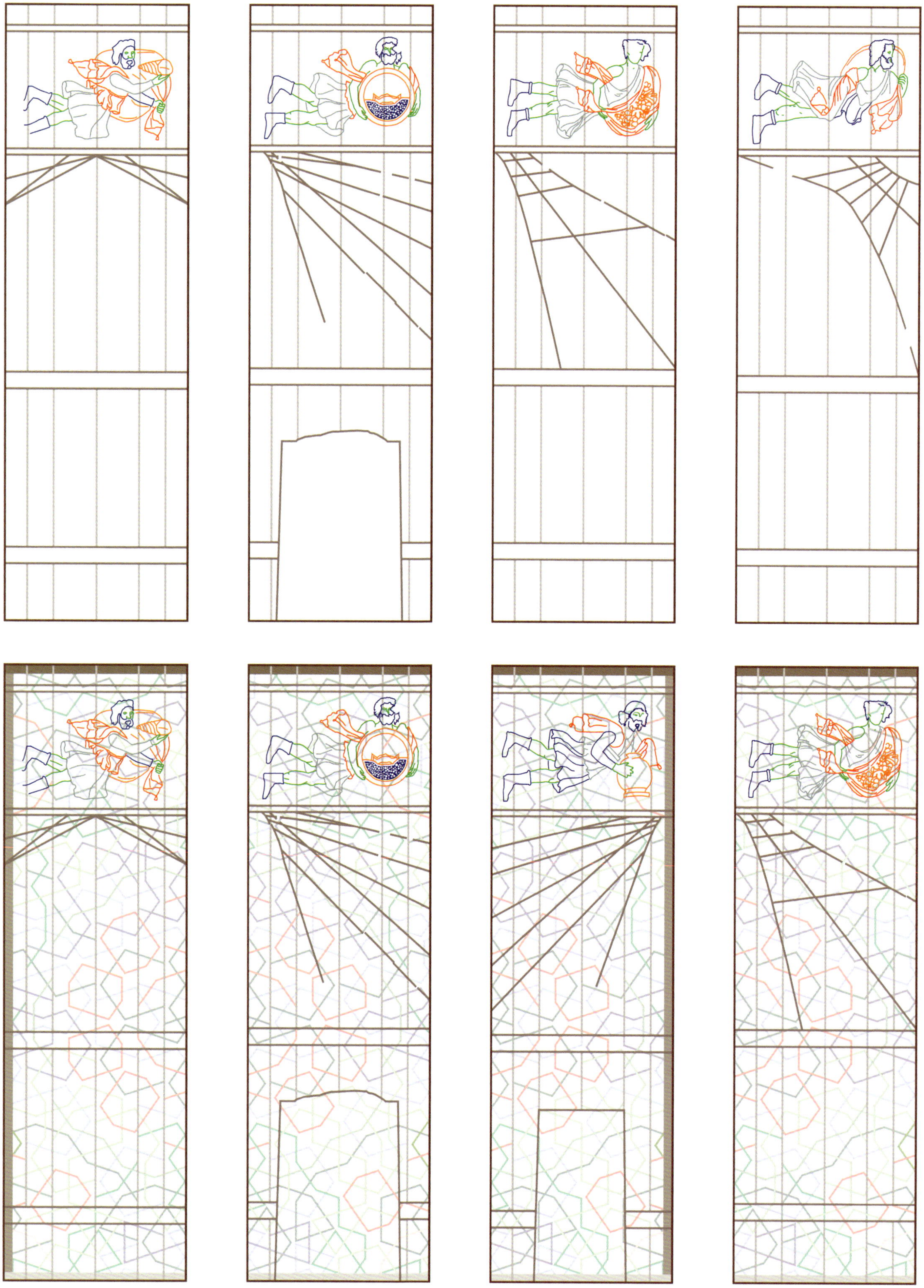

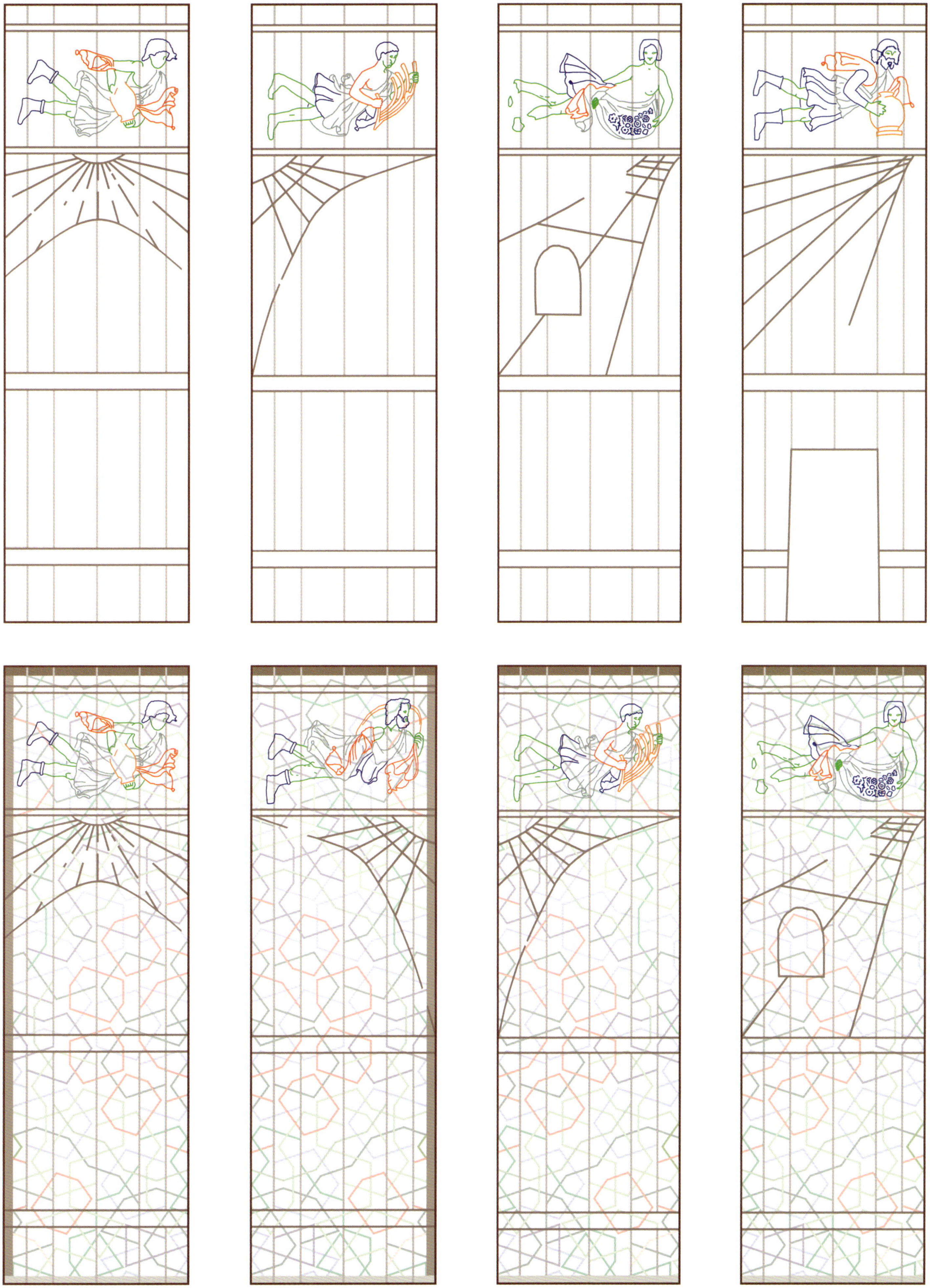

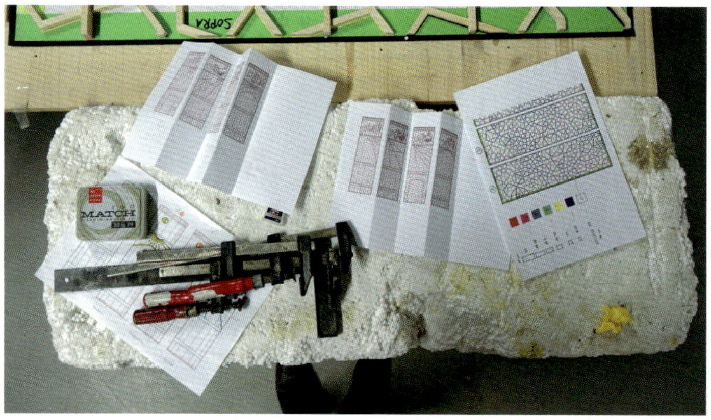

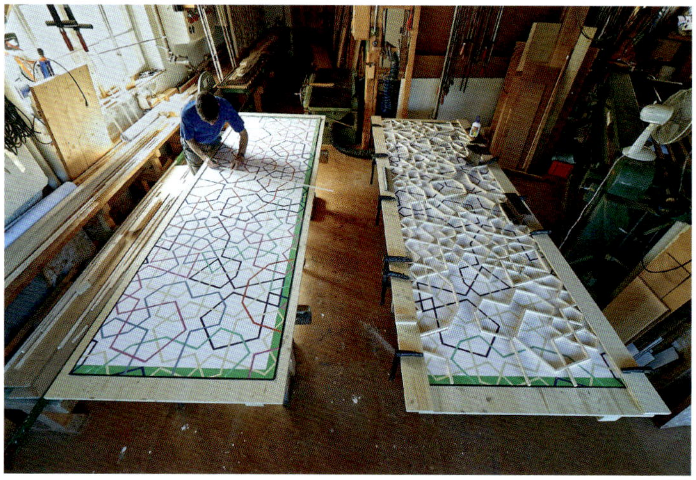

Vorherige Doppelseite: Digitale Modelle für die Realisierung des Paravents / Auf dieser Seite: Vorbereitung der Holzmodelle für die Realisierung des Paravents in Daniel Margreths Werkstatt / Previous double page: Digital models for the realization of the screen / On this page: Preparation of the wooden models for the screen in Daniel Margreth's workshop

den mittleren äusseren Bereich des Mausoleums. Das komplexe Ornament mit seinen mathematischen Implikationen hat grosse Aufmerksamkeit erlangt. Nach Carol Bier[2] folgen diese ornamentalen Muster einer langen Auseinandersetzung mit der geometrischen Ausdruckssprache, die zahlreiche prämongolische Bauten kennzeichnet. Mathematik und Baukunst greifen ineinander. Die Gestaltung des prämongolischen Ziegelsteins, der glasierten Keramik und der Stuckdekoration bringen visuelle Lösungen hervor für geometrische Probleme in Bezug auf Zahlen, Formen und die Beschaffenheit des Raums. Dies geschieht vor dem Hintergrund neuer Erkenntnisse in Algebra und Geometrie. Carol Bier verbindet erstmals die einzigartige Kombination von architektonischen Formen und Mustern des Gonbad-e Qabud mit einer lokalen ambitionierten Mathematiker-Gemeinschaft. Diese versuchte ihre theoretischen Erkenntnisse praktisch anzuwenden.

Carol Bier sah, dass die praktische Anwendung der Forschungen der zeitgenössischen Mathematiker auch an andere Bauten in dieser Region auszeichnet. Wie aber können wir diese mathematisch geprägten, geometrischen Muster deuten? Bereits André Grabar erkannte, dass geometrische Formen in der Kunst eher expressiv als repräsentativ wirken. Diese Unterscheidung ist entscheidend, um die Bedeutung von Ornamenten in der islamischen Kunst zu verstehen. Baselgia zog Hans Beltings Buch *Florenz und Bagdad: eine westöstliche Geschichte des Blicks*[3] bei, um sich einen umfassenden Einblick in die Bedeutung geometrischer Muster in der islamischen Kunst und Architektur zu verschaffen. Der deutsche Kunsthistoriker betont die unterschiedliche Sicht auf die Welt in den östlichen und westlichen Ausdrucksformen. Mithilfe der Metapher des wechselseitigen Blicks analysiert er das Aufeinandertreffen von Wissenschaft und Kunst zwischen den arabischen Kultur Bagdads und der italienischen Renaissance in Florenz. Die arabischen Mathematiker entwickelten während des Mittelalters eine Theorie der Perspektive. Erst als die Maler der italienischen Renaissance den Menschen und den menschlichen Blick ins Zentrum rückten, entwickelte sich die Perspektive im Bild. Baselgia faszinierte die Vorstellung eines Aufeinandertreffens, oder, mit Beltings Worten, eines "Blickwechsels". Er beschloss, an seinem Paravent figurative Elemente des griechischen Turms der Winde mit dem auf den iranischen Gonbad-e Qabud zurückgehenden geometrischen Muster zu verweben. Diese visuellen Elemente, die sich auf wissenschaftliches Wissen beziehen, sind das Ergebnis zweier unterschiedlicher Bildkonzepte. Das Bild in der islamischen Kultur ist etwas rein Mentales, Abstraktes, es ist expressiv; es hat nicht den bildlichen Charakter wie im westlichen Altertum und in der Renaissance. Die auf der Mathematik basierenden geometrischen Muster des Gonbad-e Qabud widerspiegeln kosmische Gesetze, die Ornamente sagen etwas aus, sie sind nicht reine

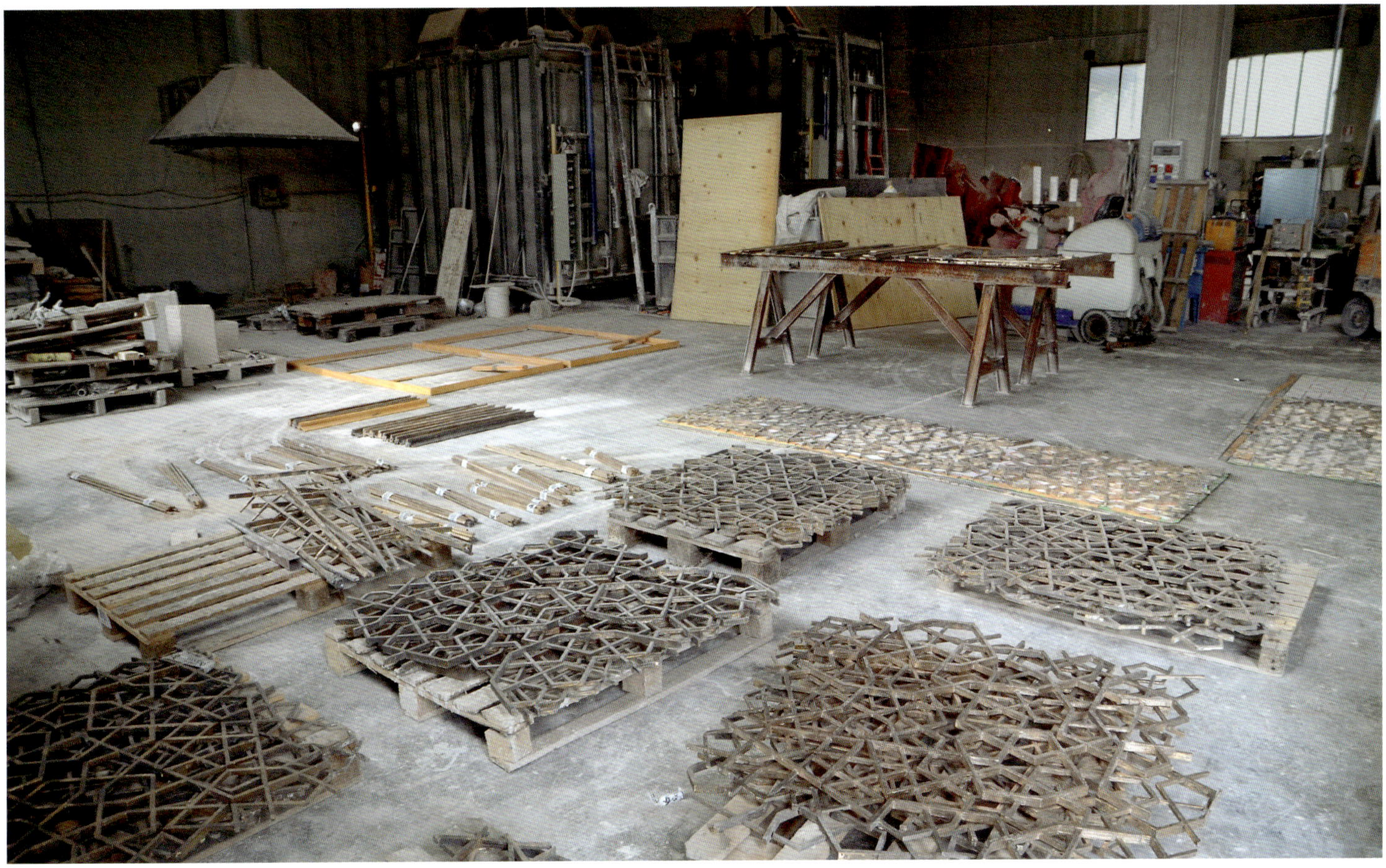

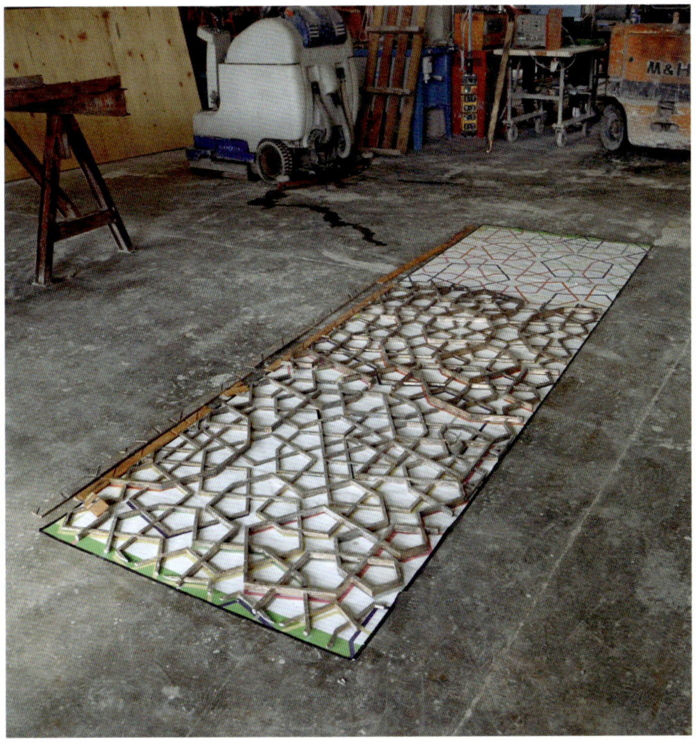

Verfahren zum Zusammenbau der verschiedenen Bronzeelemente des Paravents in der Fonderia Nolana Del Giudice / Assembling process of the various bronze elements of the screen at the Fonderia Nolana Del Giudice

middle of the section, the heart of the tree where the sap flows, a canal is carved. On this imaginary river sail boats that are carved on the tree's surface. The boats' shapes are inspired by graffiti drawn inside the Tower of the Winds, and they are metaphors of the experience of life. On this subject, it is also important to stress the impact that the visit to the sub-temple Daisen-in in Kyoto, and its dry landscape garden in 2017 had on Mirko Baselgia, and his work. This garden is divided into five small gravel and rock gardens that are all connected, and represent a metaphorical journey through life according to Zen Buddhism. In one of the gardens there is "a long boat rock" - Nagafune-ishi - sailing down the river of life, represented by the carefully raked gravel patterns. This stylized boat may symbolize how experience is accumulated during

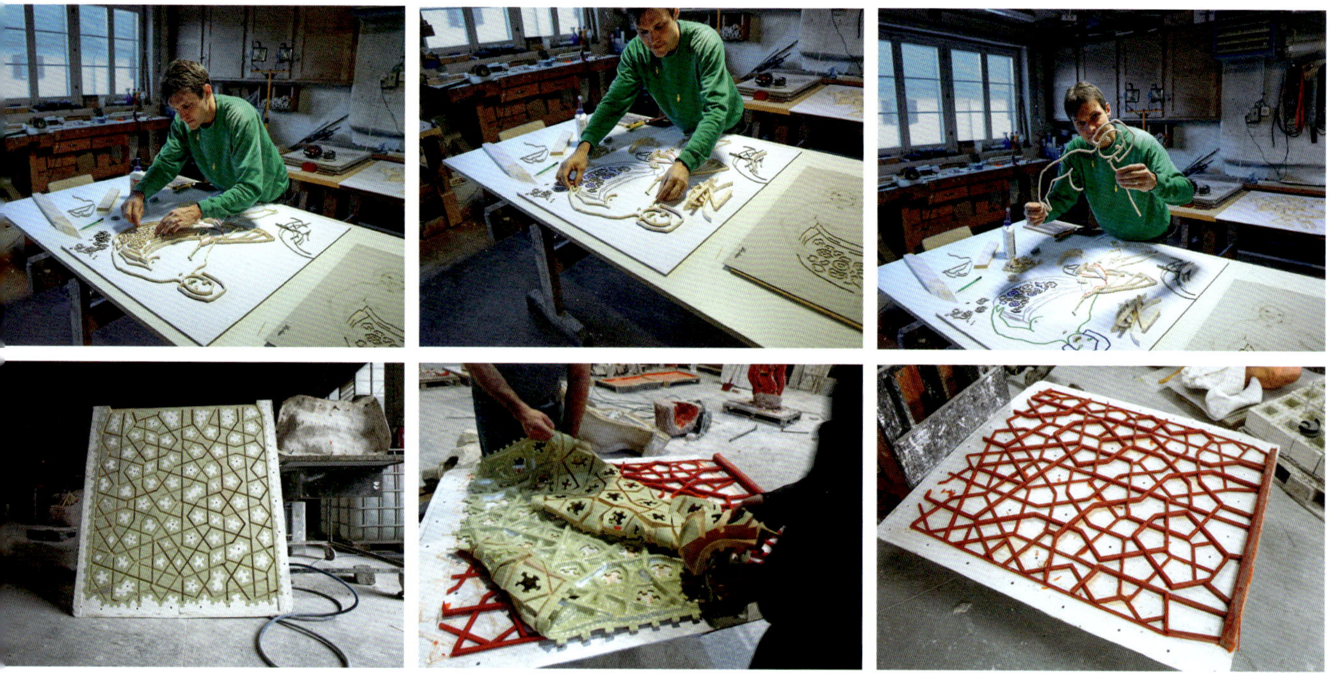

Vorbereitung der Holz- und Wachsmodelle für den Paravent in Daniel Margreths Werkstatt und in der Fonderia Nolana Del Giudice / Preparation of the wooden and wax models for the screen in Daniel Margreth's workshop and at the Fonderia Nolana Del Giudice

Dekoration. Arabische geometrischen Muster sind auf einer spirituellen, metaphysischen Bedeutungsebene fassbar, ihre abstrakte Dimension ist der Ausdruck von etwas Höherem. Der Paravent, der östliche und westliche visuelle Elemente miteinander verknüpft, wird zur physischen Metapher für das bereichernde transkulturelle Aufeinandertreffen von Ost und West. Unsere Reise setzt sich mit den beiden vertikalen Baumteilen fort, den liegenden Reliefs, die auf einem Untersatz angeordnet eine Art Bank bilden. In ihrer Mitte ist dort, wo sich das Bauminnere befindet und der Pflanzensaft fließt, ein Kanal in das Holz eingekerbt. Diesen imaginären Fluss befahren Segelschiffe, die in die Baumoberfläche eingeschnitzt sind. Ihre Form ist von den Graffiti am Turm der Winde inspiriert. Die Boote stehen für die Lebenserfahrung. In diesem Zusammenhang steht auch die große Wirkung des Untertempels Daisen-in in Kyoto mit seinem Steingarten. Im Jahr 2017 besuchte Baselgia den Tempel, was seine Arbeit prägte. Der Garten ist in fünf kleine Kies- und Felsengärten unterteilt, die miteinander verbunden sind und eine metaphorische Reise durch das Leben gemäß dem Zen-Buddhismus wiedergeben. In einem der Gärten befindet sich „ein langer Boot-Felsen“ – Nagafune-ishi –, der den Fluss des Lebens hinabsegelt, repräsentiert durch das sorgfältig ausgearbeitete Kiesmuster. Das stilisierte Boot symbolisiert, wie sich die Erfahrung im Lauf eines Lebens ansammelt. Das Boot und das Muster im Kies dienten als Vorbild für die liegenden Reliefs. Die langen Linien, die entlang der Tafel von den Jahresringen gebildet werden, geben auf natürliche Weise die parallelen Kieslinien wieder, die in dem Zen-Garten für den Fluss stehen. Baselgia ist beeindruckt von der symbolischen

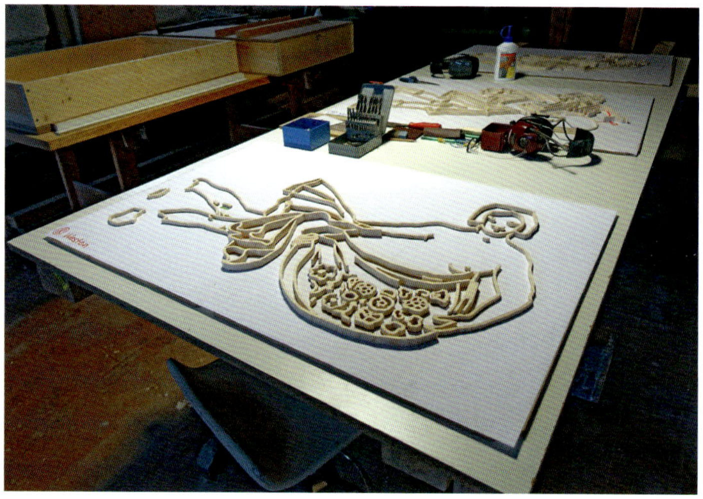

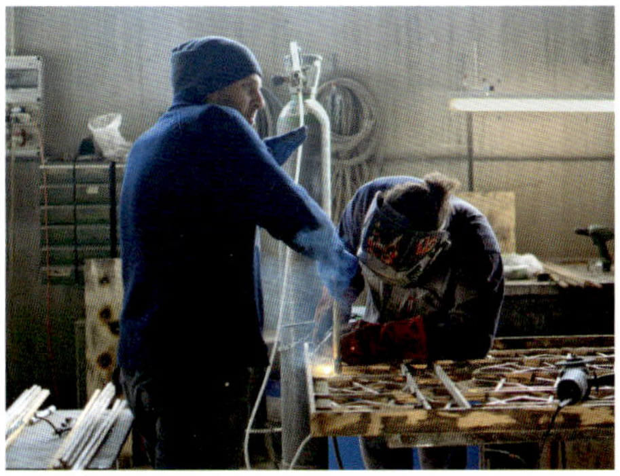

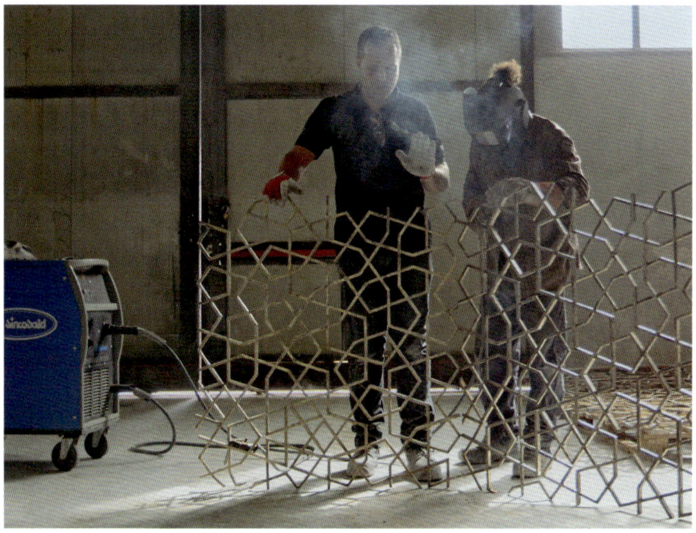

Verfahren zum Zusammenbau der verschiedenen Bronzeelemente des Paravents in der Fonderia Nolana Del Giudice / Assembling process of the various bronze elements of the screen at the Fonderia Nolana Del Giudice

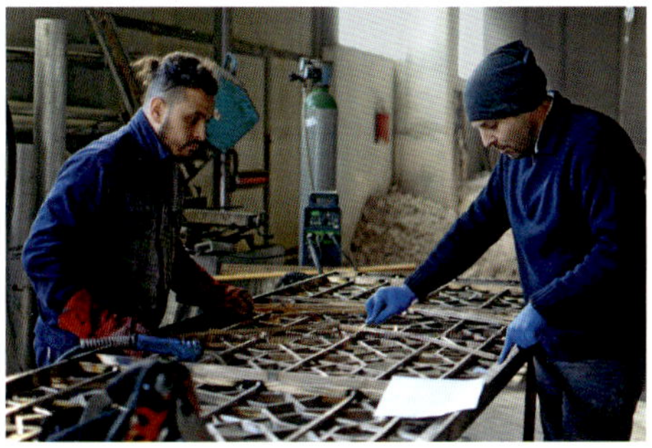

Der Grabturm Gondab-e Qabud in Maragha, Westiran (1196-97) / The tomb tower Gondab-e Qabud in Maragha, western Iran (1196-97)

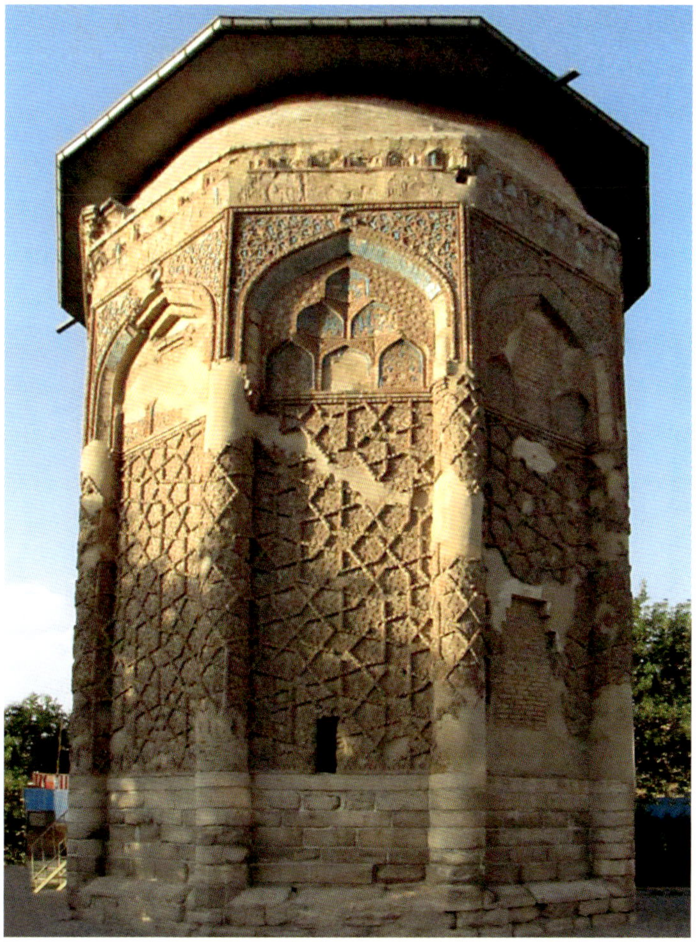

the course of life, and together with the gravel river has also been an inspiration for the horizontal reliefs. The long lines running parallel to each other along the length of the panel, which are formed by the tree growth rings, naturally echo the gravel parallel lines representing the river in the Zen garden. Baselgia is as much fascinated by the symbolical meaning of this garden as by the richness of emotions that its minimalist arrangement can unleash and the meditative atmosphere that characterized it. The meditative, and contemplative dimension is central to *The Tree of Valbella* too, especially in the horizontal reliefs. We are not only invited to observe, and feel them, but also to sit on them and take our time. Sitting on the reliefs, we can touch and closely observe their surface and the carved sail boats, and take time to look at the garden and the other elements of the ensemble, as well as the panorama surrounding the work.

At the end of the ensemble there is a space where two doors face each other. They represent the door of life and the door of death, one-way doors with no handles that we enter without exactly knowing where they take us. The door of life marks the birth, the entrance point to life. The door of

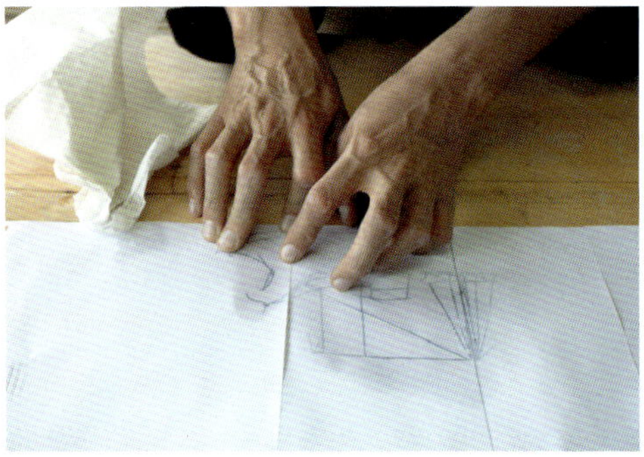

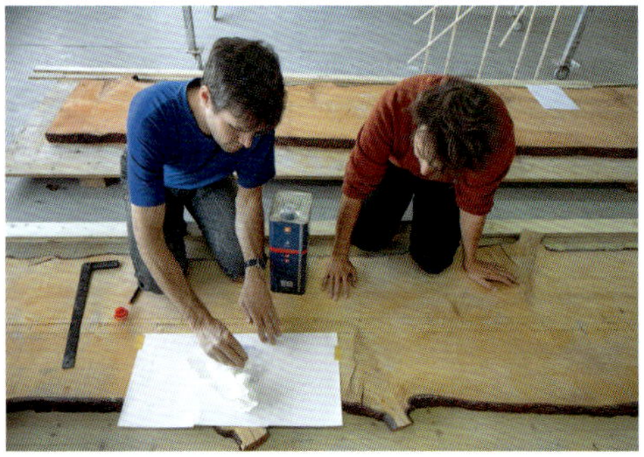

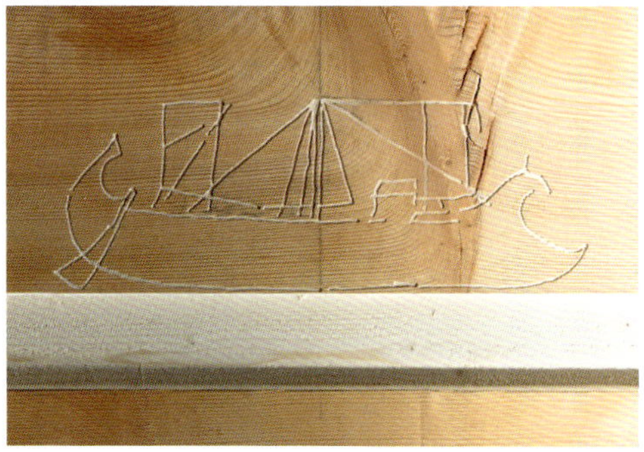

Oben: Vorbereitung des Holzmodells für das liegende Relief mit dem eingravierten Boot / Unten: Bronzegüsse der liegenden Reliefs bereit für die Endbearbeitung und den Montageprozess / Top: Preparation of the wooden model for the horizontal relief with the engraved boat / Bottom: Bronze castings of the reliefs ready for the finishing and assembly process

Bedeutung des Gartens und der Fülle an Emotionen, die das minimalistische Arrangement erzeugt, sowie von der meditativen Atmosphäre, die diesen umgibt. Diese meditative und kontemplative Dimension ist für *The Tree of Valbella* von zentraler Bedeutung, insbesondere für die liegenden Reliefs. Man ist nicht nur dazu aufgefordert, diese anzuschauen und zu berühren, sondern sich auf sie zu setzen und zu verweilen. Während man auf den liegenden Reliefs sitzt, kann man diese berühren und aus der Nähe ihre Oberfläche und die eingeschnitzten Segelschiffe erforschen, aber auch den Garten und die anderen Elemente des Ensembles in sich aufnehmen und meditieren.

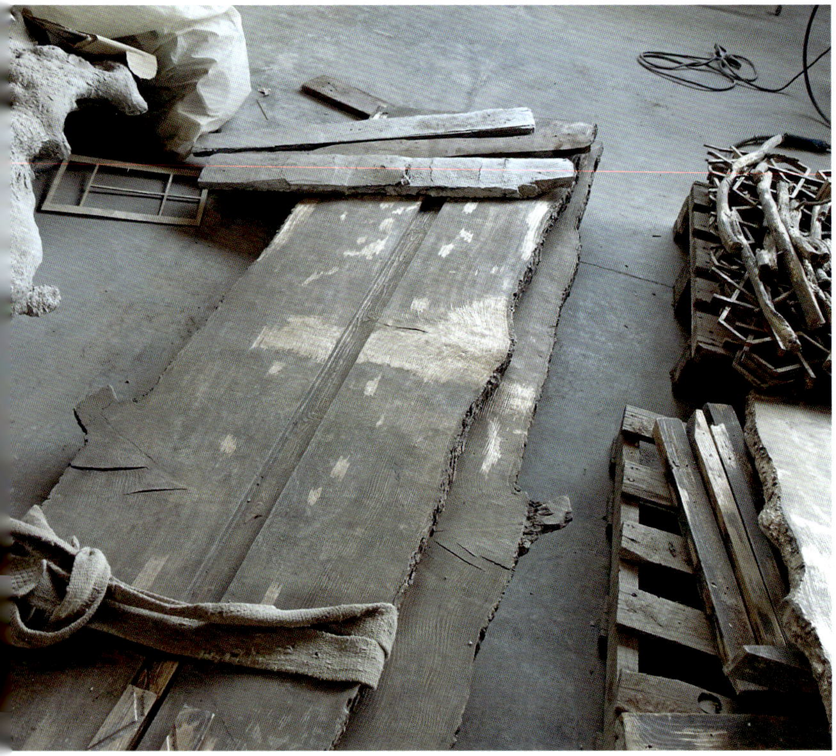

Den Abschluss des Ensembles bilden zwei sich gegenüberliegende Tore. Sie stellen das Tor des Lebens und das Tor des Todes dar. Es handelt sich um Tore, die keine Griffe besitzen und nur in eine Richtung zugänglich sind. Wir gehen durch diese hindurch, ohne genau zu wissen, wohin sie uns führen. Das Tor des Lebens ist der Geburt, dem Beginn des Lebens, gewidmet. Das Tor des Todes stellt hingegen die Schwelle dar, die das Leben vom Tod trennt, den Eintritt ins Unbekannte. Die Tore sind Reproduktionen der Tore des Turms der Winde im Maßstab 1:2 und zeichnen sich beide durch ihren skulpturalen sowie malerischen Charakter aus. Ihre Außenseiten geben den Rahmen der Tore des Turms der Winde wieder, während die Oberfläche der Tore aus einem Teil des Baums gefertigt ist und einem Bildschirm gleicht, auf dem das Leben des Baums vorüberzieht. Die Rückseiten ähneln Leinwänden mit ihren Holzrahmen; sie erinnern an diejenige im Bildvordergrund von Diego Velázquez' Meisterwerk *Las Meninas* (1656). Dieses Gemälde, eine Reflexion über den Akt des Malens und Sehens, regt dazu an, über die Grenzen zwischen Kunst und Realität und die eigene Position innerhalb des Kunstwerks nachzudenken. Victor I. Stoichita[4] nennt *Las Meninas* ein „offenes" Bild. Neben den zahlreichen Interpretationen, zeichnet es sich auch durch seine offene räumliche Komposition aus. Die Betrachter werden dazu aufgefordert, den

death represents the boundary separating life from death, access to the unknown. These doors are reproductions in scale 1:2 of the Tower of the Winds' door and are both sculptural, and pictorial surfaces. Their exterior sides reproduce the frame of the Tower of the Winds' door and the doors' surface is a section of the tree, which is like a screen showing the tree's life. The interior sides are conceived like canvases showing their wooden frames and echo the back of the canvas visible in the foreground of Diego Velázquez's masterpiece *Las Meninas* (1656). This painting is a reflection on the acts of both painting and seeing and ensures that the viewer reflects on the limits between art and reality and his or her own role within the artwork. Furthermore, as the art historian Victor I. Stoichita has pointed out[4], *Las Meninas* is an "open" painting, not only because one can interpret it in many ways, but also in respect to its spatial structure. In fact, the viewer is invited to penetrate its space and its structure of passage is underlined by the open door in the background, which is also a framing surface like the canvas in the foreground.

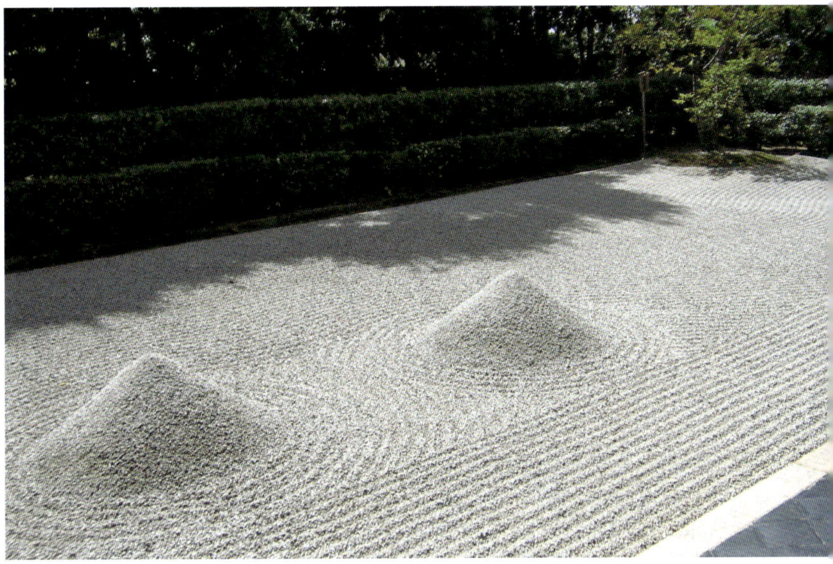

Soami, Steingarten des Untertempels Daisen-in / Dry landscape garden of the sub-temple Daisen-in, ~ 1525, Daitoku-ji, Kyoto

The complexity of Velázquez's masterpiece inspired Baselgia to add a reflection on the artistic production and its materiality, as well as the place of the viewer looking at *The Tree of Valbella*. On the interior sides, elaborations of graffiti coming from the Tower of the Winds are carved on the surface. For the artist, the small ship represents the little experience we have at the beginning of our life and the big ship is respectively the metaphor for the ample experience that we have at the end of our life. But they are even merchant ships for him, leaving empty to distant lands and returning loaded with exotic goods. Baselgia also reinterpreted the figure of the knight riding a horse, originally headless, and decided to portray his patron's face on the knight's body. In this way the artist drew on the habit originated in medieval art of frequently portraying the donors in the altarpieces or wall paintings that they commissioned.

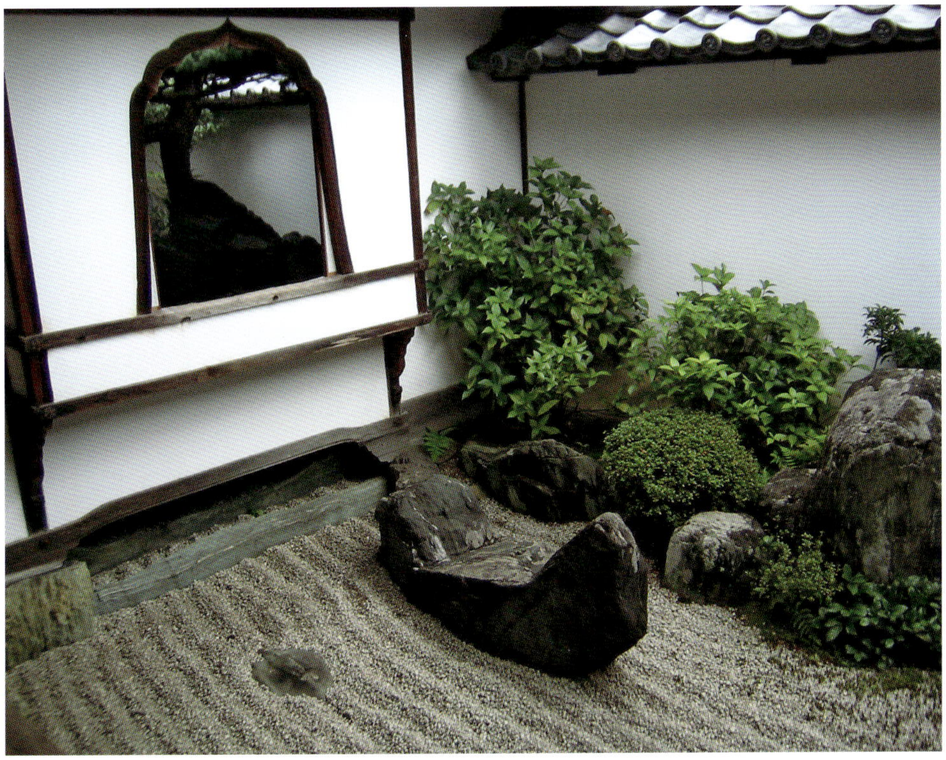

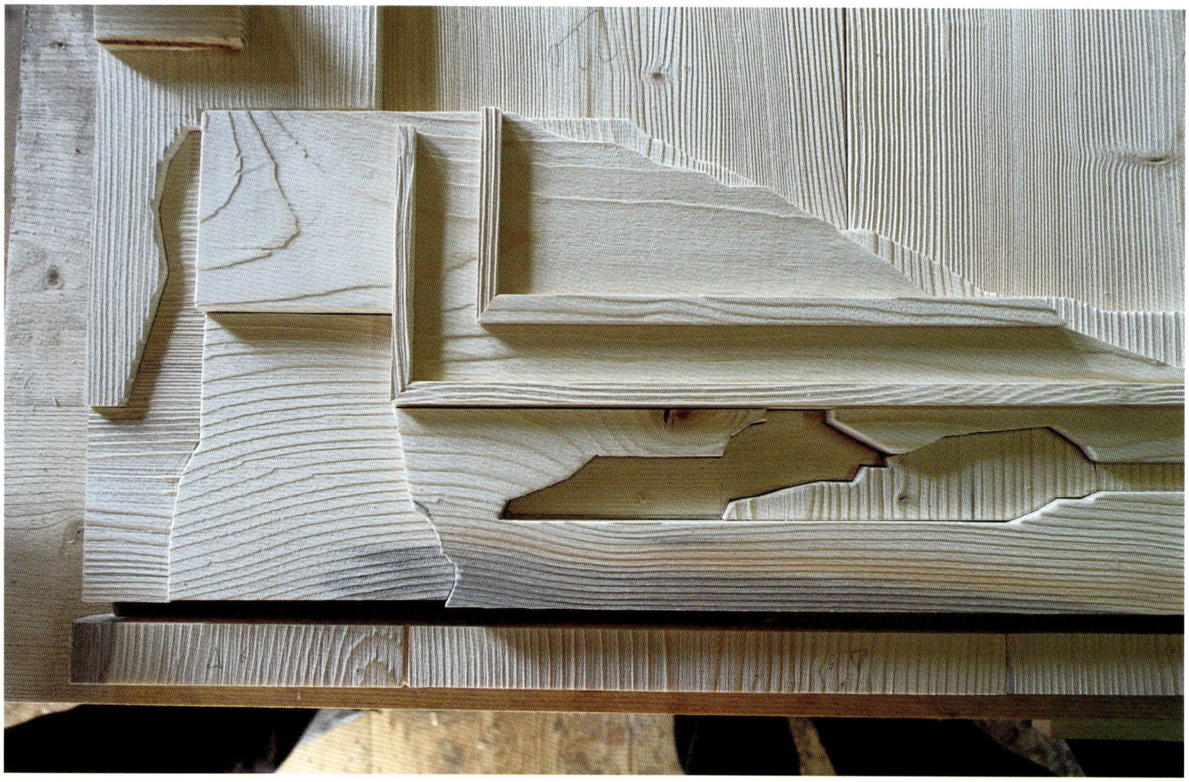

Holzmodell für eine der beiden Tore und Bronzeguss eines der Tore bereit für die Endbearbeitung in der Fonderia Nolana Del Giudice / Wooden model for one of the two doors and bronze casting of one of the doors ready for the finishing process at the Fonderia Nolana Del Giudice

unabgeschlossenen Bildraum zu ergründen, der durch die geöffnete Tür im Hintergrund unterstrichen wird, die analog der Leinwand im Bildvordergrund auch als rahmende Fläche fungiert. Die Komplexität von Velázquez' Meisterwerk inspirierte Baselgia zu einer Auseinandersetzung mit der künstlerischen Produktion und ihrer Materialität sowie über den Standort der Betrachter gegenüber *The Tree of Valbella*. Auf ihren Innenseiten sind graffitiähnliche Muster, die auf den Turm der Winde zurückgehen, eingeschnitzt. Das kleine Schiff stellt nach Baselgia die geringe Erfahrung zu Beginn unseres Lebens dar, das große Schiff hingegen veranschaulicht die umfassende Erfahrung am Lebensende. Darüber hinaus verweisen die beiden aber auch auf die Handelsschiffe, die leer in weit entfernte Länder aufbrechen und vollbeladen mit exotischen Gütern zurückkehren. Baselgia legte darüber hinaus die Figur des zu Pferd reitenden Ritters neu aus, der ursprünglich kopflos war. Er beschloss, dem Körper des Ritters das Gesicht seines Auftraggebers hinzuzufügen. Baselgia folgte damit der in der spätmittelalterlichen Kunst verwurzelten Tradition des Stifterporträts in Altarwerken oder Wandgemälden.

Im unteren zentralen Bereich dieses Raums befindet sich der Schlussstein, der sich aus dem Bronzeguss des oberen, in sechs vertikale Platten geschnittenen Teil des Baums zusammensetzt. Der obere Teil ist der jüngste des Baums, sein letzter

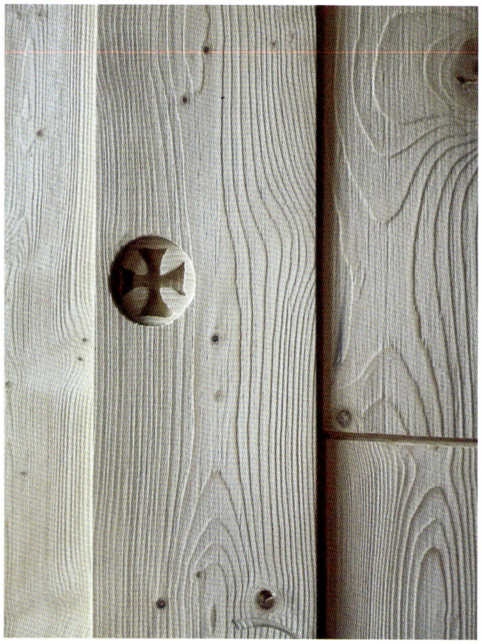

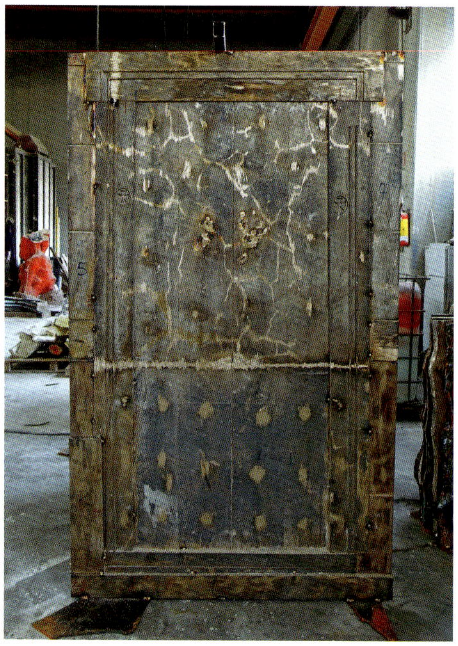

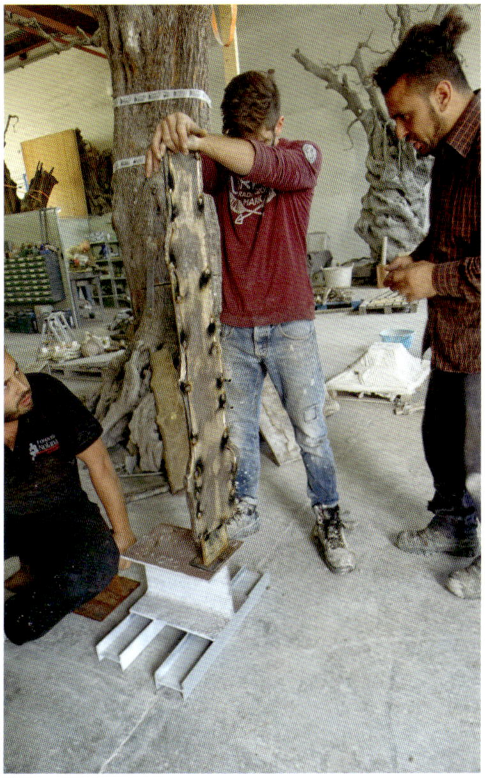

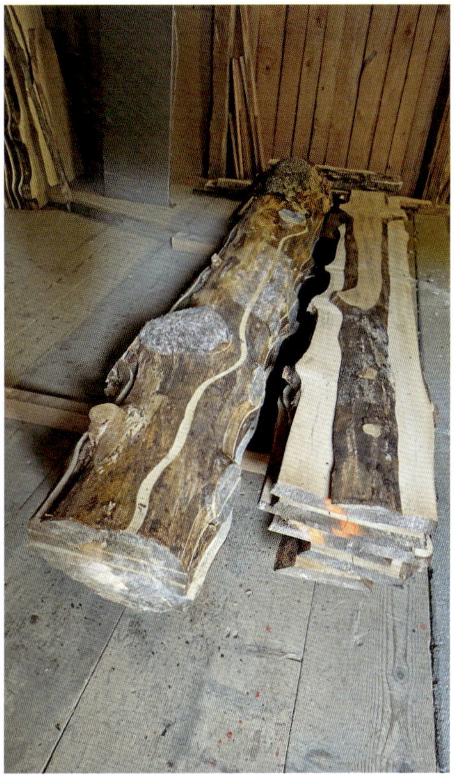

Holzmodelle für den Schlussstein und Bronzegüsse während der Endbearbeitung und des Montageprozesses in der Fonderia Nolana Del Giudice / Wooden models for the final stone and bronze castings during the finishing and assembly process

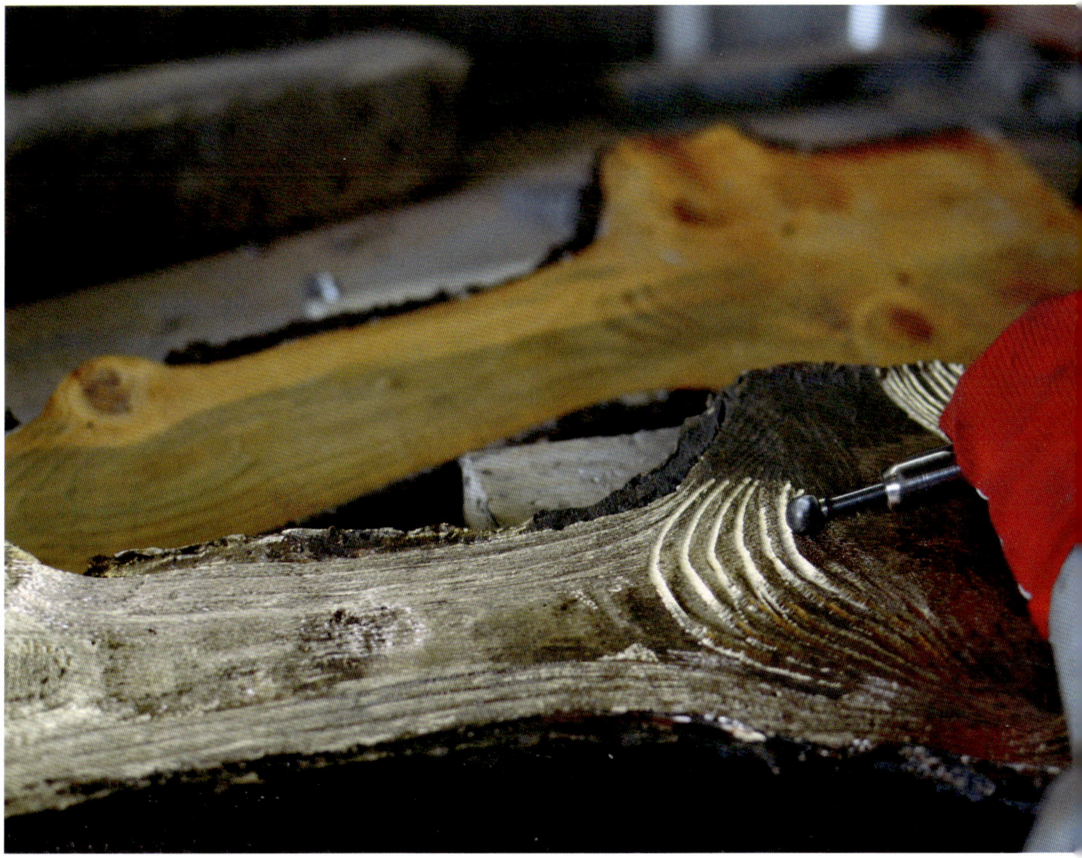

Lebensausdruck. Die sechs vertikalen Platten, die einer Abfolge von Grabsteinen gleichen, erfüllen demnach eine kommemorative Funktion. Sie stellen aber auch eine Art imaginärer Krone dar, die das Haupt des verstorbenen Baum-Königs ziert. Die Quelle ist dort positioniert, wo einst der Baum stand. Die Linie, die dieses Element mit dem Schlussstein verbindet, ist auch die imaginäre Linie, die der Baum dort gezogen hätte, wäre er nach dem Fällen auf den Boden aufgeschlagen. Da die Entfernung, die die Quelle vom letzten Element des Ensembles trennt, der Höhe der Fichte entspricht, wäre seine Krone genau dort aufgetroffen, wo sich jetzt der Schlussstein befindet. So werden die Umrisse eines fragmentierten und ausgearbeiteten Porträts des Baumes definiert und die Horizontalität der Komposition erinnert uns daran, dass die Fichte nun leblos ist.

Baselgias Arbeit ist als eine Reise konzipiert, die von Norden nach Süden führt. Das Ensemble entwickelt sich entlang einer imaginären vertikalen Linie, die das Bauminnere, die Essenz des Lebens, repräsentiert. Die Quelle, eines der Reliefs, und der Schlussstein sind entlang dieser Linie angeordnet. Die Linie vermittelt ein Gefühl von Unendlichkeit, das die gesamte Arbeit durchzieht. *The Tree of Valbella*, der sich inmitten der Natur befindet, unterliegt einem kontinuierlichen Wandlungsprozess. Die Bronze wird allmählich oxidieren. Die Sonne und das mit ihr einhergehende Spiel von Licht und Schatten werden die Oberflächen akzentuieren und immer neue Facetten zum Vorschein bringen. Der Regen wird Spiegel-Effekte erzeugen. Der Schnee wird einige Teile bedecken, während er andere herausstechen lässt. Das skulpturale Ensemble wird sich durch die Abfolge von Tag und Nacht je nach Jahreszeit und Wetterverhältnissen stetig verändern. Wir werden die Arbeit immer wieder aufs Neue entdecken. In diesem Zusammenhang klingt Lavoisiers Grundsatz[5] an „Nichts geht verloren, nichts wird geschaffen, alles verwandelt sich."

1 Karolina Tagaris, Phoebe Fronista, „Ancient Greece's restored Tower of Winds keeps its secrets", verfügbar unter der URL-Adresse: https://www.reuters.com/article/us-greece-archaeology-towerofwinds/ancient-greeces-restored-tower-of-winds-keeps-its-secrets-idUSKCN1101OS, eingesehen am 30. August 2019. Für weitere Informationen zum Turm der Winde siehe auch: Hermann J. Kienast, *Der Turm der Winde in Athen*, Wiesbaden: Reichert Verlag, 2014.

2 Carol Bier, „The Decagonal Tomb Tower at Maragha and Its Architectural Context: Lines of Mathematical Thought", in: *Nexus Netw J*, Bd. 14, Nr. 2, 2012, S. 251-273.

3 Hans Belting, *Florenz und Bagdad. Eine westöstliche Geschichte des Blicks*, München: C. H. Beck, 2008, S. 104-143.

4 Victor I. Stoichita, *L'instauration du tableau. Métapeinture à l'aube des temps modernes*, Genf: Droz, 1999, S. 328-338.

5 Antoine-Laurent de Lavoisier (1743-1794) war ein französischer Adliger und Chemiker, der einen großen Einfluss auf die Geschichte der Chemie und Biologie hatte. 1774 zeigte er, dass, obgleich die Materie ihren Zustand in einer chemischen Reaktion ändern kann, diese Gesamtmasse der Materie zu Beginn und an Ende jeder chemischen Änderung dieselbe ist. Lavoisiers Experimente stützten das Massenerhaltungsgesetz. In Frankreich wird es als Lavoisiers Gesetz gelehrt und mit der folgenden Äußerung aus seinem *Traité Elémentaire de Chimie* (1789) paraphrasiert: „Nichts geht verloren, nichts wird geschaffen, alles verwandelt sich."

In the lower centre of this space there is a final stone composed of the bronze cast of the upper part of the tree cut in six vertical plates. The upper part is the youngest part of the tree, its last expression of life. The six vertical plates are like a succession of tombstones and have therefore a commemorative dimension. But they also represent a sort of imaginary crown that adorns the head of the dead tree-king. Considering that the spring is located more or less where the tree stood, the line connecting this element to the final stone also evokes the imaginary trajectory that the tree would have drawn by falling to the ground after being felled. And, since the distance that separates the spring from the last element of the ensemble is equal to the height of the spruce, its top would have landed precisely where the final stone is. Thus, the outlines of a fragmented and elaborated portrait of the tree are defined and the horizontality of the composition reminds us that the spruce is now lifeless.

The work is conceived as a journey going from North to South, and the ensemble is articulated along an imaginary vertical line representing the tree's heart, the nucleus of life. The spring, one of the reliefs, and the final stone are installed along this line. This line gives a sense of infinity that actually permeates the whole work. Immersed in nature, *The Tree of Valbella* will be in constant evolution. The bronze will oxidize. The sun and the play of light and shadow will articulate its surfaces and always show new facets. The rain will create mirroring effects. The snow will cover some parts and then almost make some other parts stand out. The sculptural ensemble will constantly be transformed by the succession of day and night, season after season, depending on the weather conditions. We will be able to rediscover it over and over again. Lavoisier's Law[5] resonates in our ears: "Nothing is lost, nothing is created, everything is transformed."

1 Karolina Tagaris, Phoebe Fronista, "Ancient Greece's restored Tower of Winds keeps its secrets", reference available at the URL address: https://www.reuters.com/article/us-greece-archaeology-towerofwinds/ancient-greeces-restored-tower-of-winds-keeps-its-secrets-idUSKCN1101OS, consulted on August 30, 2019. For more informations about the Tower of the Winds, see also: Hermann J. Kienast, Der Turm der Winde in Athen, Wiesbaden: Reichert Verlag, 2014.

2 Carol Bier, "The Decagonal Tomb Tower at Maragha and Its Architectural Context: Lines of Mathematical Thought", in: Nexus Netw J, vol. 14, no. 2, 2012, pp. 251-273.

3 Hans Belting, *Florenz und Bagdad. Eine westöstliche Geschichte des Blicks*, München: C. H. Beck, 2008, pp. 104-143.

4 Victor I. Stoichita, *L'instauration du tableau. Métapeinture à l'aube des temps modernes*, Geneva: Droz, 1999, pp. 328-338.

5 Antoine-Laurent de Lavoisier (1743-1794) was a French nobleman and chemist who had a large influence on both the history of chemistry and the history of biology. In 1774, he showed that, although matter can change its state in a chemical reaction, the total mass of matter is the same at the end as at the beginning of every chemical change. Lavoisier's experiments supported the law of conservation of mass. In France it is taught as Lavoisier's Law and is paraphrased from a statement in his *Traité Elémentaire de Chimie* (1789): "Nothing is lost, nothing is created, everything is transformed."

FONDERIA NOLANA DEL GIUDICE: LEIDENSCHAFT FÜR DAS KOMPLEXE

LAURA GIUDICI

Die Fonderia Nolana Del Giudice ist eine innovative Gusswerkstatt, die auf die Realisierung von skulpturalen Arbeiten spezialisiert ist.[1]

Seit vier Generationen arbeitet die Familie Del Giudice Seite an Seite mit italienischen und internationalen Künstlerinnen und Künstler und unterstützt diese dabei, Skulpturen auszuführen, die im Hinblick auf Größe, Material und Komplexität variieren. Die Gießerei in Nola (Neapel/Italien) entwickelte sich dank ihres Know-hows im Bereich der Metallverarbeitung und ihrer auf die Anforderungen der Künstlerinnen und Künstler abgestimmten Techniken zu einer Anlaufstelle für die künstlerische Produktion.

In den vergangenen Jahren hat die Fonderia Nolana die Arbeiten zahlreicher renommierter, zeitgenössischer Künstlerinnen und Künstler wie Ugo Rondinone, Adel Abdessemed, Darren Bader und Latifa Echakhch umgesetzt und während des gesamten kreativen Prozesses alte Handwerkskunst mit technologischer Innovation verbunden. Die Gießerei ist bekannt für die Fertigung von monumentalen Bronzearbeiten mittels des traditionellen Wachsausschmelzverfahrens sowie für die Konzeption und Produktion von Skulpturen aus verschiedenen Metallen.

Die erfahrenen Mitarbeiterinnen und Mitarbeiter begleiten die Künstlerinnen und Künstler bei jedem Schritt des kreativen Prozesses und führen alle notwendigen Tätigkeiten aus, um ihre Ideen zu unterstützen, von den ersten Projektentwürfen, der Ausführung des maßstabgetreuen Modells, dem Konstruktiven Ingenieurbau und der Auswahl der Materialien und Patinierung bis zum Aufbau der Arbeit.

SS. / pp. 50-51
Einige Schritte des Wachsausschmelzverfahrens / Some steps of the lost wax casting process

Um das beste Ergebnis zu erzielen, erforschen und entwickeln sie jedes Mal die Produktionspraktiken, die für die spezifische künstlerische Anforderung am geeignetsten sind.

Mirko Baselgia arbeitet seit zehn Jahren mit der Fonderia Nolana zusammen, um seine Arbeiten in verschiedenen Größen und Materialien zu realisieren. Neben *The Tree of Valbella*, einem mehrjährigen Projekt, das beinahe fünf Jahre in Anspruch nahm, schuf Baselgia weitere wichtige Arbeiten in Zusammenarbeit mit der Gießerei.
Hierzu zählt *Endoderm (marmot burrows)* (2012-2013), der Bronzeguss eines Murmeltierbaus, der durch den Bau einer Straße unweit des Julierpasses (Graubünden, Schweiz) von Zerstörung bedroht war. Ein weiteres Beispiel ist *Trivialization Zylinder* (2013), ein unvollendeter Zylinder, der als Nachguss von Vesuv-Lava entstand. Mithilfe der Fonderia Nolana führte Baselgia ein erstes Experiment durch, um erstarrte Lava des Vesuvs nachzugießen. Das Ergebnis dieses Prozesses war ein Material, das sich vom ursprünglichen stark unterschied. Es wirkte beinahe glasig und konnte nur für die Ausführung von einfachen, gleichmäßigen Formen verwendet werden.

1 Für weitere Informationen siehe die Webseite der Gießerei: http://www.fonderianolana.com/en/.

FONDERIA NOLANA DEL GIUDICE: A PASSION FOR COMPLEXITY

Fonderia Nolana Del Giudice is a cutting-edge workshop, specialised in the realisation of sculptural works.[1]

Four generations of Del Giudice family have worked side by side with Italian and international artists, supporting them in the realisation of sculptures of the most varied sizes, materials, and complexity. The experience gained in metal working and the capability to use tailored techniques to satisfy every request of the artist have made this foundry in Nola (Naples, Italy) a reference point for artistic productions.

In the last years, Fonderia Nolana has worked for many important contemporary artists, such as Ugo Rondinone, Adel Abdessemed, Darren Bader, and Latifa Echakhch, combining ancient craftsmanship with technological innovation throughout the creative process. The foundry is renowned for the realisation of artistic bronzes of monumental dimension with the ancient technique of lost wax casting and for the design and production of sculptures in different metals.

The specialists of the workshop follow the artists in every step of the creative process, dealing with all the necessary activities to support their inspiration, from the first studies of the project, to the realisation of the scale model, the structural engineering, the choice of materials and coating, up to the installation of the work. A peculiar striving for excellence pushes them to study and develop each time the most appropriate production practices for the specific need of the artist.

Mirko Baselgia has been working for more than ten years now with Fonderia Nolana for the realization of works of various sizes and materials. In addition to *The Tree of Valbella*, a long-term project that lasted almost five years, the artist has created other important works in collaboration with the foundry. For example, *Endoderm (marmot burrows)* (2012-2013), a bronze casting of a real marmot burrow that was about to be destroyed for the construction of a road near the Julierpass (Graubünden, Switzerland). Another example is *Trivialization Zylinder* (2013), an imperfect cylinder made from recast Vesuvius lava. With the help of the Fonderia Nolana, the artist carried out a first experiment to recast solidified Vesuvius lava, a process that generated a different material from the original one, almost glassy and usable only for the realization of simple and regular shapes.

1 For more information, see the foundry's website: http://www.fonderianolana.com/en/.

Das Wachsausschmelzverfahren

Bronzeobjekte werden seit mindestens 5.000 Jahren mit dem Wachsausschmelzverfahren (*cire perdue*) gegossen. Obgleich sich Techniken und Materialien kontinuierlich weiterentwickeln, hat sich das Verfahren selbst seit Jahrtausenden kaum geändert. Das Wachsausschmelzverfahren ist meistens die erste Wahl, da es alle Details äußerst genau wiedergibt und die gegossenen Objekte von großer Langlebigkeit sind. Das Verfahren ist jedoch sehr arbeits- und zeitintensiv.

Das Modell, in diesem Fall ein Holzmodell, wird mit Silikongummi überzogen und durch eine feste äußere Form fixiert. Wenn die Form herausgenommen wird, bleibt sein Abdruck zurück. Hitzebeständiger Ton wird sorgfältig in den Abdruck gegeben, wodurch eine präzise Kopie des Originalmodells entsteht. Die Oberfläche des zweiten Tonmodells wird leicht abgetragen. Wenn dieses dann in die Form zurückgegeben wird, findet sich ein Hohlraum zwischen dem Modell und der Form. In diesen Hohlraum wird dann das Wachs eingegossen. Der endgültige Bronzeguss weist dann dieselbe Dicke wie der durch das Abtragen entstandene Hohlraum auf. Nachdem die Form um das Tonmodell herumgeschlossen wurde, wird heißes Wachs in den Hohlraum zwischen Modell und Form eingegossen. Das Ergebnis ist ein mit Wachs überzogenes Tonmodell, das dann originalgetreu von Hand vollendet wird. Das Wachsmodell wird dann mit *Einguss-* und *Entlüftungskanälen* versehen. Diese sorgen zuerst dafür, dass das Wachs während des Schmelzvorgangs entweicht. Danach ermöglichen sie es, dass das geschmolzene Metall gleichmäßig durch die Form fließt und Luft entweicht, wenn das Metall eingegossen wird. Bis auf eine Stelle an der Oberseite, wo die flüssige Bronze eingegossen wird, ist die Form mit einer Schicht ummantelt (eine metallene Schutzschicht), die vollkommen trocken sein muss, bevor die Bronze eingegossen wird. Die Feingussform wird dann bei einer hohen Temperatur (über 500 °C) erhitzt.

Die geschmolzene Bronze (über 1.000 °C) wird dann in die Gussform eingegossen und füllt den von dem „verlorenen" Wachs erzeugten Hohlraum aus. Wenn das Ganze abgekühlt ist, werden Beschichtung und Gussform zerschlagen, sodass das Metall zum Vorschein kommt. Die Einguss- und Entlüftungskanäle werden entfernt und die Bronzeoberfläche wird ziseliert und gefeilt, sodass ihre Spuren nicht mehr sichtbar sind. Der Prozess der manuellen Überarbeitung des Bronzegusses wird *Ziselieren* genannt. Alle Überreste des hitzebeständigen Tonmodells in dem hohlen Bronzeguss werden jetzt entfernt. Wenn das Ziselieren abgeschlossen und die Skulptur klein genug und folglich in einem Stück gegossen worden ist, erhält sie eine Patina. Größere Skulpturen werden normalerweise in Segmenten gegossen. Wenn alle Segmente gefertigt worden sind, werden sie zusammengeschweißt. Dieser Prozess heißt *brazing* (*Hartlöten*). Anschließend wird die Patinierung vorgenommen. Die Patina schützt die Skulptur und verleiht ihr darüber hinaus Farbe. Hierbei werden heiße oder kalte Oxide auf die Metalloberfläche aufgetragen, wodurch eine dünne Korrosionsschicht entsteht. Diese Schicht – in diesem Fall ist sie leicht braun – wird *Patina* genannt.

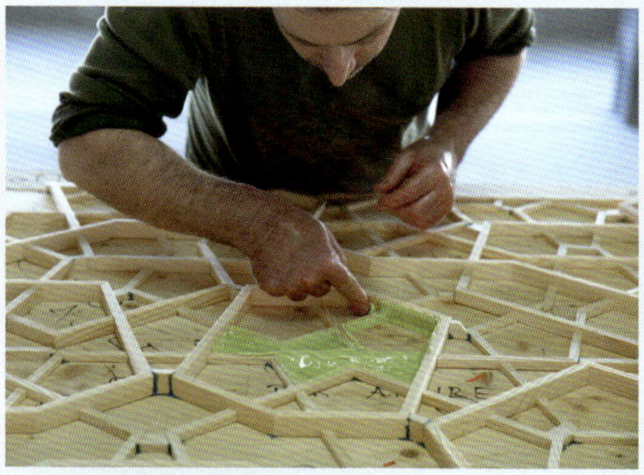
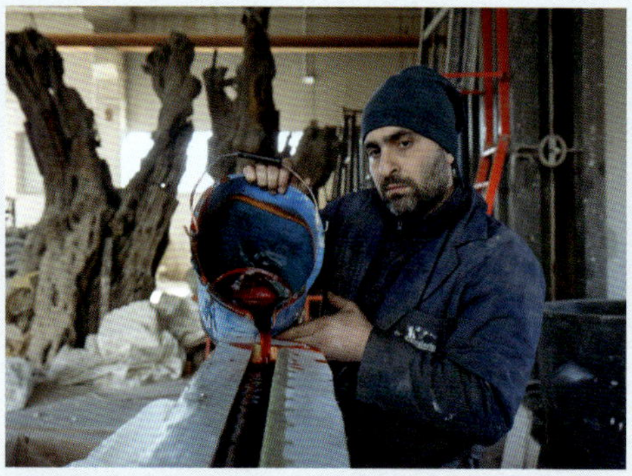
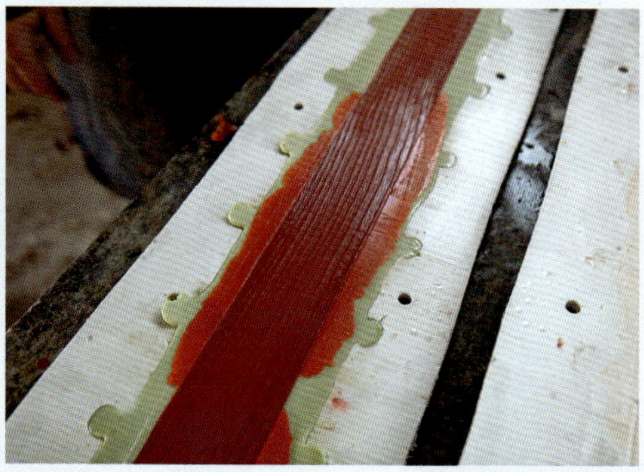
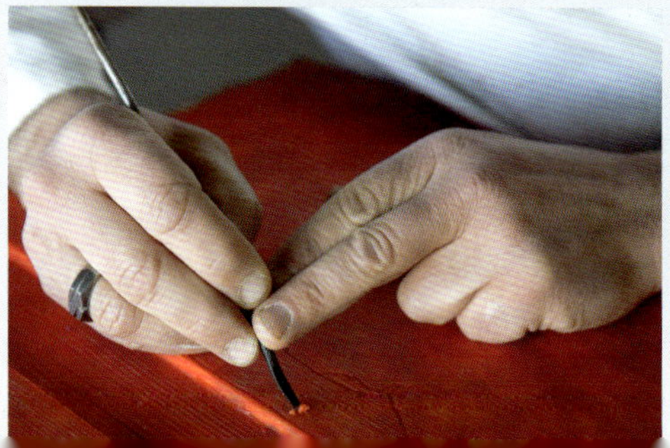
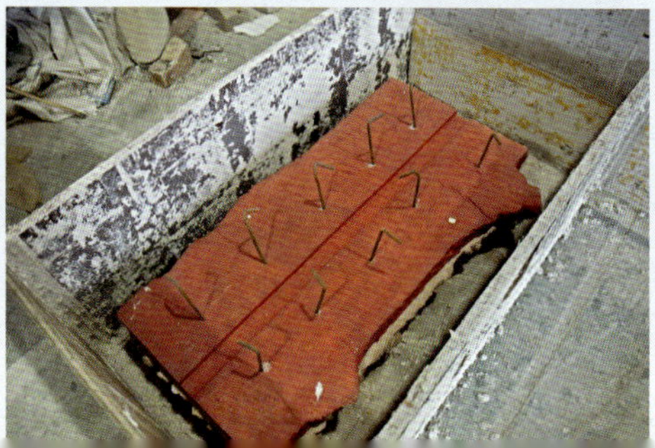
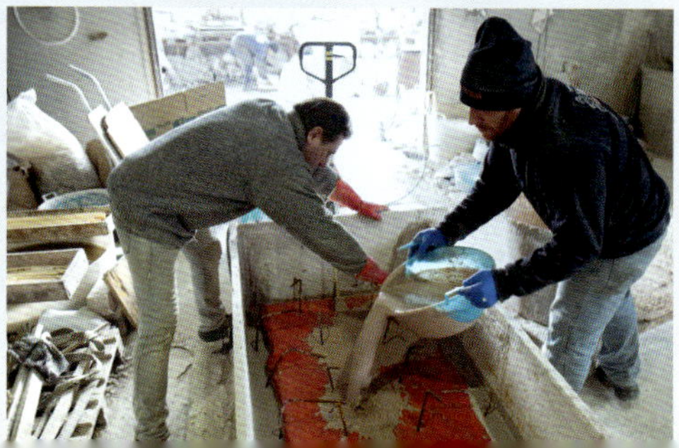

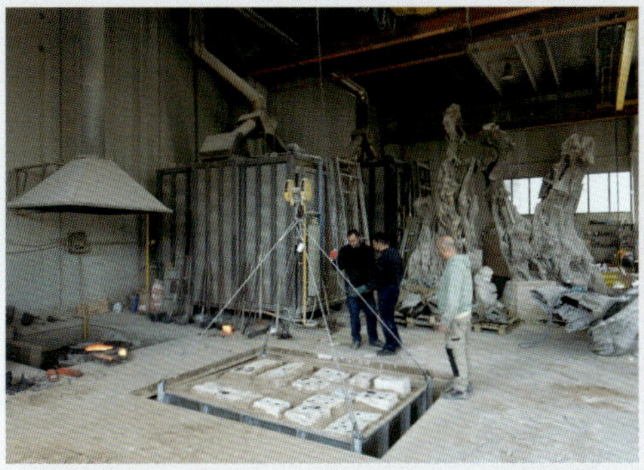
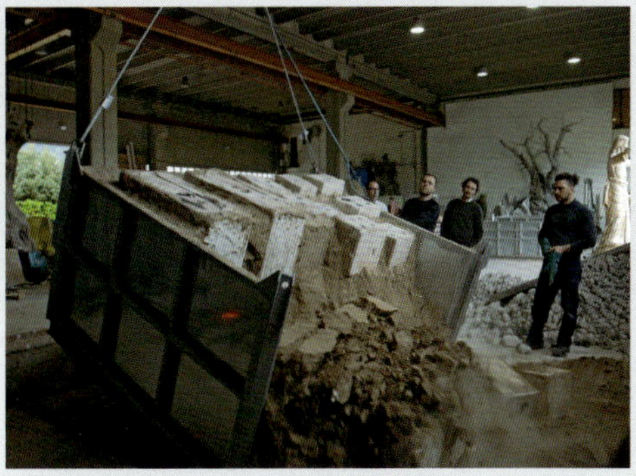
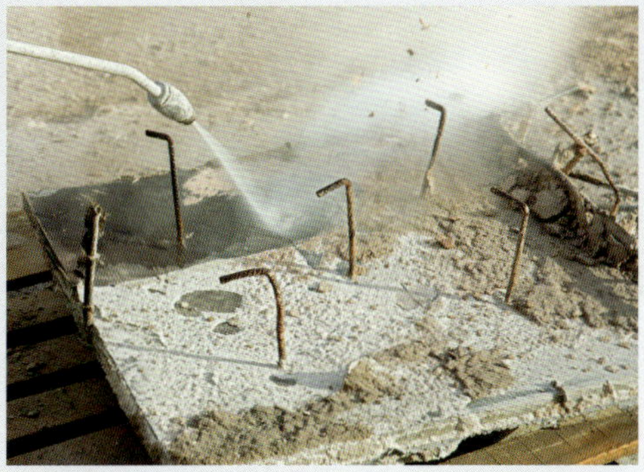
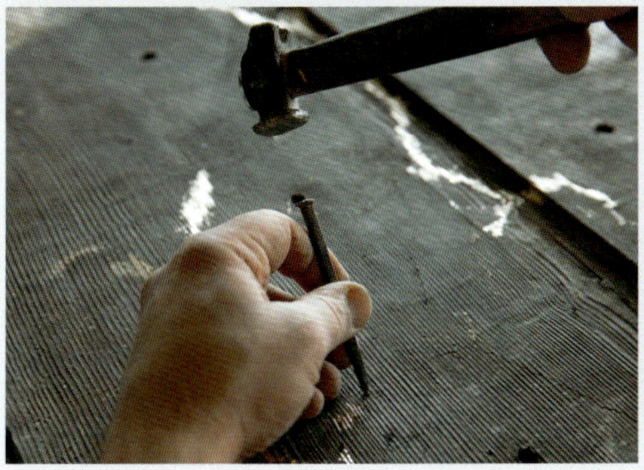
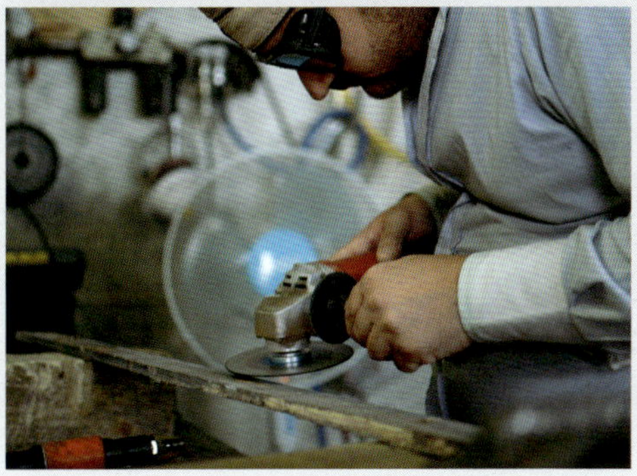
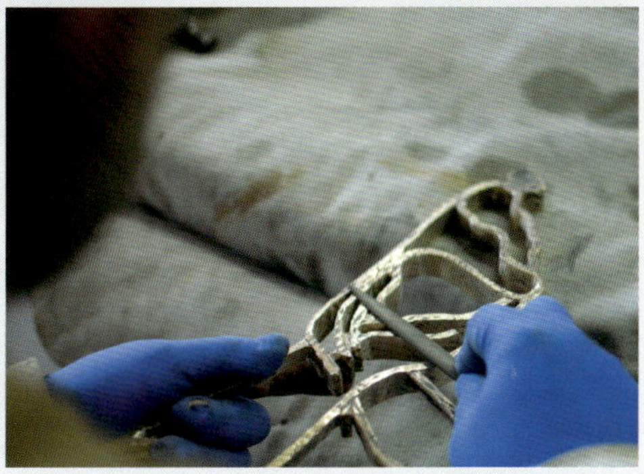

The lost wax casting process

Bronze objects have been cast using the lost wax (*cire perdue*) process for at least 5'000 years. Although techniques and materials continue to evolve, much of the process is as it was in ancient times. Lost wax casting is for many the process of choice because it is extremely accurate in replicating detail and because of the durability of the objects it creates. However, the process is very arduous and time-consuming.

The wood model, in this case, is covered with silicone rubber, held in place by a rigid outer mold. When the model is removed, its impression remains. Fireproof clay is carefully put into the impression, making a sharply defined duplicate of the original model. The surface of this second clay model is slightly scraped away. When this second model is returned to the mold, there is a gap between the model and the mold. This gap is where the wax will be poured. The final bronze will be of the same thickness as the gap that is created by the scraping. After closing the mold around the clay model, hot wax is poured into the gap between the model and the mold. The result is a clay model covered in wax, which is then hand-finished to fidelity. A network of wax pipes, called *sprues* and *gates*, is attached to the wax-covered model. These pipes first will allow the wax to escape as it melts. Later, they will enable the molten metal to flow evenly throughout the mold and will also let air escape as the metal is poured in. Except for a place to pour in the liquid bronze at the top, the mold is covered with a layer of cladding (a protective metal coating), which must be completely dry before bronze pouring begins. The investment mold is then heated to a high temperature (over 500 °C).

Molten bronze (over 1,000 °C) is then poured into the investment mold, filling the space left by the "lost" wax. When all is cool, the cladding and investment mold are broken and the metal appears. The network of sprues and gates is then removed and the surface of the bronze is chiseled and filed so that no trace of them can be seen. This process of hand-finishing the bronze to perfection is called *chasing*. Any remains of the fireproof clay model left inside the hollow bronze are removed now. When the process of chasing is finished, iif the sculpture is small enough to have been cast in one piece, the work is given a patina. Larger sculptures are generally cast in segments, and after all segments have been made, they are joined together, a process called *braising*. After braising, the artwork would proceed to patination. A patina not only protects the sculpture, but also gives it color. It is a step in the making of the finished bronze wherein hot or cold oxides are applied to the surface of the metal, creating a thin layer of corrosion. This layer – in this case slightly brown – is called the patina.

PASQUALE DEL GIUDICE

LAURA GIUDICI

Laura Giudici: Pasquale, du bist der Vertreter der dritten Generation der Fonderia Nolana Del Giudice. Deine vier Kinder arbeiten heute alle in der Gießerei. Erzähle uns etwas über den Beginn und die Geschichte dieses Familienabenteuers.

Pasquale Del Giudice: Ich kann die Entstehung der Gießerei nicht mit ein paar Worten umreißen. Es ist eine lange Geschichte. Soweit ich mich erinnern kann, begann alles mit meinen Onkeln, die Graveure waren, das heißt, sie ziselierten geprägtes Silber. Ich kann die Geschichte der Gießerei ab dem Jahr 1956 [Del Giudice war damals 5 Jahre alt] erzählen, da ich in der Gießerei auf die Welt kam. Ich habe Leben, Tod und Wunder erlebt. Ich habe Statuen gesehen, die Personen angefertigt haben, die heute siebzig Jahre alt sind. Die Gießerei entstand langsam. Meine Großeltern gründeten sie. Die Gießerei Chiurazzi in Neapel, die sehr bekannt ist, wurde von den Arbeitern meines Großvaters ins Leben gerufen. Seit dem Krieg durchlief die Gießerei unterschiedliche Phasen und Änderungen. Eine Gießerei benötigt Kontinuität. Es ist ein Handwerk, bei dem du nicht improvisieren kannst. Es wird weitergegeben. Die Kinder machen das, was der Vater macht. Für mich begann daher alles, als ich ein Kind war und das Handwerk erlernte. Ich wuchs mit diesem auf. Meine Kinder setzten die Arbeit dann fort. Ich glaube, weil sie mit meinem Handwerk aufgewachsen sind, verinnerlichten sie dieses, ohne es notwendigerweise auszuüben. Ich habe ihnen niemals gesagt, dass sie in der Gießerei arbeiten müssen. Wie du aber siehst, erkannten sie selbst, wie faszinierend diese Arbeit ist und Respekt verschafft. Nicht jeder kann Bronze bearbeiten. Eine Arbeit darf niemals jemandem aufgedrängt werden. Meine Kinder hatten die Freiheit, sich ihre Arbeit auszusuchen. Aus diesem Grund gehen sie heute gerne dieser Arbeit nach und halten die Gießerei am Laufen. Wir können uns glücklich schätzen, wenn die Kinder meiner Kinder die Aktivität fortsetzen. Dieselbe Geschichte, die ich gerade erzähle, ereignete sich vor mir und meinen Kindern.

LG: Die Gießerei hat sich in den letzten Jahren stark weiterentwickelt und mehrere führende zeitgenössische Künstlerinnen und Künstler haben sich entschieden, mit euch zusammenzuarbeiten. Was waren die Herausforderungen dieser jüngsten Entwicklung und wie fallen die Prognosen für die Zukunft aus?

PDG: Die Hauptherausforderung dieser Entwicklung lag darin, dass man sich in unserem Beruf nur sehr langsam einen Ruf erwirbt, von einer Arbeit nach der anderen. Und man muss die Möglichkeit haben, wichtige Arbeiten zu realisieren. Wir haben die neue Gießerei ins Leben gerufen, da sie zuvor rein handwerklich ausgerichtet war, und es darüber hinaus zu wenig Platz gab. Ich habe etwa 10 Jahre verloren, während der ich bereits das Land besaß, aber nichts machen konnte, vor allem wegen der italienischen Bürokratie [*lacht*]. Letztendlich war ich ein industrieller Handwerker und baute die heutige Anlage auf, die es uns ermöglichte, ein Image zu kreieren. Die erste Herausforderung war dann eine monumentale Arbeit in Israel, die die zwölf Apostel mit Jesus darstellt und in nur drei Monaten ausgeführt wurde. So forderten wir die Welt heraus, da es Gießereien in Spanien und England gab, die diese Arbeit hätten machen können. Und da wir mit einer anderen Gießerei zusammenarbeiten mussten, um die Arbeit in so kurzer Zeit zu bewerkstelligen, und ich noch meine alte Gießerei besaß, arbeiteten die beiden Gießereien zusammen. Diese Erfahrung half uns dabei zu verstehen, welche Richtung wir einschlagen konnten. Dann führten wir Zidanes Skulptur aus [Adel

PASQUALE DEL GIUDICE

Laura Giudici: Pasquale, you are the representative of the 3rd generation of the Fonderia Nolana Del Giudice and today your four children all work in the foundry. Tell us a little about the birth and history of this family adventure.

Pasquale Del Giudice: The birth of the foundry cannot be told in three or four words; it is actually a novel. As I remember, it all started with my uncles, who were engravers, they were involved in the chiselling of embossed silver. I can tell you the history of the foundry from 1956 onwards [when he was 5 years old], because I was born in the foundry. I have seen life, death and miracles, I have seen statues that were made by people who are now about seventy years old. The foundry developed slowly. My grandparents started the foundry. Among other things, the famous Chiurazzi Foundry in Naples, was founded by my grandfather's workers. Since the war, the foundry has experienced different periods and changes. Foundries need continuity, it is a job in which you cannot improvise, handed down from one generation to the next, so the children continue to do what the father does. For me it all started when I was a child and learned the craft and growing up with it. My children then continued, I think because they were born to it; they have always had in them the art of their father without necessarily practicing it. I never told them to work in the foundry, but you can see that they themselves have recognized the charm of this work and the respect it inspires in people, because not everyone can work bronze. A profession must never be obligatory, and my children have had the freedom to choose. This makes it possible for them to work with pleasure today, and for the foundry to continue. Now we must hope that my children's children will continue this activity. The story that I am telling you now, started a long time before me and my children.

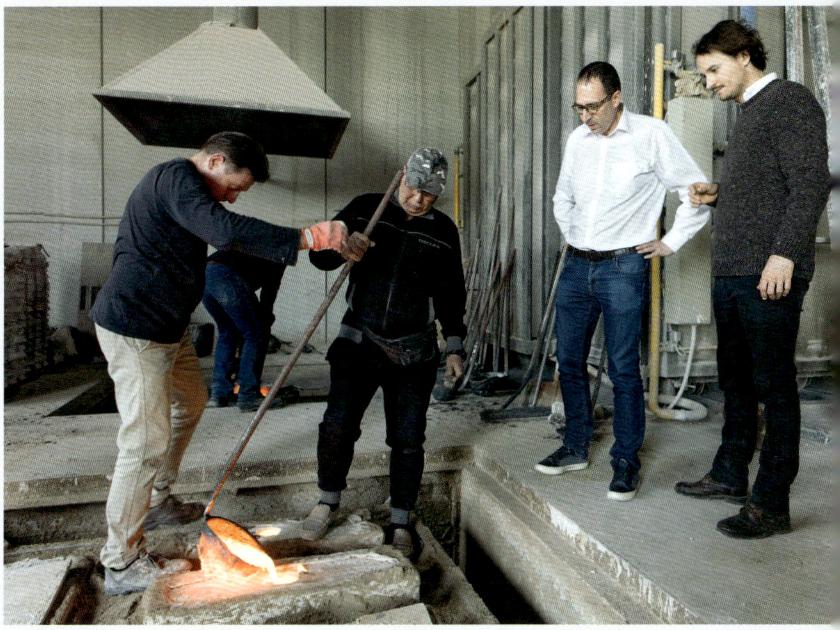

Mario Liccardo, Pasquale Del Giudice, Thomas Abegg und Mirko Baselgia (von links nach rechts) während des Bronzegießens / Mario Liccardo, Pasquale Del Giudice, Thomas Abegg and Mirko Baselgia (from left to right) during the bronze pouring

LG: The foundry has experienced great development over the last few years and several leading contemporary artists have decided to collaborate with you. What have been the challenges of this recent evolution and what are the future prospects?

PDG: The main challenge of this evolution has been that, in our profession, we acquire a reputation very slowly, piece by piece, and we must have the opportunity to do important works. We started the new foundry; it used to be completely artisanal and there was little space. I lost about 10 years, in which I already had the land, but I couldn't do anything with it, mainly because of the Italian bureaucracy [laughs]. In the end, I was an industrial-artisan and I built the current structure, which allowed us to create an image. The first challenge was

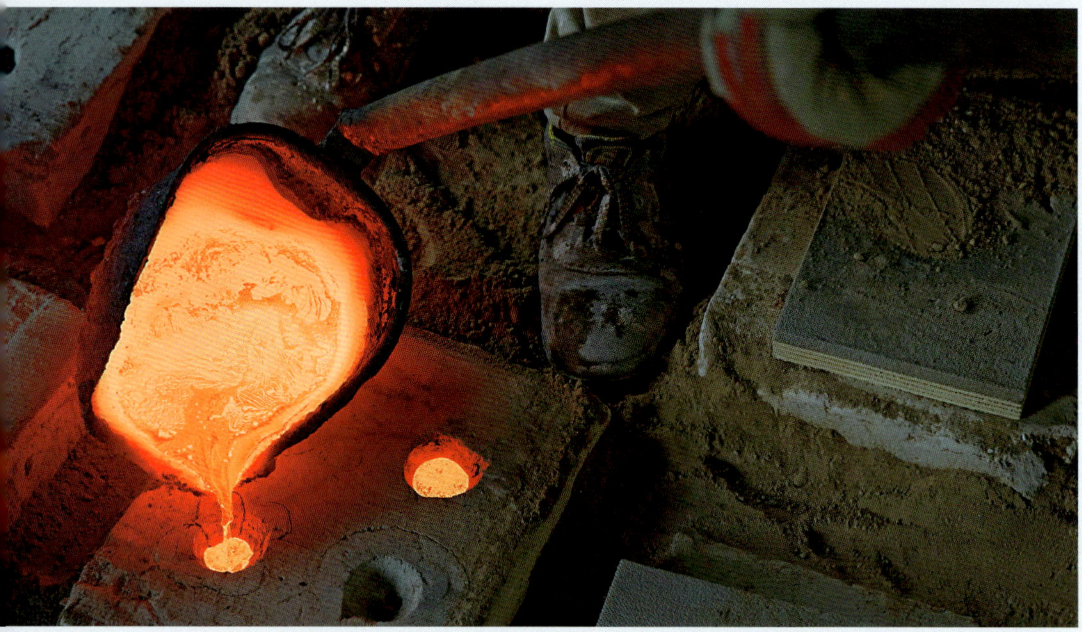

Geschmolzene Bronze (über 1.000 °C) wird in die Form gegossen / Molten bronze (over 1,000 °C) is poured into the investment mold

Abdessemeds Monumentalskuptur *Coup de tête* aus dem Jahr 2012], eine weitere große Herausforderung. Wir erhielten diesen Auftrag, da es Sommer war und sonst niemand zur Verfügung stand. So machten wir den nächsten Sprung, der es uns ermöglichte, neues technisches Know-how zu erwerben. Danach arbeiteten wir an einer Restaurierung im Vatikan, Pericle Fazzinis Skulptur *Die Auferstehung* in der vatikanischen Audienzhalle. All diese Arbeiten dienen als Leistungsausweis für die Gießerei. Dann gab es da noch die Zusammenarbeit mit Ugo Rondinone, dem eine besondere Rolle für unsere Entwicklung zukommt. Diese Arbeiten sind oft schwierig. Je schwieriger sie aber sind, desto mehr Zufriedenheit verschaffen sie uns. Wie die Madonnina-Statue in Mailand, die uns große Resonanz verschaffte. Es ist wie Punkte sammeln. Jede Arbeit bringt einen Extrapunkt, und das verhilft der Gießerei dazu, den nächsten Schritt zu tun. Wir unterscheiden uns vielleicht von den anderen Gießereien darin, dass wir immer versuchen, einen Schritt weiter zu sein. Als die anderen noch neapolitanische Figuren produzierten, die sich nicht mehr so gut verkauften, haben wir bereits zur Monumentalskulptur gewechselt. Als die anderen dann auf das Monumentale setzten, begannen wir bereits für zeitgenössische Künstlerinnen und Künstler zu arbeiten etc. Was die Zukunft angeht, liegt diese nicht in meinen Händen, sondern in denen meiner Söhne. Das Einzige, was ich hierzu sagen kann, ist, dass man niemals mit der Arbeit innehalten darf, wenn man eine Gießerei betreibt. Du musst immer einen Extrasprung voraus sein. Eine Gießerei kann viele neue Dinge angehen. Du darfst dich nie mit dem zufriedengeben, was du gerade machst. Eine Idee kann viele neue hervorbringen. Du brauchst eine Vision, um dich immer ein Stück weiterzuentwickeln.

LG: Wie stellst du dir die Gießerei in 20 Jahren vor?

PDG: Ein bisschen ruhiger. Man soll verstehen, dass hier Kunst gemacht wird. Oft verstehen es die Leute nicht, was es bedeutet, Kunst zu schaffen. Sie glauben, dass man die Dinge von einem Tag auf den anderen machen kann, während man Ruhe zum Kunstschaffen braucht. Kunstwerke sind für die Ewigkeit bestimmt, daher ist es sinnlos, die Dinge zu übereilen. Das ist eine Gewohnheit, die wir uns angeeignet haben, da wir sehr schnell arbeiten. Und dann ersticken wir in Arbeit. Ich möchte, dass sich die Gießerei der Kunst widmet, aber auf eine gelassene Art, und vor allem müssen wir auch Zeit haben, unser Leben zu leben. Wir mussten oft an Sonntagen arbeiten, um Verpflichtungen nachzukommen, die beinahe unmöglich waren, die wir aber möglich gemacht haben. Man kann aber nicht über einen längeren Zeitraum hinweg auf diese Weise arbeiten. Man braucht Ruhe. Das wünsche ich mir. Sonst liegt alles in den Händen meiner vier Kinder. Ich vertraue ihnen, vorausgesetzt, dass sie weitermachen. Im Leben ist alles möglich. Ich glaube aber, dass das der Fall sein wird. Die Arbeit hält sie so beschäftigt, dass es gar nicht anders sein kann [*lacht*].

a monumental work in Israel that represents the 12 apostles with Jesus, constructed in just 3 months. So, we kind of challenged the world, because there were other foundries in Spain and England that could have done this work. And since we needed to collaborate with another foundry to make the work in such a short time, and I still had my old foundry, the two foundries worked together. This experience allowed us to understand where we could go. Then we made Zidane's sculpture [Adel Abdessemed's monumental sculpture *Coup de tête*, made in 2012], another big challenge. We managed to get this job because it was summer and there was no one else willing to do it. So, we took another step forward, which allowed us to acquire new technical knowledge. We then worked on a restoration in the Vatican, the *Resurrection* of Pericle Fazzini in the Paul VI Hall. All these works serve as documentation for the foundry. There is also the collaboration with Ugo Rondinone who played a particular role in our evolution. Often these works are difficult, but for us, the more difficult they are, the more we derive satisfaction from them. For example, the Madonnina in Milan, which brought us a lot of publicity. You could say that it's a question of scoring, in which case each work is an extra point, and this allows the foundry to move forward. Perhaps what distinguishes our foundry from the others is that we always try to be one step ahead. When the others produced Neapolitan figurines that were no longer selling so well, we had already switched to monumental sculpture. When the others launched themselves into the monumental, we had already started working for contemporary artists, and so on. At this point, concerning our prospects, the future is not in my hands, but in those of my boys. The only thing I can say is that, to run a foundry, you must never stand still. You always have to make an extra leap. There are many other things that the foundry can do, you can't be satisfied with what you're already doing. Many more things can develop from one thing, and you need to have vision to be able to move forward.

LG: What would you like the foundry to look like in 20 years' time?

PDG: A little calmer. That is to say, to understand that one is making art. Often people don't understand what it means to create art, they believe that things can be made from one day to the next, while to make art you have to be able to take your time. The artworks remain forever, and it is useless do things in a hurry. It's a practice that we have learned, because by nature we are very fast. As a consequence, we end up being overwhelmed by the work. What I would like is a foundry dedicated to artwork, but with tranquillity, and above all we must also have time to live our own lives. In fact, we have often had to work on Sundays to keep commitments, which were almost impossible, but we did it. But you can't work like that in the long term, you have to be calm. That's what I wish. For the rest, everything is in the hands of my 4 children, and I have confidence in them, provided that they continue to get along, because in life you never know. But I think it will be the case, because the work will keep them so busy it can't be otherwise [*laughs*].

ANTONIO DEL GIUDICE

LAURA GIUDICI

Laura Giudici: Antonio, du bist der älteste Sohn und selbst Künstler. Hattest du je Zweifel, die Familientradition fortzusetzen? Aus welchen Gründen hast du diesen Weg gewählt?

Antonio Del Giudice: Wie ich immer sage, das Gusshandwerk ist Teil unserer DNA. Ich hatte schon immer eine Leidenschaft für das Abformen und allgemein für das Gießen und die Gießerei. Als ich ein Kind war, gab es verschiedene Systeme in der Gießereitechnik. Im Laufe der Zeit entwickelten sich die Materialien, Techniken und Maschinen weiter. Vielleicht gab mir dies den Anreiz, kontinuierlich nach innovativen Materialien zu suchen, und folglich in der Gießerei ein Wachstumspotenzial zu sehen. Neben der Technik interessierte mich aber auch das Verhältnis zu den Kunden, und die Möglichkeit, geeignete Kunden für unsere Gießerei zu finden. Aus diesem Grund beschloss ich, meine Studien zuerst an der Kunstschule und dann an der Kunstakademie fortzusetzen. Die Kunstakademie war eine gute Anlaufstelle für mich und die Gießerei. Ich begriff, welche Gemeinsamkeiten es zwischen der Gießerei und den Künstlerinnen und Künstlern geben könnte. Vor allem aber hatte ich die Möglichkeit, mich der zeitgenössischen Kunst anzunähern. Die Auseinandersetzung mit der zeitgenössischen Kunst ermöglichte es mir später, Ugo Rondinone zu treffen, einer der ersten Künstler, der mit der Gießerei zusammenarbeitete. Es war Ugo Rondinone, der mir dann Mirko vorstellte, da wir beide an einem seiner Projekte arbeiteten. Ich glaube, das war vor mindestens zehn Jahren. Wenn damals Ugo Rondinones Arbeiten die schwierigsten für uns waren, dann sind es heute die von Mirko [*lacht*].

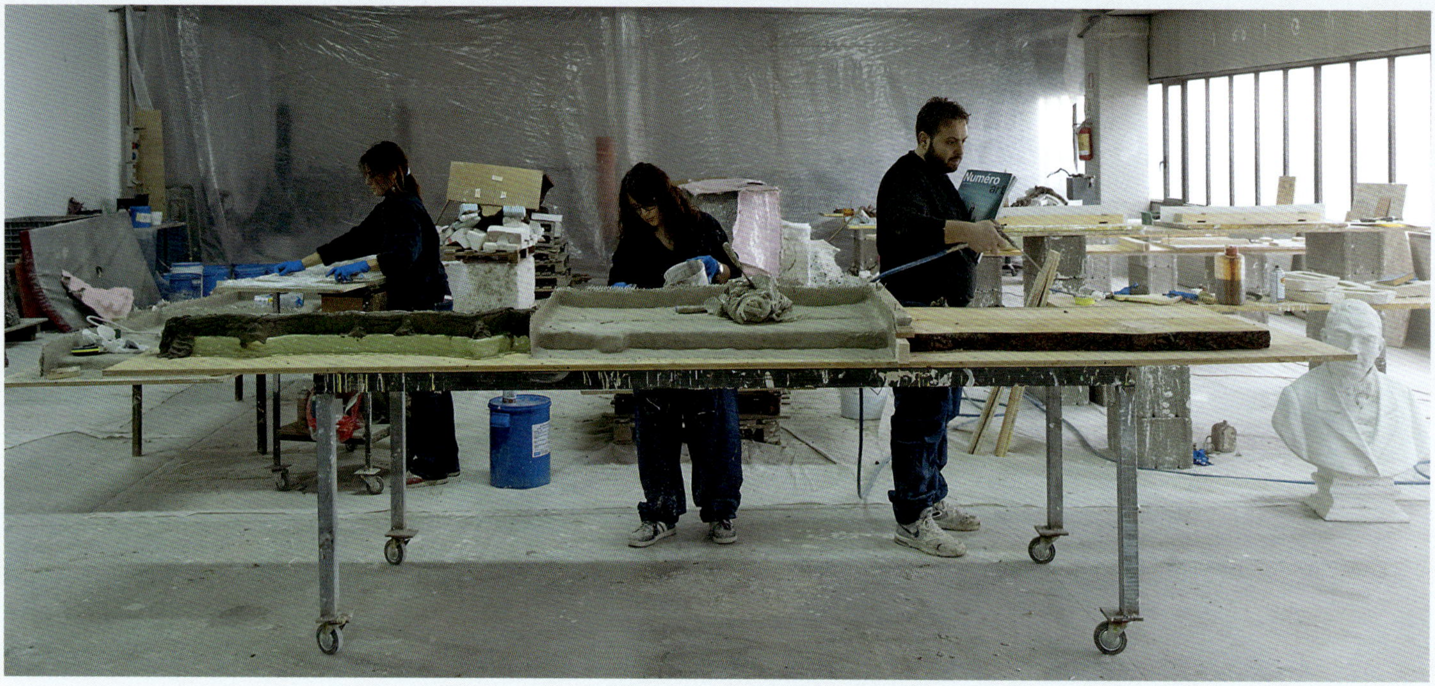

ANTONIO DEL GIUDICE

Laura Giudici: Antonio, you are the eldest son and you are an artist yourself. Has continuing the family tradition ever been a doubt for you? What were the reasons that led you to continue along this path?

Antonio Del Giudice: As I've always said, it's part of our DNA. I have always had a passion for moulding, and also for casting and foundry in general. Consider that when I was a child there were different systems in the foundry technique, and over time there has been an evolution in materials, techniques and machinery. Maybe this was my stimulus, to always go in search of innovations in materials, and to see a potential for growth for the foundry. In addition to the technique, I was also stimulated by the relationship with customers, and the fact that I had to find suitable customers for our foundry. For this reason, too, I decided to continue my studies, first at art college and then at the academy of Fine Arts. The academy of Fine Arts was a good reference point for me and the foundry. Let's say that I understood well what could be in common between the foundry and the artists, and above all I had the opportunity to deal with contemporary art. This confrontation with contemporary art later allowed me to meet Ugo Rondinone, one of the first contemporary artists to collaborate with the foundry. It was Ugo Rondinone who introduced me to Mirko, as we were both working on one of his projects. I think it was at least ten years ago. In this regard, if at the time the works of Ugo Rondinone were the most difficult for us, I can say that now they are those of Mirko [*laughs*].

LG: How would you define Mirko's work? What are the aspects that you particularly appreciate and, maybe, those that you find hardest to perceive?

ADG: I like Mirko's work because it brings together nature and technique. I really appreciate

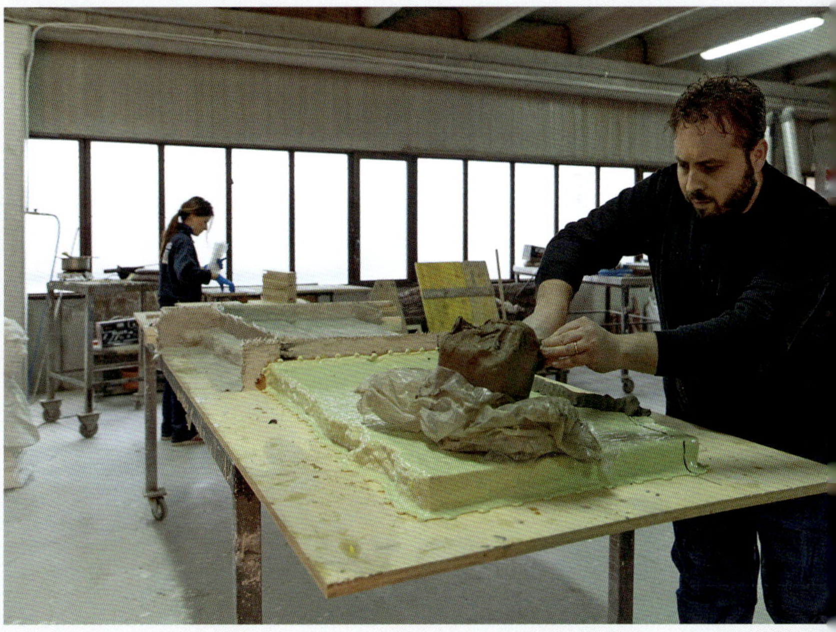

Links: Antonio Del Giudice und zwei Mitarbeiterinnen der Gießerei bei der Vorbereitung der Silikonformen für die liegenden Reliefs / Left: Antonio Del Giudice and two collaborators of the foundry during the preparation of the silicone rubber molds for the horizontal reliefs / Auf dieser Seite: Antonio Del Giudice beim Herstellen einer starren Außenform auf der Silikonkautschukschicht / On this page: Antonio Del Giudice creating a rigid outer mold on the silicone rubber layer

his works and they represent a challenge for us every time, and I think for him too. It almost seems that he's willing to conceive works that push us to our limits with regard to the technique and the realization [*laughs*]. But so far these challenges have all been successfully overcome.

I appreciate all of Mirko's work, and I don't find it difficult to perceive his basic themes. I find that over time he has also found his own line of action. And what can I say, for me his work is simply beautiful.

LG: Tell us about the installation of the sculpture in Valbella. What are the aspects that had to be taken into account? Have there been any particular difficulties?

LG: Wie würdest du Mirkos Arbeiten beschreiben? Welche Aspekte sprechen dich besonders an und welche kannst du nur schwer nachvollziehen?

ADG: Ich mag Mirkos Arbeiten, da sie Natur und Technik vereinen. Ich schätze seine Werke sehr. Sie stellen uns jedes Mal vor eine Herausforderung, und auch ihn, wie ich glaube. Ich habe den Eindruck, dass er seine Arbeiten so konzipiert, dass sie auch uns im Hinblick auf Technik und Ausführung auf die Probe stellen [*lacht*]. Bisher aber konnten wir alle Schwierigkeiten erfolgreich meistern.

Ich mag alle Arbeiten von Mirko. Ich finde es nicht schwierig, seine Grundthemen zu erfassen. Meiner Ansicht nach hat er im Laufe der Zeit seine eigene Vorgehensweise gefunden. Ich bewundere seine Arbeiten.

LG: Beschreibe die Installation der Skulptur in Valbella. Welche Aspekte mussten berücksichtigt werden? Gab es besondere Schwierigkeiten?

ADG: Es gab keine besonderen Schwierigkeiten. Ganz im Gegenteil. Mirko versteht sich darauf, den Auftraggeber, die Arbeiter und alle Beteiligten, einschließlich dich, einzubeziehen.

Wir sahen uns nicht mit besonderen Schwierigkeiten konfrontiert, die Arbeit war aber sehr langwierig. Der Kranführer arbeitete sehr effizient. Wir fanden alles ordentlich vor, sodass die Arbeit reibungslos über die Bühne ging, auch wenn es anstrengend war. Vor ihrer definitiven Aufstellung war die Arbeit bereits aufgebaut worden, in Genf und in der Gießerei selbst. Daher wussten wir, wie wir vorzugehen hatten.

LG: Dieses Projekt nahm sehr viel Zeit und Arbeit in Anspruch. Was waren die größten technischen Herausforderungen, die ihr in Angriff nehmen musstet?

ADG: Da wir die Arbeit ruhig angehen, war die Ausführung nicht so schwierig für uns. Bevor wir die Arbeit produzierten, waren wir jedoch monatelang mit der Planung beschäftigt, um die beste Vorgehensweise zu finden. Gerade die Holztafeln bestanden aus lauter Segmenten, schmalen und breiten. Die einzige Schwierigkeit lag darin, all diese Formen in Bronze zu gießen. Die Tafeln wurden dann in drei Teilen gefertigt und mehrere Male reproduziert, in Wachs und schließlich in Bronze. Als schwierig gestaltete es sich, dass man bei jedem Schritt dasselbe Ergebnis erhalten musste. Schließlich hatten wir Erfolg. Wir mussten auch versuchen, dem Holzmodell möglichst treu zu bleiben, auch aus Respekt für Daniel, der wie wir sehr viel Mühe in diese Arbeit gesteckt hat. Wir haben gute Arbeit geleistet. Es war eine große Herausforderung.

ADG: I would say there have been no particular difficulties. On the contrary, going back to the previous question, it's nice the involvement that Mirko creates with the client, with the operators and with all people involved, including you.

Although there were no particular difficulties, it was a very long job. The crane operator was very efficient, however, and we found everything in order, so there were no particular difficulties there, but it was tiring. We must also consider that, before the final installation, the work had already been installed other times, in Geneva and in the foundry itself, so the procedure was very clear.

LG: This project took a lot of time and work. What are the main technical challenges you had to face?

ADG: I have to say that, perhaps because we take the work much more lightly, it wasn't difficult for us. In any case, before putting the work into production, it took months of planning to figure out the best way to do it. Above all, you have to consider that the wooden panels were a network of segments, where narrower and wider segments were alternating, and therefore the main difficulty was how to take up all these forms with bronze. The panels were then made in three parts, and were reproduced several times, in wax and bronze. The difficulty was that at each step you had to get to the same result, and in the end, we managed to get it. We also had to try to be as faithful as possible to the wooden model, also out of respect for Daniel, who like us has put a lot of effort into this work. It was a good job; it was a good challenge.

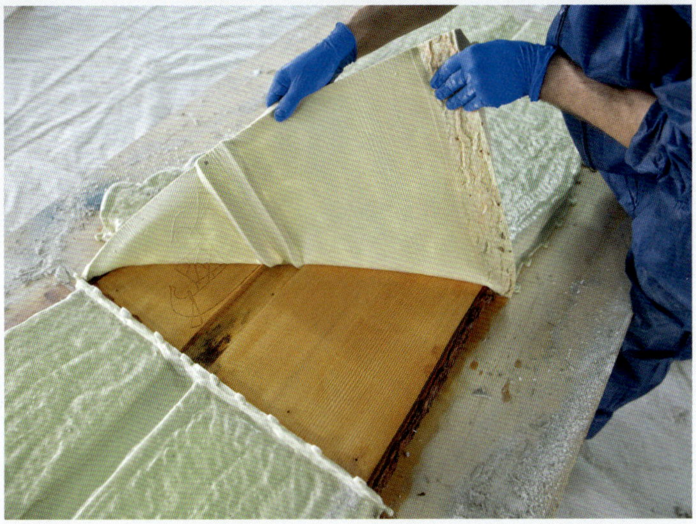

Die Silikonkautschukschicht auf einem der liegenden Reliefs / The silicon rubber layer on one of the horizontal reliefs

MARCELLO DEL GIUDICE

LAURA GIUDICI

Laura Giudici: Marcello, du koordinierst die täglichen internen und externen Aktivitäten der Gießerei. Was ist dein Geheimnis für eine harmonische und effiziente interne Kommunikation?

Marcello Del Giudice: Ein Familienunternehmen ist voller Fallstricke. Man muss das Familienleben von der Arbeit trennen. Weder Ruhephasen noch Momente familiärer Spannung dürfen das ultimative Ziel des Unternehmens beeinflussen: die Bedürfnisse der Künstler zu erfüllen.

Die Kommunikation sollte immer den Aufgaben berücksichtigen, denen jeder von uns in seinem Kompetenzbereich nachkommt. Wir versuchen, jeden Einzelnen zu stimulieren, an dem gemeinsamen Projekt zu arbeiten und die Künstlerinnen und Künstler zufriedenzustellen.

LG: Die Zusammenarbeit mit Mirko begann vor vielen Jahren. Wie nahm sie ihren Anfang und wie entwickelte sie sich im Lauf der Zeit?

MDG: Ich habe Mirko ein paar Jahre nach seinem ersten Projekt in unserem Unternehmen getroffen. Seine künstlerische Entwicklung in Bezug auf die technischen Schwierigkeiten seiner Projekte und die anspruchsvolleren Produktionsbedürfnisse hatte keinen Einfluss auf sein Verhalten. Mirko fordert komplexe Projekte, kommuniziert aber mit uns auf eine leicht verständliche Art. Ich glaube, dass sich seine Freundlichkeit und Bescheidenheit infolge seiner Arbeit weiterentwickelt haben.

LG: Kannst du uns eine Anekdote über ein großes Missverständnis erzählen, dass dir mit Mirko unterlaufen ist, oder einen ausgefallenen Wunsch von seiner Seite oder spannungsreiche Momente zwischen euch beiden?

MDG: Es gab keine Spannungen zwischen uns. Ich kann mich hingegen an einige ausgefallene Wünsche erinnern. Hierzu zählt das Projekt der Lavaschmelze. Wir trugen uns mit dem Gedanken, einen aktiven Vulkan aufzusuchen, mit Gussformen, um die Lava zu sammeln (das war natürlich Mirkos Idee). Wir endeten in der Gießerei mit Lavasteinen, die wir zum Schmelzen brachten. Es war ein wunderbares Experiment, sowohl aus künstlerischer als auch aus technischer Sicht. Und es hat sich meiner Meinung nach ausbezahlt.

LG: Dieses Projekt nahm sehr viel Zeit und Arbeit in Anspruch. Was waren die größten technischen Herausforderungen, die ihr meistern musstet?

MDG: Der Paravent war sicherlich ein herausfordendes Projekt. Von der Aufteilung der Arbeit für das Modell aus Wachs bis zur Montage. Es handelte sich um eine Art Arbeit, die in jeder Phase Schwierigkeiten bereitet, und für jede Phase des Projekts wurde daher eine Strategie gewählt, um systematisch vorzugehen. Der Erfolg einer Arbeit im Wachsausschmelzverfahren liegt in einer stringenten Arbeitsmethode in den einzelnen Phasen. Aufgrund seiner Komposition musste der Paravent in jedem einzelnen Schritt auf eine beinahe fanatische Art und Weise bearbeitet werden. Der technische Teil ging Hand in Hand mit der mentalen Annäherung an die Arbeit, die auf jedes einzelne Detail des Prozesses fokussiert war.

MARCELLO DEL GIUDICE

Laura Giudici: Marcello, you coordinate the daily activity of the foundry inside as well as outside. What are the secrets for a harmonious and efficient internal communication?

Marcello Del Giudice: A family business always hides pitfalls. You need to be careful not to mix the aspects of family life and work. Moments of relaxation or family tension should not affect the ultimate goal of the company: to satisfy the artist in his requests.

In this way communication is always established with respect for the roles of each one of us in their own field of competence. We try to encourage every member of the team to collaborate for the common project in order to satisfy the artist's requests.

LG: The collaboration with Mirko started many years ago now. How did it start and how has it evolved over time?

MDG: I met Mirko a few years after his first project in the company; his artistic evolution both in terms of technical difficulties of the projects and more demanding production needs did not affect his way of being. Mirko requires complex projects but he interfaces with us in the simplest possible way. I believe that kindness and simplicity have evolved as his work progresses.

LG: Would you have an anecdote to tell about a big misunderstanding that you had with Mirko or an extravagant request from him or maybe also an episode of particular tension between you two?

MDG: I don't think we had episodes of particular tension between us. I can count a few more extravagant requests instead. One of the projects I like to talk about is certainly the lava fusion. We started thinking about going to an active volcano, with casts ready to collect lava (Mirko's idea of course...). We ended up in the foundry with lava stones to melt. And we did it. It was a beautiful experiment, both artistic and technical, and I think it paid off.

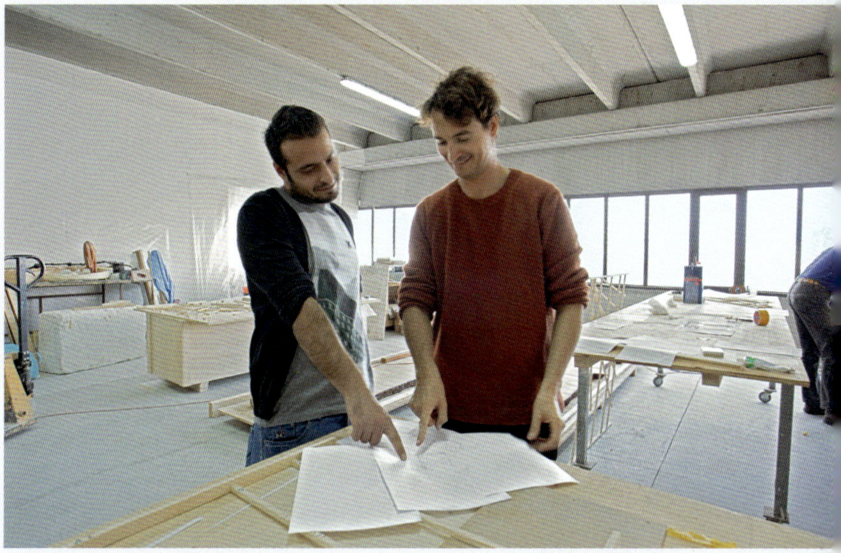

Links: Holzmodelle für den Paravent in der Werkstatt der Fonderia Nolana Del Giudice / Left: Wooden models for the screen in the workshop of the Fonderia Nolana Del Giudice / Auf dieser Seite: Marcello Del Giudice und Mirko Baselgia im Gespräch über den Produktionsprozess des Paravents / On this page: Marcello Del Giudice and Mirko Baselgia discussing the production process of the screen

LG: This project took a lot of time and work. What are the main technical challenges you had to face?

MDG: Certainly, the screen was a project with many pitfalls. From the division of the work for the model from wax to the assembly. It is a type of work that presents difficulties in each phase and for each phase of the project a strategy was chosen to work in an orderly manner. The success of a lost-wax casting work lies in the good working method of the individual phases. For its composition, the screen had to be dealt with almost obsessively in every single step. The technical part went hand in hand with a mental approach to the work that was focused on every single detail of the process.

LUCA DEL GIUDICE

LAURA GIUDICI

Laura Giudici: Luca, du warst hauptsächlich für die Erstellung der Wachse zuständig. War das schon immer so? Wie werden die Rollen zwischen euch Brüdern aufgeteilt? Und wie seid ihr zu der aktuellen Konstellation gelangt?

Luca Del Giudice: Anfangs war es nicht so. Im Laufe der Jahre aber erhielt jeder von uns eine präzise Aufgabe: einer von uns ist für das Abformen verantwortlich, der andere für das Finish und ich für die Wachse. Hier erhalten wir die positiven Wachsmodelle aus den Formen. Darauf folgt eine Reihe von Arbeits- und Vorbereitungsprozessen. Anschließend wird die Wachskopie im Brennofen gebrannt. Jeder Teil erfordert eine unterschiedliche Vorbereitung. Es handelt sich daher um einen Beruf, bei den man durch Erfahrung und in vielen Arbeitsjahren lernt, alles zu bewerkstelligen. Auch wenn jeder von uns Brüdern eine spezifische Aufgabe hat, kann jeder alles machen. Ab und zu kümmere ich mich um das Abformen, im Laufe der Zeit wurde aber klar, dass ich mich besonders für die Vorbereitung der Wachse und Formstoffe eignete, Antonio für das Abformen und Giuseppe für Finish. Mit der Zeit haben wir die Aufgaben gefunden, die am geeignetsten für uns sind. Letztendlich kann jeder von uns alles machen, jeder hat aber seine spezifischen Aufgaben.

LG: Inwieweit war Mirko in den Produktionsprozess eingebunden? Habt ihr viel diskutiert?

LDG: Als wir Mirko das erste Mal trafen, war er Ugo Rondinones Assistent. Wir trafen uns beim MUSAC [Museo de Arte Contemporáneo de Castilla y León] in Spanien. Die Chemie zwischen uns stimmte sofort, auch wenn wir die Gießerei waren und er der Assistent. Vielleicht entwickelte sich schon bei dieser Gelegenheit ein freundschaftliches Verhältnis zwischen uns. Im Laufe der Zeit wurde Mirko selbst ein wichtiger Künstler, und wir begannen, direkt mit ihm zusammenzuarbeiten. Im Gegensatz zu anderen Künstlern, die vielleicht ein wenig extravagant sind, ist es einfach, mit Mirko ohne große Diskussionen die richtige Lösung abzuwägen. Wir können die Lösung sofort finden, und in diesem Fall laden wir den Künstler ein, uns zu treffen und die verschiedenen Arbeitsschritte zu besprechen. Wir bringen beide Seiten zusammen. Es gibt Künstler, die jeden Produktionsschritt verfolgen möchten. Mirko aber vertraut der Gießerei und den Leuten, die dort arbeiten und macht von dieser Möglichkeit keinen Gebrauch. Auf jeden Fall versuchen wir, den Personen, die mit uns arbeiten, Vertrauen zu vermitteln, und ihnen nahezubringen, mit welch große Leidenschaft wir unserer Arbeit nachgehen. Wenn sie dann sehen, dass wir eine bestimmte Sache souverän ausführen, sind sie automatisch beruhigt. Der Dialog macht den Unterschied, aber auch der Wunsch, zu verstehen, was die Künstlerinnen und Künstler möchten. Das ist ein Vorteil für uns, aber auch für sie.

LG: Habt ihr öfter mit solch großen und komplexen Projekten zu tun oder stellte dieses Projekt eine außergewöhnliche Erfahrung dar?

LDG: Jedes Projekt, das wir erhalten, besitzt seine eigene Faszination. Mirkos Projekt war sehr ausgefeilt. Für diese Art Arbeit waren sehr viel Ruhe und, vor allem, Erfahrung notwendig. Es war zeitlich ein ziemlich aufwendiges Projekt, das Arbeitsaufteilung, Wachse, Teile etc. erforderte. Dieses Projekt war eine echte Herausforderung.

Alles, was wir tun, stellt jedoch eine Herausforderung für uns dar. Jedes neue Projekt, das eingeht, ist immer eine Realität für sich. Mirkos

LUCA DEL GIUDICE

Laura Giudici: Luca, you're mainly in charge of the realization of the waxes. Has it always been like this? How is the division of roles between you brothers and how did you get to the current configuration?

Luca Del Giudice: At the beginning it wasn't like that, then with the passing of the years each of us had a very precise role: someone is in charge of the moulding, someone is in charge of the finish and I took care of the wax department. Here we recover the positive waxes from the forms. Then there are some preparation processes and subsequently we can proceed with the baking of the dough. Each piece has a different preparation from the others. It is therefore a profession that, partly with experience and partly with the passing of the years, one can learn to assemble everything. Among us brothers, even if each of us has a specific role, everyone knows how to do everything. Every now and then, for example, I too take care of moulding, but the passage of time has made us understand that I was particularly suited to take care of the wax and dough preparation, Antonio for the moulding and Giuseppe for the finish department. So, let's say that over time we have gravitated towards the roles that best suit us. In the end we all know how to do everything, but each of us has his specific field.

LG: How much is Mirko involved in the production process? Do you discuss a lot?

LDG: When we first met Mirko, he was working as an assistant for Ugo Rondinone and we met him at MUSAC [Museo de Arte Contemporáneo de Castilla y León], in Spain. There was immediately this relationship of complicity between us, even though we were the foundry and he was the assistant. Perhaps already on that occasion a relationship of friendship and brotherhood between us was established. Over time, he too became an important artist and we began to collaborate directly. I must say, every time Mirko comes and we have to discuss some work, unlike other artists who may be a bit 'extravagant, with him you can always find the right solution without too much discussion, but by thinking and reflecting together. It happens that we can find the solution immediately, and in this case, we help the artist to understand the various steps. Together we can find a common ground between the two parts. There are artists who want to follow the production step by step, but Mirko has confidence in the foundry and in the people, who work there and does not feel this need. In any case, we try to inspire trust in the people who work with us, to make them understand the love we put into our work. Then, when they see us serene about the realization of a certain thing, they

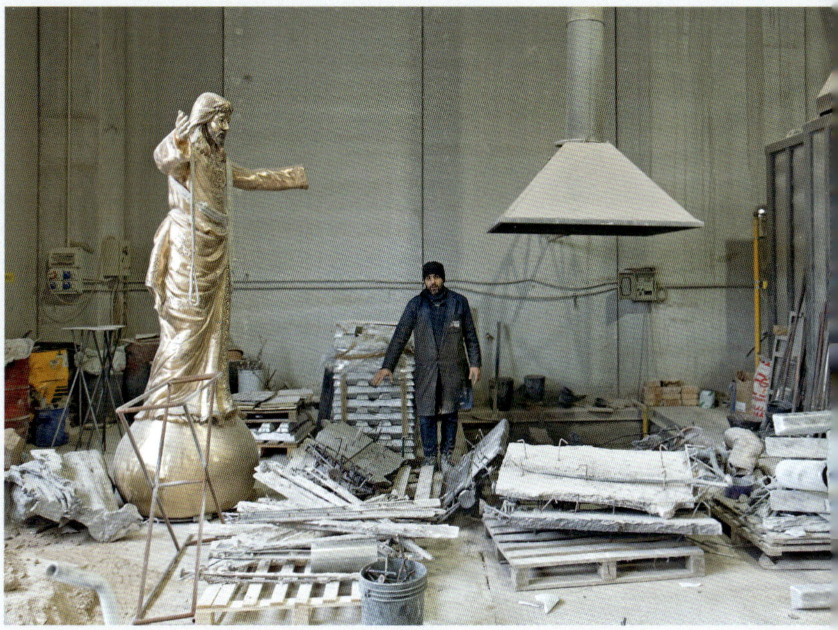

Luca Del Giudice bei der Sandgrube in der Werkstatt der Gießerei / Luca Del Giudice by the sand pit in the foundry's workshop

Projekt war wirklich gut. Es war bis ins letzte Detail ausgearbeitet und die Arbeit daran war sehr langwierig. Manche Teile bereiteten Schwierigkeiten. Je weiter wir jedoch mit dem Projekt vorankamen, desto besser gelang es uns, die damit verbundenen Probleme zu lösen. Das Projekt war eine große Herausforderung. Zum Glück haben wir es bewältigt. Mirko ist damit zufrieden, ebenso all jene, die die Arbeit gesehen haben. Und das ist unsere größte Genugtuung.

Luca Del Giudice bei der Vorbereitung der Gußkanäle aus Wachs, die am mit Wachs überzogenen Modell befestigt werden / Luca Del Giudice preparing the network of wax pipes to be attached to the wax-covered model

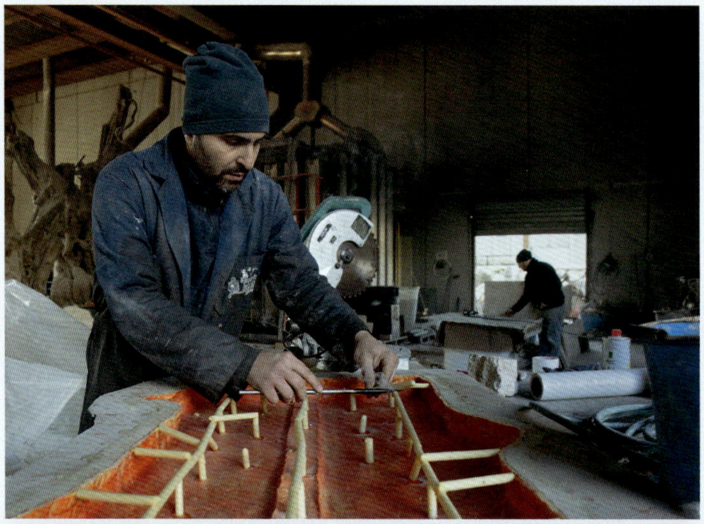

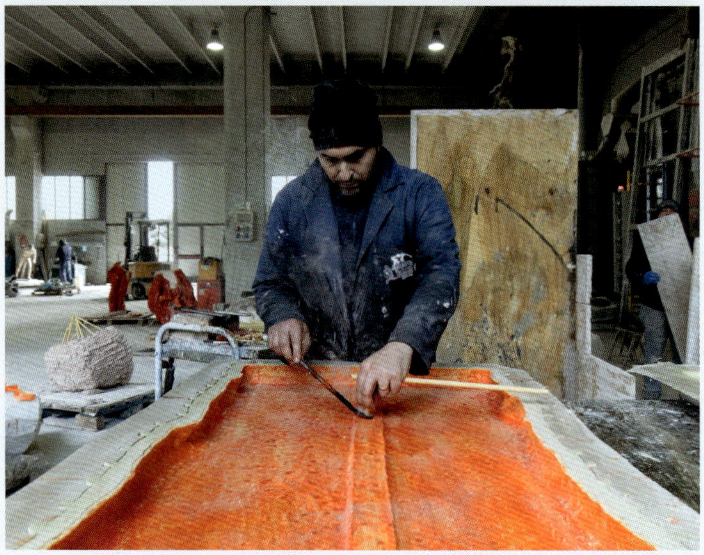

LG: Dieses Projekt nahm viel Zeit und Arbeit in Anspruch. Was waren die wichtigsten Herausforderungen, denen ihr euch stellen musstet?

LDG: Was die technischen Herausforderungen betrifft, bin ich der Meinung, dass, wenn man sich seiner Sache sicher ist und überzeugt davon ist, seine Aufgabe zu bewältigen, man mit keinerlei Problemen zu rechnen hat. Ganz im Gegenteil, je schwieriger sich die Aufgabe gestaltet, desto mehr Leidenschaft und Engagement steckt man in die Sache hinein, um sie zu meistern, insbesondere wenn es einmal schwierig gewesen wäre, wir uns aber im Laufe der Zeit die für die Ausführung notwendige Erfahrung angeeignet haben. Ich erinnere mich nur daran, dass es während der Verlegung der Wachsformen der Gitter in die Schale eine kleine Bewegung gab, die nach dem Gießen zu einer vergrößerten Form führte. So mussten wir das Ganze wiederholen. Da wir den Schaden aber zum Glück sofort beheben konnten, stellten wir sicher, dass die Arbeit so fortgesetzt wurde, als ob es dieses kleine Missgeschick niemals gegeben hätte.

are automatically serene too. Let's say that maybe it's this dialogue that makes the difference, but also our desire to understand what the artists want. This is an advantage for all concerned

LG: Are you used to such large and elaborate projects or was working on this project a rather exceptional experience?

LDG: Every project that comes to us has its own charm. Mirko's project was really a very elaborate one, which took a long time and above all experience because of the type of work. It was a fairly long project, including subdivision, waxes, pieces and everything else. So, it was really a challenge.

Everything we do is challenging, so every new project that comes to us has different requirements. Mirko's project was a really interesting one, studied in detail. It took a long time to work on his project. Sometimes, for example, there were pieces that didn't go well, but nevertheless, as we progressed, we managed to solve the problems as they arose. So, this project was a great challenge, but luckily everything went well. Mirko is happy, as are the people who saw the work, and that is our greatest satisfaction.

LG: This project took a lot of time and work. What are the main technical challenges you had to face?

LDG: Look, what I can tell you about the technical challenges is that, when we are serene about something and we are sure we can do it, we don't encounter any particular problems. On the contrary, the more difficult a thing is to do, the more there is that passion and that desire to succeed in achieving it, especially if in the past it could have been difficult, but, as the years go by, we have gained the experience necessary to do it. Perhaps the only thing that comes to my mind is that, during the movement of the wax forms of the grids in the box, there was a small movement, following the casting, which caused the expansion of the form. So, we had to redo the piece, but fortunately, we could resolve the problem immediately, and made sure that the work continued as if that little hitch never happened.

GIUSEPPE DEL GIUDICE

LAURA GIUDICI

Laura Giudici: Giuseppe, du beschäftigst dich hauptsächlich mit dem Bronzeguss. Kannst du uns etwas über deine Ausbildung und Spezialisierung erzählen?

Giuseppe Del Giudice: Ich näherte mich dem Bronzeguss bereits in meiner Kindheit an, als ich meinen Vater zur Gießerei meines Großvaters begleitete. Die Leidenschaft, die mich zu dieser Arbeit antreibt, entspringt der Hingabe meines Vaters und seiner konstanten Auseinandersetzung mit dem Gusshandwerk.

Jede Arbeit trägt dazu bei, Erfahrung zu schaffen, der die tägliche Arbeit mit den Künstlerinnen und Künstlern. Unsere Neugier regt auch zu neuen Experimenten an. Die jahrhundertelange Reise der Familie Del Giudice begann als Silberziselierer bis hin zur heutigen Tätigkeit der Gießerei.

LG: Schildere uns den Aufbau des Skulpturenensembles in Genf. Welche Aspekte mussten berücksichtigt werden? Gab es besondere Schwierigkeiten?

GDG: Wir mussten verschiedene Probleme in Bezug auf die Installierung an einem öffentlichen Ort berücksichtigen. Wir mussten im Boden verankerte Metallbasen anfertigen, um eine solide Struktur zu schaffen. Der Platz ist unterschiedlich hoch, sodass es nicht möglich war, das Werk abzusichern. Die einzelnen Teile wurden per Hand bewegt, da es nicht möglich war, die passenden Maschinen vor Ort zu bringen. Wir führten jedes Teil vor Ort aus In vier Stunden gelang es uns, das gesamte Werk aufzubauen und zu installieren.

LG: Die Produktion von Bronzegüssen mittels Wachsausschmelzverfahren ist eine sehr alte Technik. Beeinflussen neue Technologien dieses Verfahren? Wenn ja, auf welche Weise?

GDG: In der Vergangenheit wurde Steinkohle verwendet, um die Brennöfen anzuheizen, in denen die Metalle geschmolzen wurden. Die neuen Gas- und Schmelzöfen beschleunigen hingegen die erste Arbeitsphase, die Produktionszeiten sind jedoch dieselben. Wie uns die Tradition lehrt: „Gut Ding will Weile haben."

Heute verwenden wir in unserer Gießerei die besten Maschinen der neuesten Generation, die uns erlauben, präzise und grosse Projekte zu verwirklichen: 3D-Scanning, Prototyping, Lasergravieren, 3D-Printing, Kunstguss und Feinguss Kunststoffe, Vergrößerung von Skulpturen und Restaurierungstechniken.

LG: Dieses Projekt nahm sehr viel Zeit und Arbeit in Anspruch. Was waren die größten technischen Schwierigkeiten, die ihr in Angriff nehmen musstet?

GDG: Die Arbeit war sehr aufwendig und erforderte ein Maximum an Präzision. Jeder Teil wurde rechtwinklig angeordnet und positioniert. Die Zusammensetzung war zeit- und arbeitsintensiv. Die größten Herausforderungen lagen in der Präzision, der Reinigung und der Montage der Arbeit vor Ort. Bronze kann mithilfe der Patinierung auf unterschiedlichste Weise vollendet werden, indem das Material glänzend, leuchtend, braun oder grün wird.

GIUSEPPE DEL GIUDICE

Laura Giudici: Giuseppe, you are mainly involved in bronze casting. Tell us about your training and specialization.

Giuseppe Del Giudice: My relationship with bronze casting began at an early age, when I used to go with my father to see my grandfather's foundry as a child. The passion that drives me to do this work comes from my father's dedication and constant observation of the foundry practice. Each work contributes to creating that experience that is formed thanks to daily work with the artists and the curiosity that stimulates experimentation. The century long journey of the Del Giudice family began as silver chiselers until today's foundry work.

LG: Tell us about the installation of the sculptural ensemble in Geneva. What are the aspects that had to be taken into account? Were there any particular difficulties?

GDG: We had to take into account various problems related to the installation in a public space. It was necessary to create metal bases anchored to the ground to create strong structures; the square had differences in height that made it impossible to secure the work. The works were moved manually because it was not possible to bring the appropriate machinery into the square. We made every single piece on site and in four hours we were able to set up and install the entire work.

LG: The production of bronzes with the technique of lost wax is very old. Have new technologies had an influence on this technique? If yes, in what way?

GDG: In the past, hard coal was used to power the furnaces in which the metals were melted. Today, with gas and smelting furnaces, the manual process for the first phase of setting up the work has been speeded up, but the production times have remained the same. In fact, as tradition teaches us: "It takes a long time to do things well".

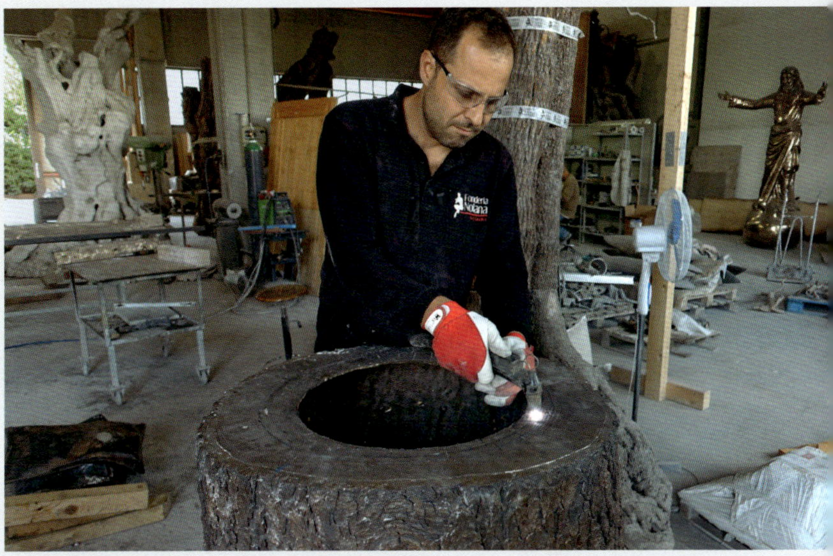

Giuseppe Del Giudice bei der Endbearbeitung der Quelle / Giuseppe Del Giudice during the finishing of the spring

Today, in our foundry, we use the best machines of the latest generation that allow us to do detailed and laborious work such as: 3D scanning, prototyping, laser engraving, 3D printing, artistic casting and micro fusion casting, synthetic materials, sculptures' enlargement and restoration techniques.

LG: This project took a lot of time and work. What are the main technical challenges you had to face?

GDG: The work was very laborious and of maximum precision. Each piece was squared and positioned. Its assembly took a lot of time and dedication. The main challenges were the precision, cleaning and assembly of the work on site. Bronze can be finished in a variety of ways using patinas that make the material shiny, bright, brown or green.

Auf dieser Seite und rechts: Einige Schritte der Endbearbeitung und der Patinierung der Bronzegüsse / On this page and left: Some steps of the finishing process and patination of the bronze castings

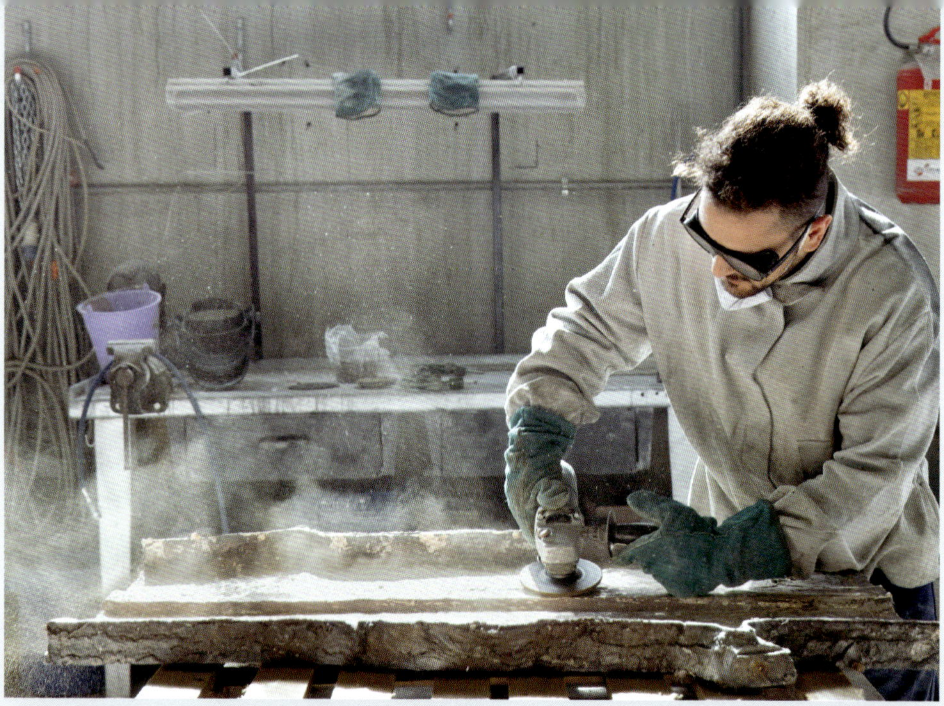

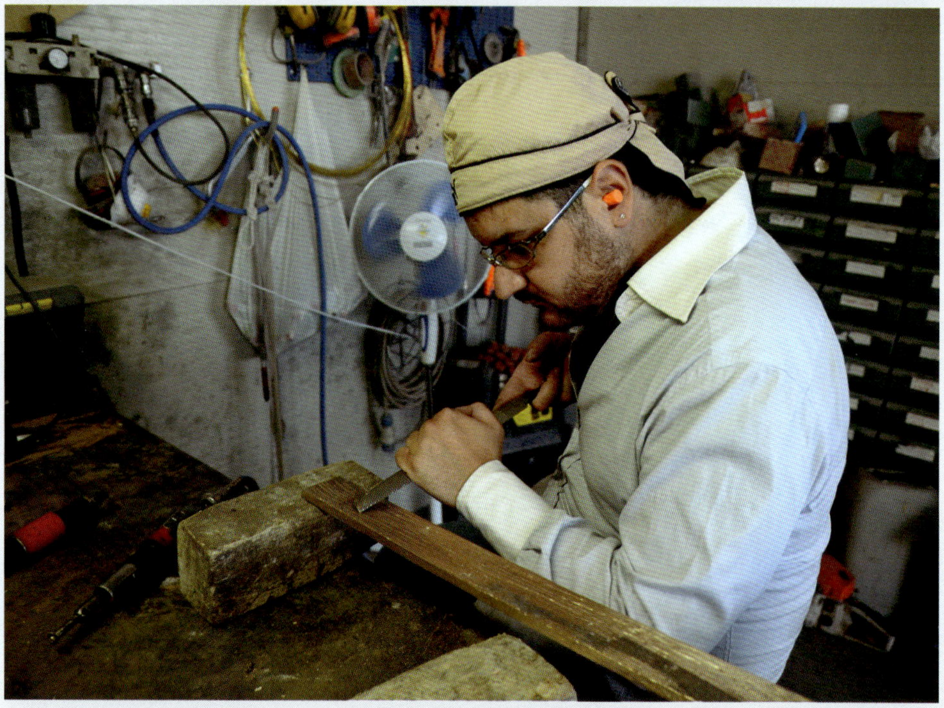

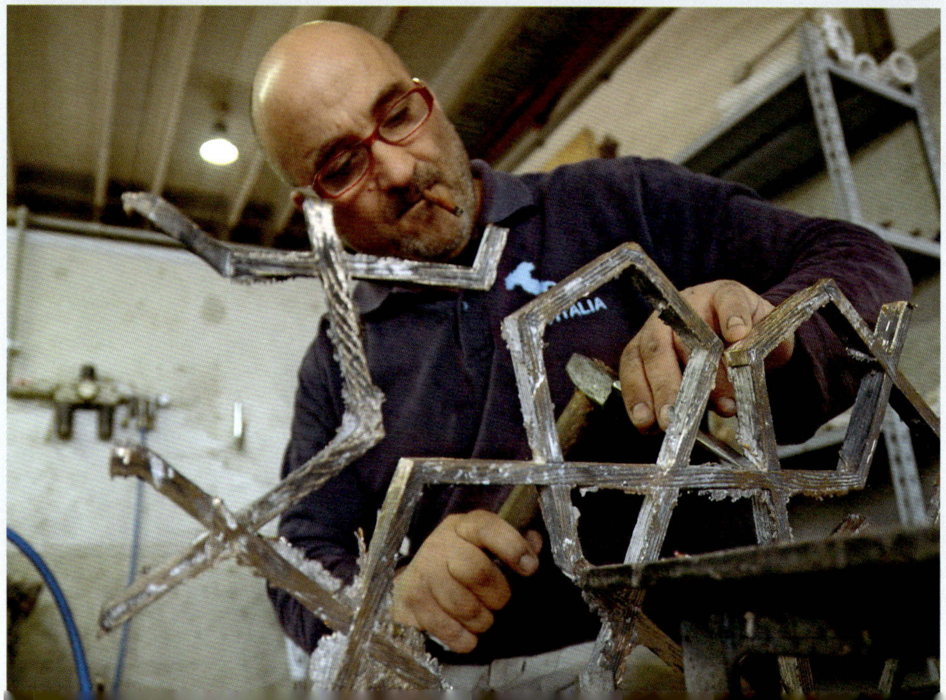

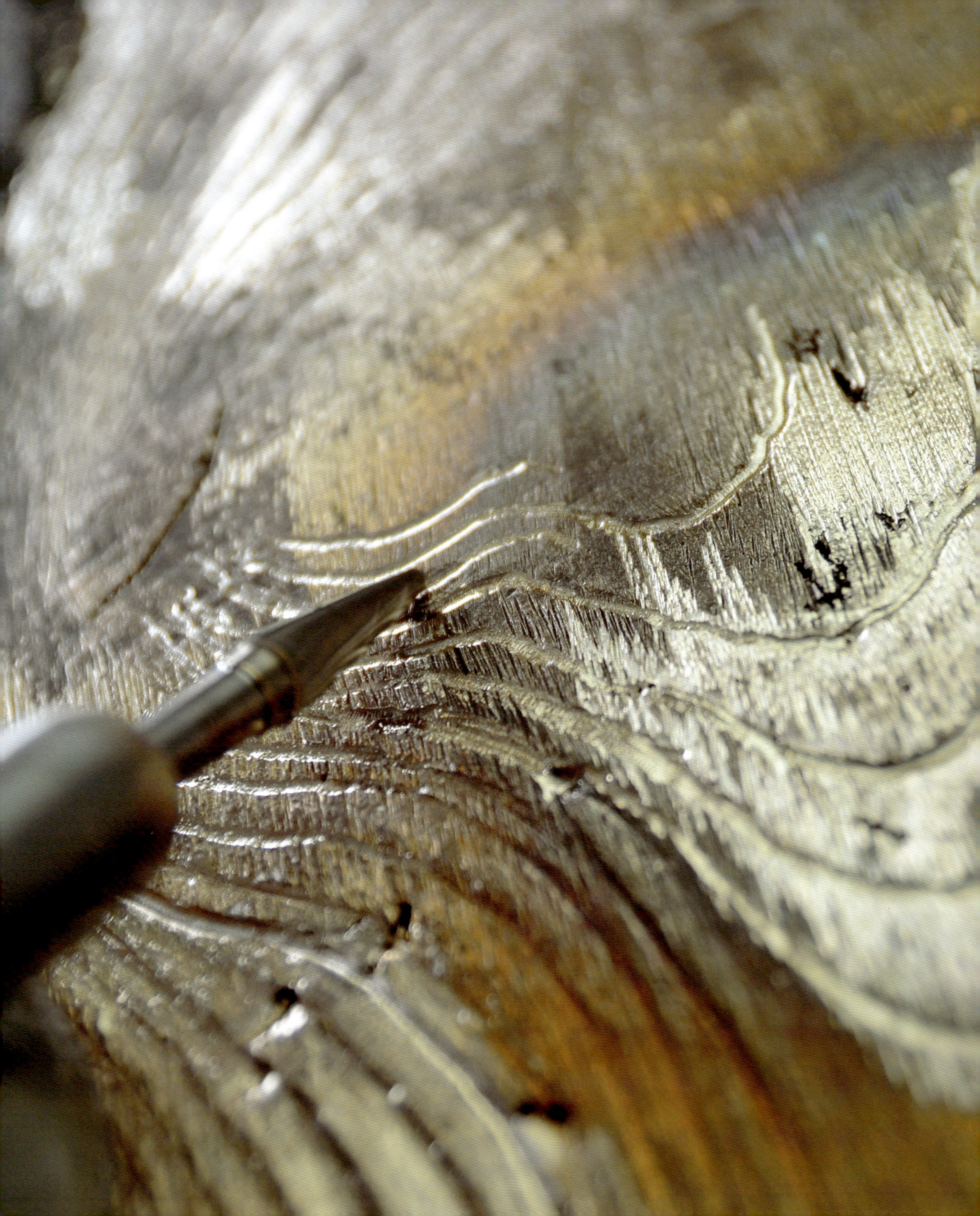

DANIEL MARGRETH IM GESPRÄCH MIT LAURA GIUDICI

Laura Giudici: Wie und wann hast du beschlossen, Schreiner zu werden?

Daniel Margreth: Das stand nie zur Debatte. Mein Großvater war schon Schreiner, einige meiner Onkel sind Schreiner. Die Schreinerei liegt mir im Blut. Es war kein Thema. Es war immer klar. Wie eine Berufung.

LG: Wann hast du begonnen, mit Mirko zusammenzuarbeiten? Wie würdest du eure Zusammenarbeit beschreiben?

DM: Ich arbeite mit Mirko seit Ende 2016 zusammen. Dieses Projekt war unser erstes gemeinsames. Zur damaligen Zeit war ich anderweitig beschäftigt, und ich dachte mir, dass die Zeit für einen Wechsel gekommen sei. So begann ich, mich mit meinen Interessen auseinanderzusetzen. Ich habe mit Mirko gesprochen und dann meinen Job gekündigt, obwohl ich noch keine Arbeit von ihm bekommen hatte. Aber ich dachte mir: „Jetzt mache ich Kunst." Einige Zeit später erhielt ich eine Anfrage für dieses Projekt, das mich natürlich fesselte, da es genau das war, was ich immer machen wollte. Selbstverständlich sagte ich sofort zu. Die Zusammenarbeit mit ihm war wirklich positiv. Mehr oder weniger [*lacht*]. Für mich jedenfalls. Mirko ist ein Pedant, er weiß ganz genau, was er will. Genauso wie ich. Wir haben uns gefunden. Wir arbeiten wirklich gut zusammen.

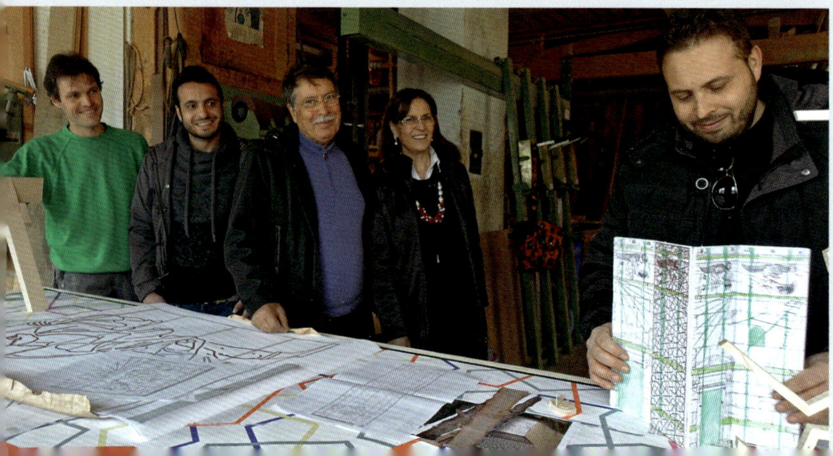

LG: Was waren die Herausforderungen bei der Produktion von *The Tree of Valbella*?

DM: Eine bestand darin, das Projekt zu realisieren [*lacht*]! Und die andere, mit dem Material zu arbeiten, das uns zur Verfügung stand. Das heißt, mit dem Baum, mit dem wir alles machen mussten, was Mirko wollte. Es genügte uns. Wir mussten es aber gut aufteilen, damit das Holz für alle Erfordernisse ausreichte. Als wir 3,3 Meter lange Teile benötigten, mussten wir alle Bretter in Augenschein nehmen und fanden dann nur eines, das wirklich passte. Letztendlich schafften wir es, aber es war nicht einfach. Schwierig war es anfangs auch, dass ich den Kostenvoranschlag ausgehend von einer Idee und ein paar Zeichnungen erstellte, sich dann die Ausgangsidee aber unglaublich weiterentwickelte. Aus diesem Grund sah es bei uns am Ende finanziell ziemlich knapp aus. Wir mussten uns auch entscheiden, ob die Tore einfacher gestaltet werden sollten. Wenn du sie jetzt betrachtest, sind sie in Wahrheit alles andere als einfach... [*lacht*]. Es hat mir wirklich Spaß gemacht, das Projekt auszuführen. Die ganze Filigranarbeit des Paravents. Ich habe stundenlang daran gearbeitet, aber es war wirklich zufriedenstellend. Als normaler Schreiner kommt man überhaupt nicht an solche Arbeiten. Daher wollte ich so arbeiten, und es hat mir Spaß gemacht. Es gab viele Herausforderungen, du musst dir aber einfach nur sagen: „Ich bin froh darüber, es zu tun." Und dann gelingt es auch.

LG: Arbeitest du auch für andere Künstlerinnen und Künstler? Worin genau unterscheidet sich die Produktion eines Kunstwerks vom normalen Schreinerhandwerk?

DM: Was die erste Frage betrifft, leider nein. Aber vielleicht kann das noch kommen. Ich

DANIEL MARGRETH IN INTERVIEW WITH LAURA GIUDICI

Laura Giudici: How and when did you decide to become a carpenter?

Daniel Margreth: That was never a question for me. Well, my grandfather is a carpenter, some of my uncles are carpenters too. It's in the blood. That was not an issue at all. It was always clear, like a vocation.

LG: When did you start working with Mirko? How would you describe your collaboration?

DM: Well, I've been working with Mirko since the end of 2016, and this project was the first time I collaborated with him. At that time, I was employed somewhere else and I thought it was time to change. So, I started to think about my interests, talked with Mirko about art and then I decided to quit, even though I had no work from him. But I thought: "Now I'm going to make art." Some time later I got the request for the project, and of course I was excited about it, because it is exactly what I always wanted to do. Of course, I accepted immediately, and working with him is very pleasant. More or less, actually [*laughs*]. For me it is. Mirko is pedantic, he knows exactly how everything has to be, but so am I. We found each other, I think. We work really well together.

LG: What were the specific challenges in the production of *The Tree of Valbella*?

DM: One was to get it done [*laughs*]! And the other was to work with the material we had. This means the tree, with which we had to be able to make everything Mirko desired. It was enough, but we had to share it well, to be sure that the wood was enough for what we needed. When we needed 3.3 meters long pieces, we had to look through all the boards and eventually we only found one that really fit. In the end we managed it, but was not so easy. What was also difficult was that at the beginning I made an offer from an idea and a few drawings and then the basic idea developed enormously and so we had the problem of being financially too tight in the end. We also had to decide to make the doors easier to realize. If you look at them now, they are in reality anything but simple… [*laughs*]. I really enjoyed implementing the project. For the whole filigree of the screen, for example, I worked for hours, but I really enjoyed it. As a normal carpenter, you can actually forget such work. That's why I wanted to work like that and it was fun. There were many challenges, but you simply have to say: "I'm happy to do it." And then it comes good.

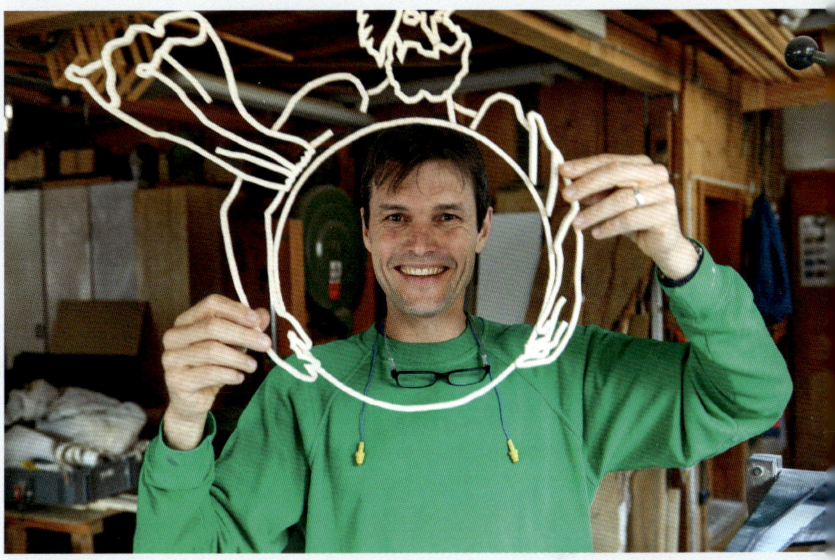

Daniel Margreth mit dem Holzmodell von Kaikias, dem Nordostwind des Paravents / Daniel Margreth with the wooden model for Kaikias, the northeast wind of the screen

S. / p. 70
Daniel Margreth, Marcello, Pasquale, Antonietta und Antonio Del Giudice in der Schreiners Werkstatt in Seewis / Daniel Margreth, Marcello, Pasquale, Antonietta and Antonio Del Giudice in the carpenter's workshop in Seewis

LG: Do you work for other artists? In what way is the production of a work of art different from normal carpentry?

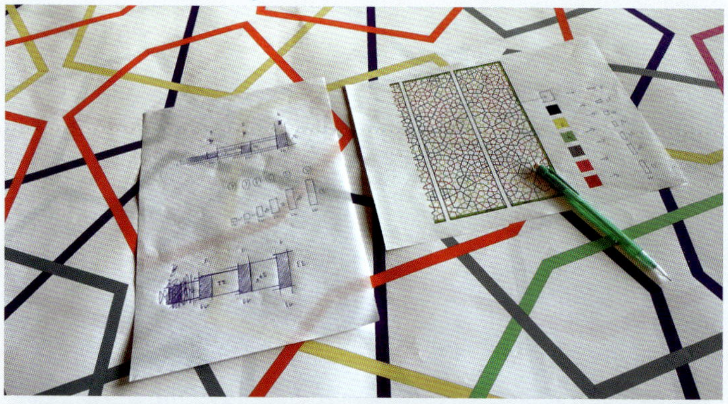

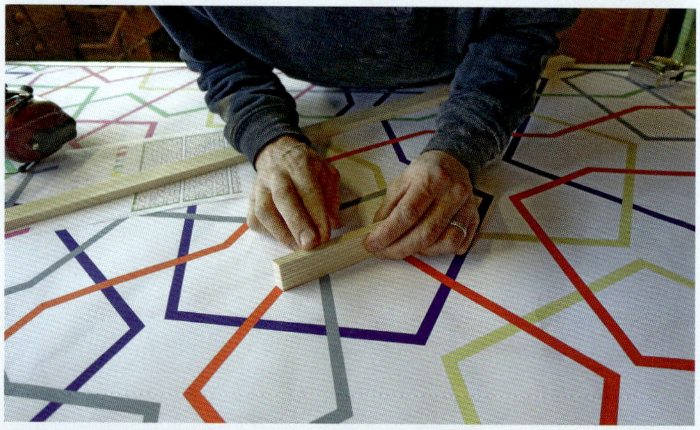

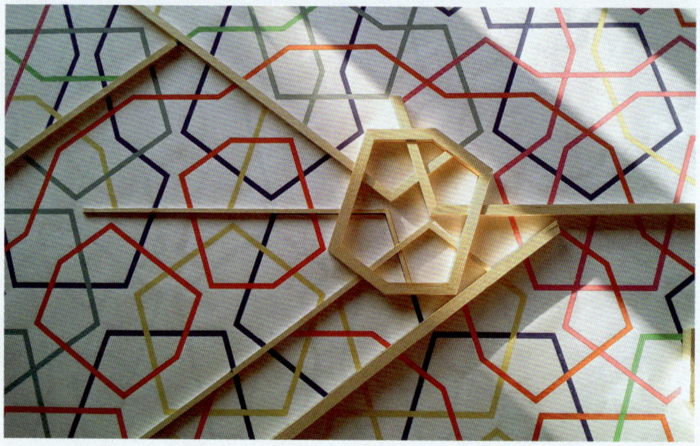

Auf dieser Seite und rechts: Einige Schritte der Realisieung der Holzmodelle für den Paravent / On this page and right: Some steps of the realization of the wooden models for the screen

SS. / pp. 74-75: Daniel Margreth beim Zusammenbau des Holzmodells einer der Tafeln des Paravents / Daniel Margreth assembling the wooden model of one of the panels of the screen

habe weitere Arbeiten für Mirko ausgeführt. Was die zweite Frage betrifft, habe ich diese bereits teilweise beantwortet. Wenn man ein Kunstwerk realisiert, kann man sich wirklich ganz den Details widmen, und dieses, so wie man es möchte, ausführen. Es nimmt mehr Zeit in Anspruch, es ist aber zufriedenstellend, so etwas zu machen. Es ist schwierig, die normale Schreinertätigkeit zu beschreiben. Ich war in mehreren Schreinereien tätig. Es handelt sich um eine vielfältige Arbeit. Das Beste, was man tun kann, ist, ständig etwas anderes zu machen. Es wäre wirklich großartig, noch mehr solcher Projekte auszuführen, wofür man aber auch Geld benötigt... [*lacht*].

LG: Wie war die Zusammenarbeit mit der Fonderia Nolana? Was waren die besonderen Herausforderungen?

DM: Ich hatte eigentlich nicht so viel mit der Gießerei zu tun, da ich mein Modell erstellte, und nachdem ich es abgeschlossen hatte, nach Neapel schickte. Ich war dort nur einmal mit Mirko, um einige letzte Änderungen vorzunehmen. Zu Beginn kamen der Vater und die Brüder Del Giudice in meine Werkstatt und wir besprachen einige Dinge, beispielsweise wie die verschiedenen Teile des Paravents nummeriert werden sollten, damit sie diese zusammenmontieren konnten. Schließlich einigten wir uns darauf, dass ich jedes Teil nummerieren würde, was jedoch nicht ausreichte. Ich musste mit Mirko nach Neapel fahren, um den Mitarbeitern dort alles genau zu erklären. Letztendlich habe ich nur zwei große Teile ausgeführt, aus denen sie acht Teile erstellen mussten. Die rückseitigen Teile mussten später hinzugefügt werden. Es dauerte ein wenig, ihnen zu erklären, wie sie alles zusammensetzen sollten, vor allem weil es nicht immer einfach war, auf Deutsch und Italienisch zu kommunizieren. Wir mussten die Details mehrmals durchgehen. Mir wurde klar, dass ich seit Monaten an diesem Projekt arbeitete und jedes Detail kannte, für die Leute in Neapel aber alles vollkommen neu war und sie Zeit brauchten, das Ganze zu verstehen. Schließlich aber ging alles gut über die Bühne. Ich war beeindruckt, als ich die Bronzeskulptur das erste Mal in Genf sah. Die Arbeit, die dahintersteckt, ist unglaublich. Tausende von Teilen... der reinste Wahnsinn! Das Ergebnis ist großartig!

LG: Was ist dein Lieblingselement von *The Tree of Valbella*?

DM: Eigentlich alle [*lacht*]. Besonders genoss ich die Arbeit an den Windgöttern, da dies der diffizilste Teil war. Leider befinden sie sich so weit oben, man kann nicht alle Details sehen...

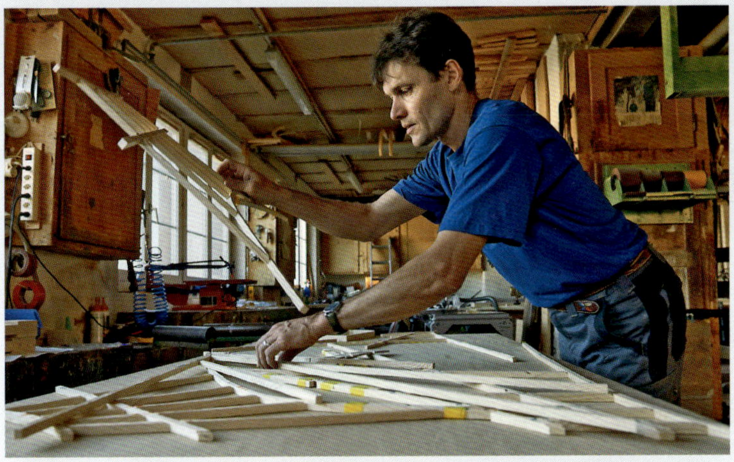

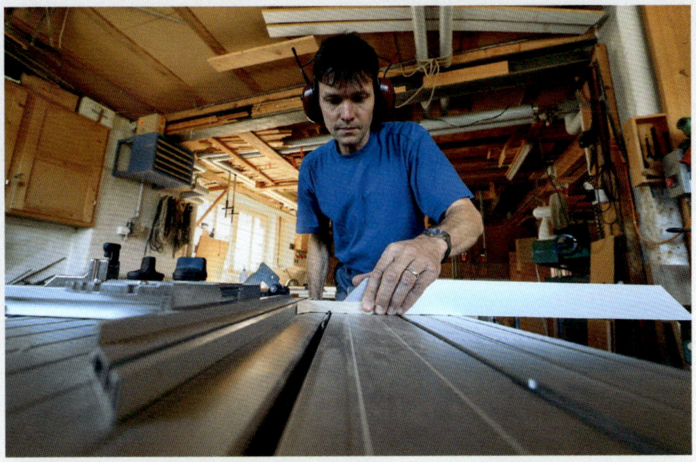

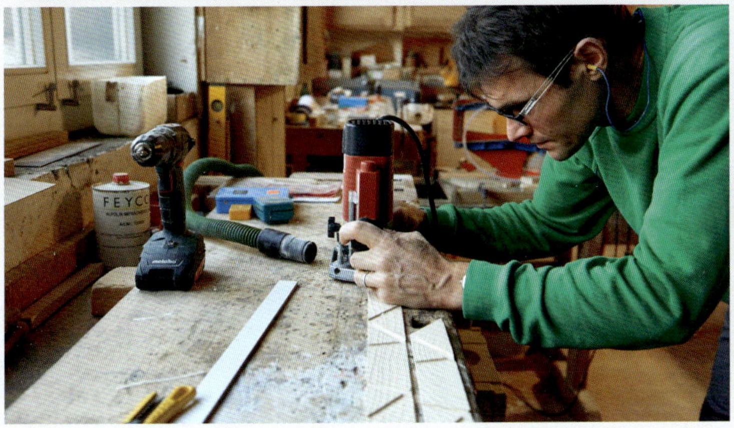

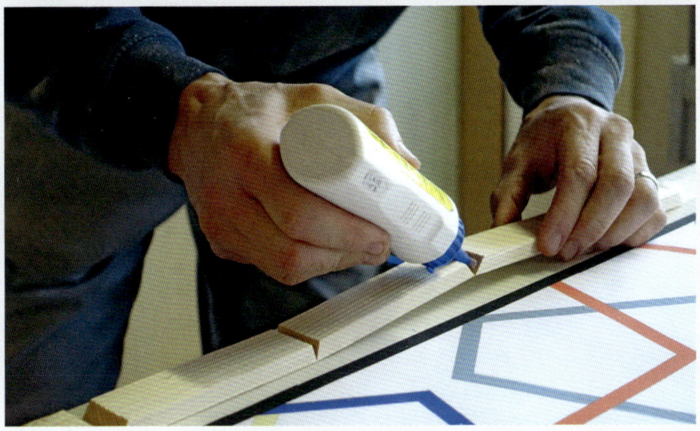

DM: Concerning the first question, no, unfortunately not. But it can still happen. Anyway, I have made a couple of other works for Mirko. And concerning the second question, I have already partly answered. In the production of a work of art you can really go into details and make it the way you want it. It takes longer, but it's nice to make something like that. Normal carpentry work is actually difficult to define. I have worked in many carpentries and each one is different. It is such a versatile job. The best thing to do is to change, change and change, look at everything and choose. It would be great to be able to do even more of these things, but this also requires money… [*laughs*].

LG: How was the collaboration with the Fonderia Nolana? Were there any special challenges?

DM: Actually, I didn't work very much with the foundry because I made my model and when it was finished, I sent it to Naples. I just went there with Mirko after that to make some final modifications. In the beginning the father and the Del Giudice brothers came to my workshop and we discussed some things, such as how to number the different parts of the screen so that they could put them together. Finally, we agreed that I would number each part, but it was not enough anyway. I had to go with Mirko to Naples to explain in detail to the people there how it all worked. In the end I had only made two big pieces and they had to make eight pieces out of them. The back parts had to be added later and explaining how everything had to be put together took a bit of time, especially because with German and Italian, communication was not always easy. So, we had to discuss the details several times and I also realized that I had been working on this project for several months and knew every part, but for the people in Naples everything was completely new and they needed time to understand how everything worked. But in the end, it worked very well. I was amazed when I saw the bronze sculpture for the first time in Geneva. The work behind it is incredible. Thousands of pieces… madness! And the result looks great!

LG: What is your favorite part of *The Tree of Valbella*?

DM: Well, actually all of them [*laughs*]. But maybe my favorite was working on the wind gods, because it was the most delicate work. Unfortunately, they are too high up to see them well…

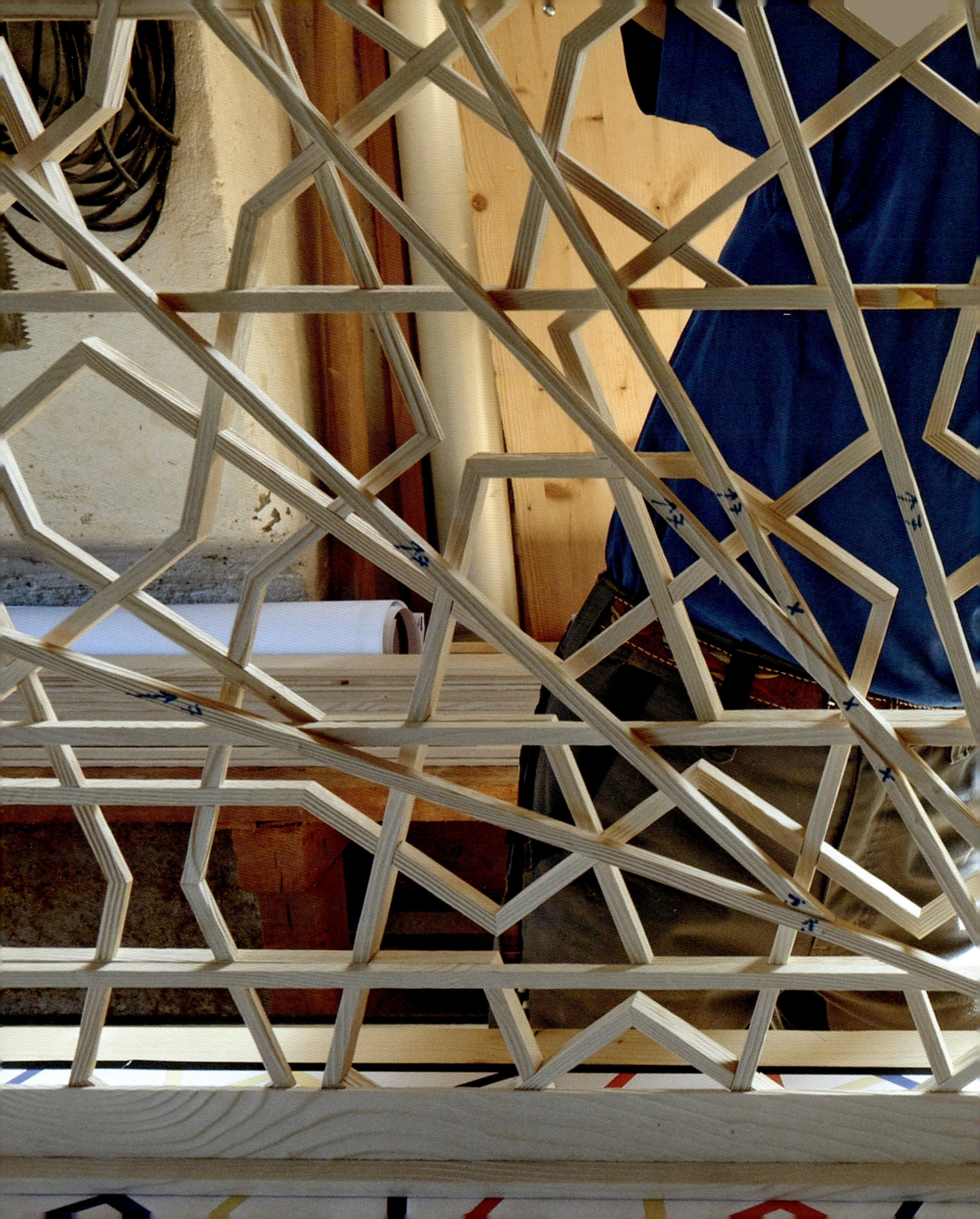

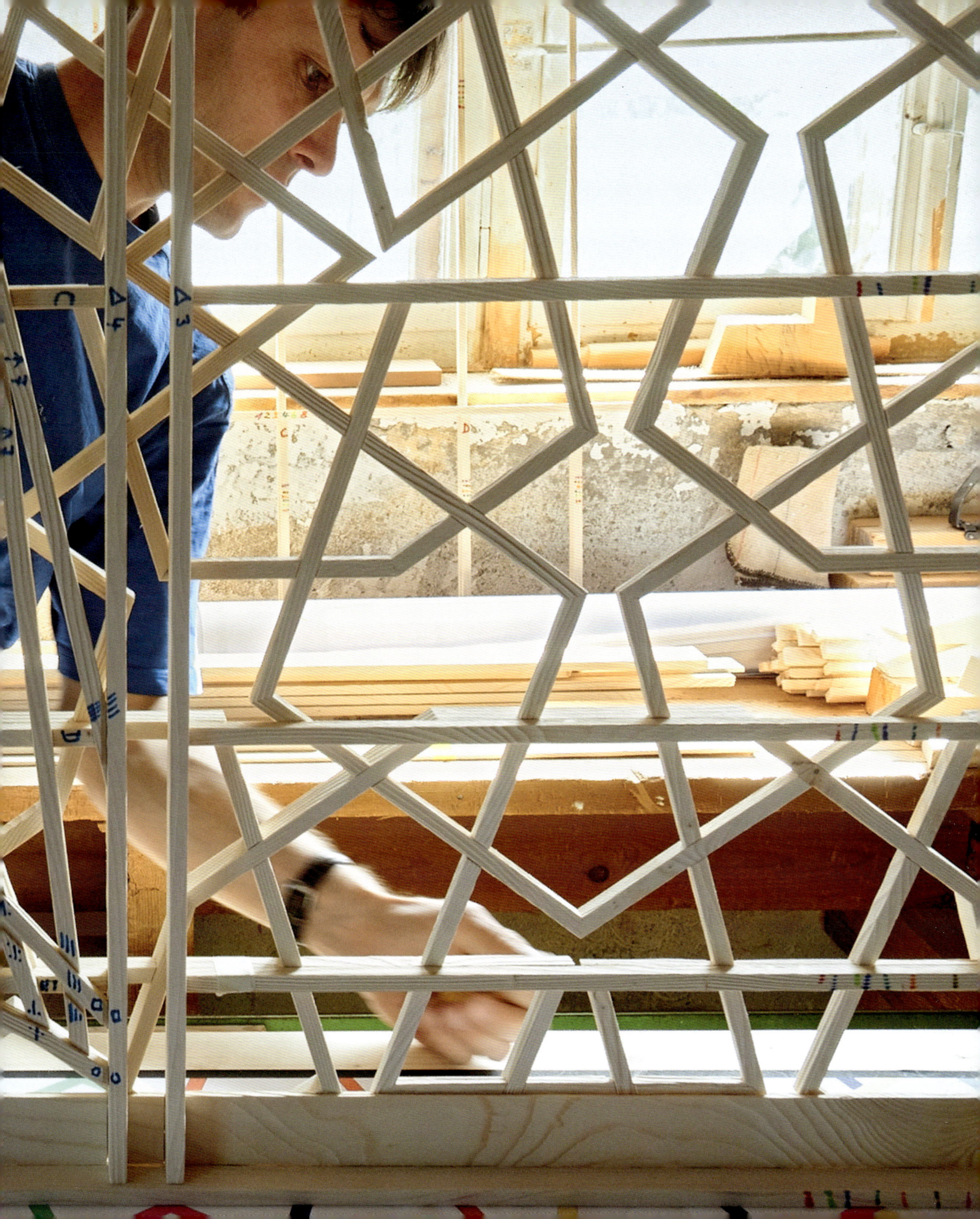

KUNST ALS META-NATUR ÜBER MIRKO BASELGIA

JÉRÔME NEUTRES

Wenn man die Persönlichkeit und die Kunst von Mirko Baselgia wirklich verstehen und würdigen möchte, muss man sich nach Tiefencastel in Graubünden begeben, wo der 38-jährige Künstler arbeitet, nur wenige Kilometer vom kleinen Ort Lenz entfernt, in dem er aufgewachsen ist.

In diesen friedlichen schweizerischen Bergen, in denen die Natur die Landschaft beherrscht, lebt Mirko Baselgia im Einklang mit dem Reich der Natur und schafft im und ausgehend vom Ökosystem, das ihn umgibt, eine Kunst, die so einzigartig wie kraftvoll ist. So hat ihm die Beobachtung der Bienen die Materie – das Sujet und das Material – für eine Serie geliefert, die repräsentativ für seine Arbeit ist. Das Studium der Murmeltierbauten ist das Sujet einer anderen Werkserie mit Videos und Skulpturen. Wenn man durch sein Atelier schreitet, erblickt man Leinwände, die mit Harz gemalt wurden, das den Werken eine ungewöhnliche und äußerst raffinierte Textur und Lichtqualität verleiht. Hier sind Schildkrötenpanzer, die dem Künstler die Form für weitere *natürliche Skulpturen* vorgeben, als Ode und Hommage an die Schönheit der Natur und des Tierreichs. Dort bringt die mit Keramik wiedergegebene Zeichnung einer Baumrinde ein ungewöhnliches, farbiges Basrelief hervor. Da ist es wiederum ein einfacher Tannenzapfen aus Bronze, der ein intensives visuelles – und taktiles – Erlebnis beschert. Denn für Mirko soll Kunst visuell sein, aber auch den Tast- und den Geruchssinn anregen, und er sucht bezüglich dieser Sinnesvielfalt ohne Unterlass nach neuen Medien in der Natur – ah, der aromatische Duft von Bienenwachs… „Ich liebe es mit dem zu experimentieren, was ich in der Natur finde. In der Kunst wie in der Küche", erklärt Mirko. Vegetarier in seiner Seele und in seiner Imagination, ernährt sich der Künstler von lokalen Produkten, so wie er seine Kunst mit den Wunderdingen der Natur speist, denen er auf den Bergpfaden begegnet. Das Menü unseres Aperitifs: Brennnessel- und Birnenchips, die der Künstler nach einem Besuch in seinem Garten am Morgen erfunden hat. Für Mirko muss Kunst allumfassend oder gar nicht sein. Jeder Gestus des Lebens, jede Handlung, muss einen Teil Kunst enthalten, vom Atelier bis zur Küche, und ein zusammenhängendes persönliches Universum in Symbiose mit der Natur bilden.

„Die Natur ist das schönste Spektakel", sagt uns dieser Künstler, der zunächst ein Philosoph ist, einer dieser Schöpfer, für die Kunst nicht nur zur Betrachtung, sondern auch zum Denken anregen soll. Inmitten der Menge an Kunstwerken, die das Atelier bevölkern, findet man bei den Bildern und Kisten Bücherregale, die mit den Werken der bedeutendsten Denker der Moderne gefüllt sind: Bourdieu, Derrida, Foucault, aber auch die Klassiker fehlen nicht, Hume, Wittgenstein, Nietzsche (der im Übrigen in Graubünden geschrieben hat und auch von dieser Natur inspiriert wurde), bis zum Sufi-Mystiker Rumi. Neben diesen grundlegenden metaphysischen Werken findet man natürlich auch eine Sammlung mit Abhandlungen und Lexika zu Botanik und Biologie sowie Geographiebücher. Konsequent und mit glücklicher Hand vereinigt der Künstler Natur und Kunst. Mit einer an Voltaire erinnernden Weisheit, scheint er Kunst hervorzubringen, wie andere ihren Garten kultivieren. Sein von der Stille der Berglandschaft umgebenes Arbeitszimmer ist mit einem großen Glasfenster ausgestattet, durch das man, wie in einem Breitwandfilm, eine Landschaft mit dramatischen Erhebungen bewundern kann, die dem Atelier eine äußerst romantische Färbung verleiht. Dieser grüne Horizont der heiteren Ruhe ist der Raum für die

ART AS META-NATURE APROPOS OF MIRKO BASELGIA

To understand and fully appreciate the art and personality of Mirko Baselgia, one needs to go to Tiefencastel, in the Swiss canton of Graubünden, where the 38-year-old artist works just a few kilometres from his hometown of Lenz.

In the peace of the Swiss Alps, where nature dominates the landscape, Baselgia communes with the natural world and creates art as unique as it is powerful, in and from the ecosystem that surrounds him. His observation of bees has thus given the matter—both topic and medium—of an iconic series of his artistic output. Studying marmot burrows was the inspiration for another body of work, giving rise to videos and sculptures.

Surveying his studio, one sees canvases coated with tree resin, which give his work a unique and highly refined luminosity. Off to one side, tortoise shells provide the artist with moulds for the creation of other *natural sculptures*, homages to the beauty of nature and of the animal kingdom. In another corner, a drawing of tree bark reproduced in ceramics provides us with an astonishing basrelief covered in colours. And over there is a simple bronze pinecone that evokes an intense visual—and tactile—emotion. Because for Mirko, art must be visual but also appeal to the senses of touch and smell, and he is constantly seeking new natural media that will create this multisensory effect—ah, the delicious perfume of beeswax…

'I like to experiment with what I find in nature… in art as well as in cooking', Mirko explains. A vegetarian in his heart and in his imaginatio,n the artist eats local products just as he nourishes his art with natural wonders found on mountain paths. On the menu for our aperitif: nettle-and-pear chips, invented by the artist after a stroll through his garden that morning. For Mirko, art must be all-embracing, or not exist at all. Every gesture in one's life, every action, must have an artistic dimension, from the studio to the kitchen, and form a coherent personal universe in symbiosis with nature.

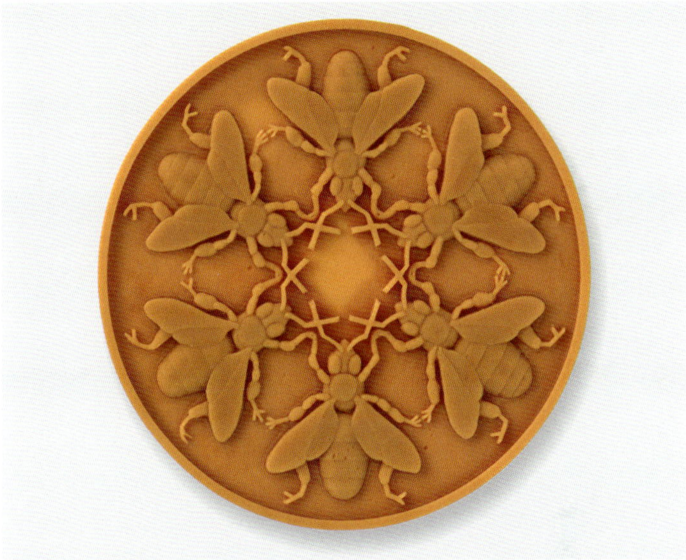

Mirko Baselgia, *Antupada - The Bee dreams up the Flower and the Flower dreams up the Bee*, 2012, Bienenwachs / Beeswax, Ø 55 cm, 3.3 cm deep, edition of 1 + 5 AP

'Nature is the most beautiful spectacle', says Baselgia, who is above all a philosopher, one of those creators for whom art should speak not only to the eyes, but to the mind as well. Near the frames and boxes in the art storeroom adjacent to his studio, one finds a bookshelf lined with works by the greatest modern thinkers—Bourdieu, Derrida, Foucault—but also the classic minds: Hume, Wittgenstein, and Nietzsche (who wrote in the canton of Graubünden and was also very much inspired by nature), as well as the thirteenth-century Persian Sufi mystic, Rumi. Next to these essential metaphysical works, one also finds a collection of botanical and biological treatises and dictionaries, along with books about geography.

Mirko Baselgia merges nature and art with joy and rigour. Endowed with Voltairean wisdom, he

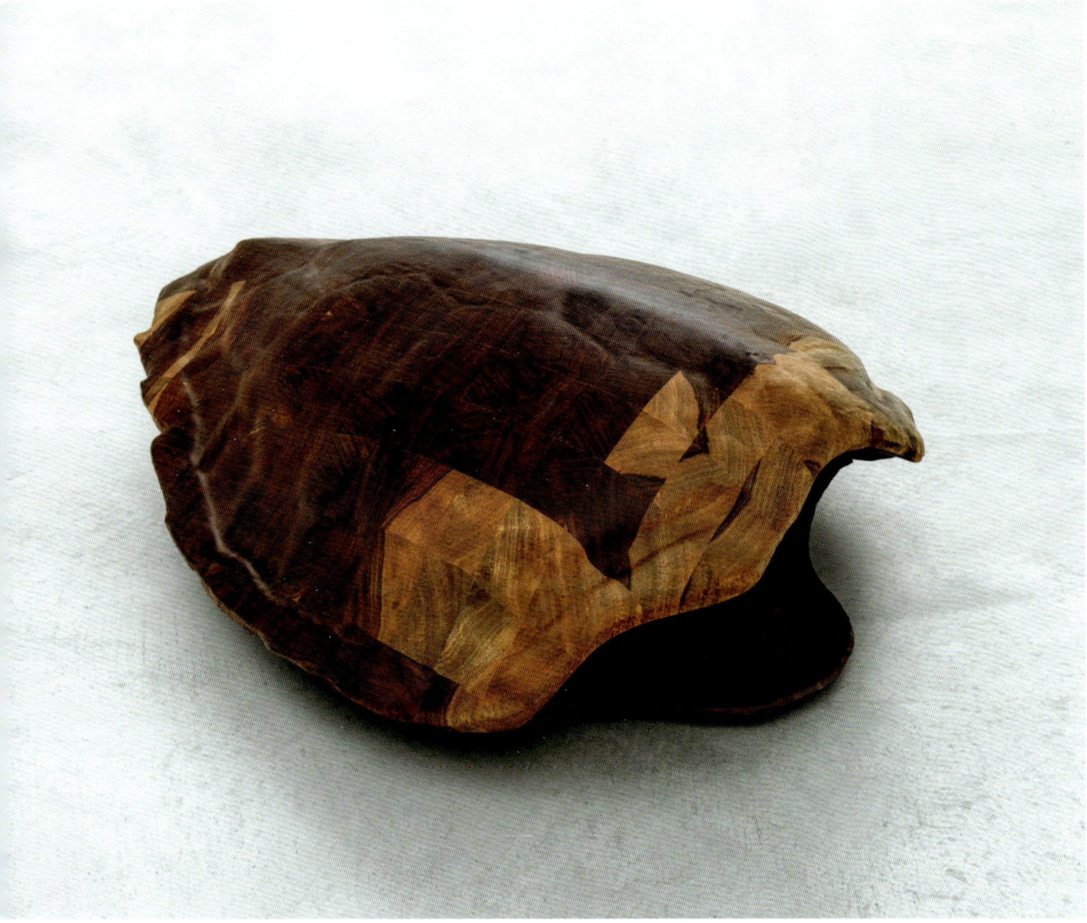

Mirko Baselgia, *Tartaruga*, 2018, Bubinga Holz / Bubinga wood, 24.5 x 77.5 x 65.5 cm

Mirko Baselgia, *Las flours digl gôt*, 2015, Weißbronze / White bronze, Grösse / Size 1:1 - 15 x 5 x 5 cm, edition of 5 + 1 AP

p. 81
Mirko Baselgia, *La pel digl gôt (greenyellow)*, 2015, Keramik, glasiert mit Pigmenten / Ceramic, glazed with pigments, 44 x 33 cm

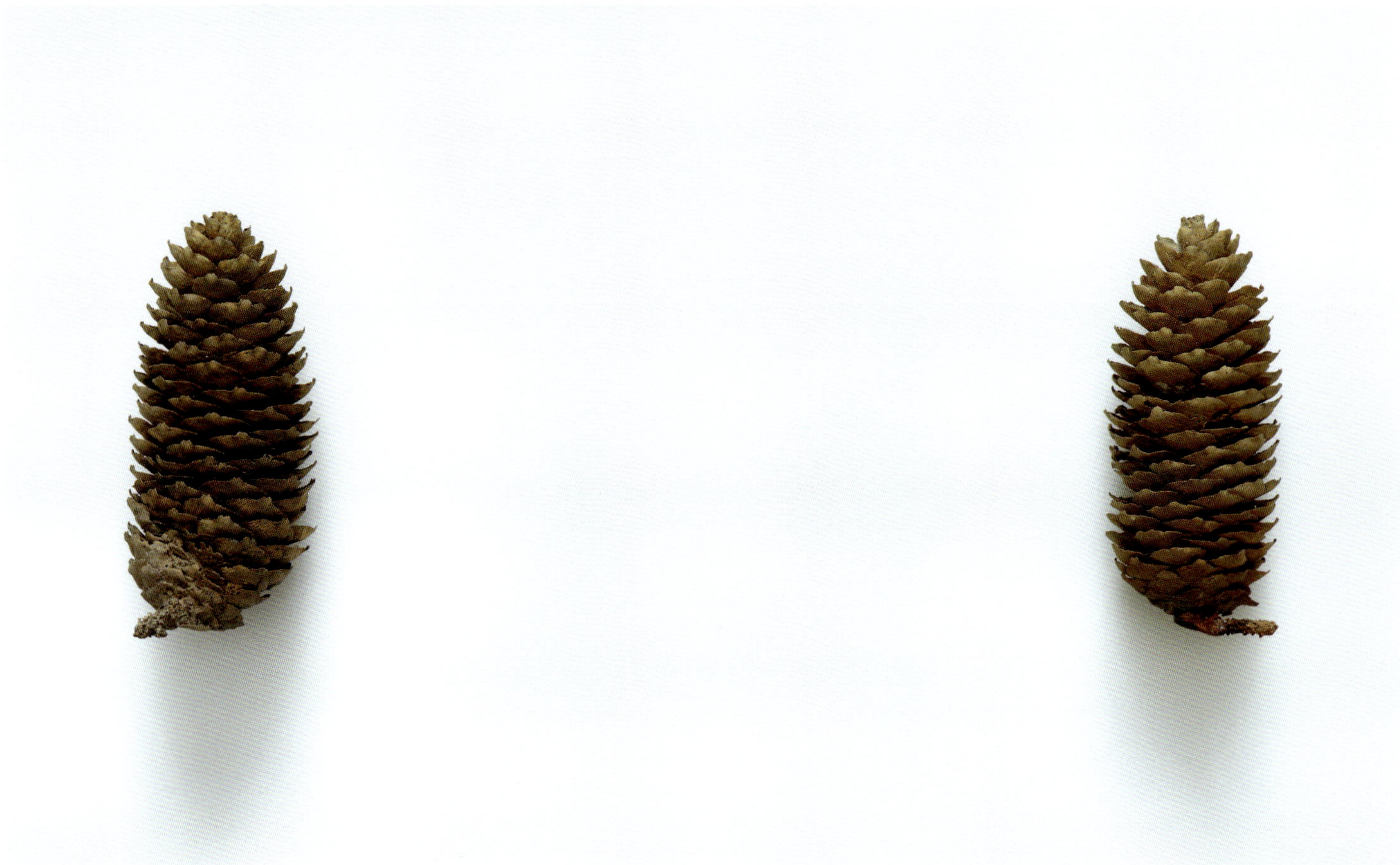

seems to produce art the way other people cultivate their gardens. In the silence of the mountains, the view out of the picture window from his desk allows him to contemplate, as if in Cinemascope, a landscape of dramatic, sharp outlines that suffuse the studio with thoroughly romantic hues. It is this same serene, green horizon that is the source of inspiration for Baselgia's entire oeuvre. To create his magnificent drawings, the artist, like a Renaissance painter, makes his own pencils with natural pigments and local wax. Mirko's entire artistic process is dependent upon the ecosystem of the region: wood, resin, wax, frames—all the materials he uses are local products. And his entire oeuvre is inspired by the same surroundings. In this way, Mirko's creations are an extension of the work of the pioneers of Land Art, particularly Environmental Art, a movement taking shape in the late 1960s and the early 1970s, with artists such as Robert Morris, Nils Udo, and Agnes Denes. But his predecessors concentrated primarily on works on a natural scale, installations placed directly in nature or integrating 'nature' into urban spaces. They weren't speaking about nature, but rather incorporating their art into it.

Mirko Baselgia develops a world suited to the scale of his studio or expressed in more traditional formats—sculptures, paintings, drawings—to offer us a vision of nature and of the limitless richness of his inspiration. He motivates us to discover nature as a source of ideas, of beauty, of tastes and smells that no cultural environment can surpass. Viewing Mirko's works, one has the impression that nature is *thinking* and is itself a great artist. He thus creates an original artistic ecosystem inspired by the larger one surrounding him, in which he has lived and learned since his childhood.

Baselgia rejects the label of *eco-artist*, a term he feels too narrow and circumscribed. Instead, he incorporates the logic of his artistic process into a lifestyle that requires his commitment just as much as it influences his art. The desire to create eco-responsible works has led him to become interested in salvage and even industrial waste, which, in turn, furnish material to be transformed into art. One work generates another. Is this the natural progression of art?

This is the spirit behind the sawdust that the artist makes us contemplate and touch, and from which he hopes to create a new work. 'You gave me your mud, and from it I made gold', said Baudelaire in defining the act of creating art. Mirko Baselgia embodies a contemporary variation of this Baudelairean concept in developing an oeuvre that is essentially ecological, that is to say inspired by and created from natural substances, with an eye to taking responsibility for and protecting nature.

Returning to Baudelaire, Mirko is one of the clairvoyant artists who 'understand the language of flowers and silent things.' Another theorist who influenced him is Ernst Haeckel, creator of the concept of *Oecologia*, which led to modern ecology but to which the vision of this thinker-naturalist cannot be reduced. For Haeckel, nature was replete with works of art, and part of the German biologist-philosopher's work involved drawing parallels between art and nature, particularly in his *Art Forms in Nature* (1899-1904). Mirko belongs to the school of thinkers who interweave art, biology, and philosophy. He was strongly influenced by the work of the Chilean scientists Francisco Varela and Humberto Maturana, who call themselves 'biosophers' because they approach philosophy through biology. And one can say that Mirko Baselgia approaches philosophy in and through his artistic process.

Through the meta-nature that his oeuvre embodies, Mirko Baselgia invites us to return to a fundamental and more philosophical vision of the relationship between culture and nature. He introduces a new artistic vision that gives fresh meaning and another role to the artist and to a work of art. This orientation is the key principle of his artistic process. It is not by chance that the artist entitled one of his pieces, inspired by the work of marmots, *L'origine du monde - Marmot burrows*. Mirko Baselgia's art and life are based on complete awareness of the philosophy that guides him and that he wants to convey. *Meta-nature*: perhaps it's the way forward for the committed modern artist.

Inspiration und den gesamten Entstehungsprozess der Werke Mirko Baselgias. Der Künstler stellt die Wachsmalstifte für seine wundervollen Zeichnungen wie ein Renaissancemaler selbst aus natürlichen Pigmenten und lokalem Wachs her. Die gesamte Produktionskette von Mirkos Kunst fügt sich in ein regionales Ökosystem ein: Holz, Harz, Wachs, Rahmen, alle verwendeten Materialien sind lokale Produkte. So wie alle Sujets seines Werks einer Inspiration entspringen, die in diesem Terroir gesammelt wurde. In diesem Sinne setzt Mirko die Arbeit der Pioniere der *Land Art* fort, insbesondere der *Environmental Art*, einer Bewegung, die Ende der 1960er-, Anfang der 1970er-Jahre entstand, mit Vertretern wie Robert Morris, Nils Udo und Agnes Denes. Aber diese Vorläufer konzentrierten sich vor allem auf Arbeiten im Maßstab der Natur, Installationen inmitten der Natur oder solche, die ein Stück „Natur" in den urbanen Raum integrieren. Sie sprachen nicht von der Natur, sie integrierten ihre Kunst in die Natur. Mirko Baselgia entwickelt seine eigene Welt, in seinem Atelier übersetzt in Artefakte eher traditioneller Art – Skulpturen, Malereien, Zeichnungen... –, um uns seine Vision von der Natur und des unendlichen Reichtums an Inspiration, die ihr innewohnt, darzubieten. Mirko lässt uns die Natur als Quelle von Konzepten, Schönheit, Aromen und Düften entdecken, die keine kulturelle Umgebung je übertreffen könnte. Wenn man Mirkos Arbeiten betrachtet, bekommt man den Eindruck, dass die Natur *denkt* und selbst eine große Künstlerin ist. So erschafft Mirko ein künstlerisches Ökosystem, das von dem größeren Ökosystem angeregt wird, welches ihn umgibt, in dem er seit seiner Jugend lebt und lernt. Er, der die Bezeichnung Öko-Künstler als zu reduktiv und formatiert ablehnt, macht aus der Logik seiner Arbeitspraxis einen Lebensstil, der ihn so sehr verpflichtet, wie er seine Kunst beeinflusst. Dem Wunsch, ein nachhaltiges Werk zu schaffen, entspringt das Interesse für Recyclingmaterialien und Abfälle bestimmter Produktionen, die wiederum Material liefern und zu Kunst werden.Ein Werk zieht das nächste nach sich – ein natürlicher Kreislauf der Kunst? So wie diese Sägespäne, die wir betrachten und berühren können, aus denen der Künstler hofft, ein neues Werk zu schaffen. „Du gabst mir deinen Dreck und daraus machte ich Gold": Mit diesen Worten hat Baudelaire den künstlerischen Gestus beschrieben. Mirko Baselgia verkörpert eine zeitgenössische Variante von Baudelaires Begriff, mit einem Werk, das im Wesentlichen ökologisch ist, das heißt, es entsteht ausgehend von und fabriziert mit natürlichen Gegenständen, mit einem verantwortungsvollen, schützenden Blick auf die Natur. Um nochmals Baudelaire zu zitieren, kann man sagen, dass Mirko zu den sehenden Künstlern gehört, die „die Sprache der Blumen und der stummen Dinge" verstehen. Zu Mirko Baselgias Bezugspunkten gehört auch Ernst Haeckel, der Schöpfer des Begriffs *Oecologie*, der der modernen Ökologie zugrundeliegt, auf den man die Ideen dieses naturwissenschaftlichen Denkers allerdings nicht reduzieren kann. Für Haeckel ist die Natur von Kunstwerken erfüllt, er stellte Parallelen zwischen der Kunst und der Natur her, insbesondere in *Kunstformen der Natur* (1899-1904). Mirko fühlt sich in der Praxis zu Hause, in der sich Kunst, Biologie und Philosophie vermischen. Er wurde stark von der Arbeit der chilenischen Forscher Francisco Varela und Humberto Maturana beeinflusst, die sich als „Biosophen" bezeichnen, da sie Philosophie über die Biologie betreiben. Und man kann sagen, dass Mirko Baselgia seinerseits Philosophie über seine und in seiner künstlerischen Arbeit praktiziert.

In der Meta-Natur, aus der also Mirko Baselgias Werk besteht, lädt uns der Künstler ein, zu einer essentiellen und mehr philosophischen Vision der Beziehung zwischen Kunst und Natur zurückzukehren. Mirko Baselgia führt eine neue künstlerische Praxis ein, die dem Künstler und dem Kunstwerk eine neue Bedeutung und Funktion gibt. Diese Positionierung ist ein Postulat. Es ist kein Zufall, wenn der Künstler eines seiner Werke, das von der Arbeit der Murmeltiere inspiriert wurde, *L'origine du monde – Marmot Burrows* nennt. Mirko Baselgia wirkt in seiner Kunst und in seinem Leben im vollen Bewusstsein der Philosophie, die ihn leitet und die er weitergeben möchte. *Meta-Natur*: Vielleicht ist das der moderne Weg für den engagierten Künstler.

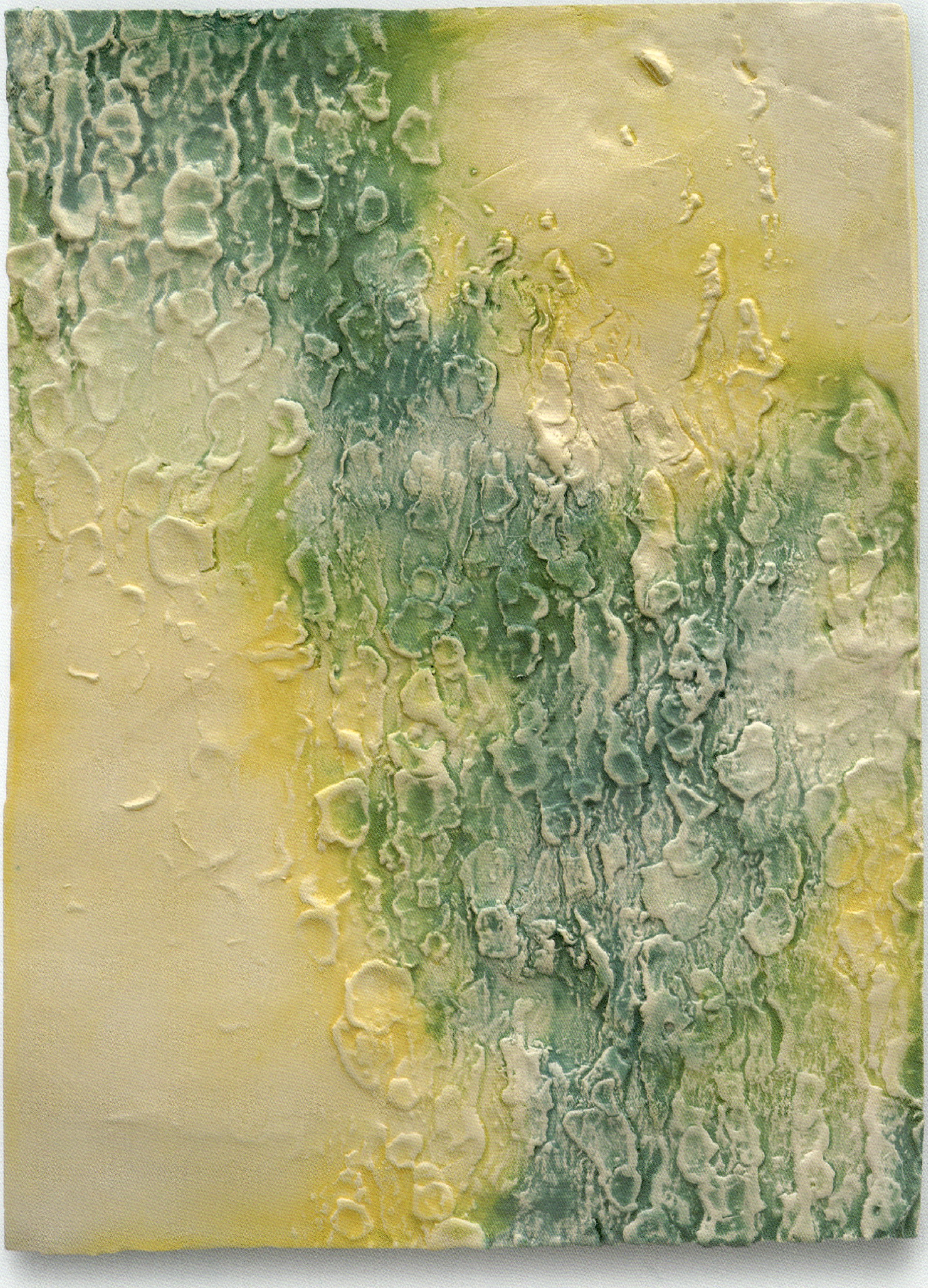

DER BAUM VON VALBELLA ANTHROPOMETRIE EINES SKULPTURALEN ENSEMBLES

JÉRÔME NEUTRES

In Targû Jiu in Rumänien hat Constantin Brâncuşi 1937-1938 ein „skulpturales Ensemble" geschaffen, das die Geschichte der modernen Skulptur und der plastischen Installationen im Freien geprägt hat. Die monumentale Installation setzt sich aus drei großen Gruppen von Skulpturen aus Stein und Bronze zusammen: Der *Table du silence* (*Tisch des Schweigens*), die *Porte du baiser* (*Tor des Kusses*) und die *Colonne sans fin* (*Endlose Säule*), die fast dreißig Meter hoch ist, wobei die beiden letztgenannten Werke eine Art Apotheose wiederkehrender, grundlegender Figuren im Œuvre des Künstlers sind.

Das zur Erinnerung an die Toten des ersten Weltkriegs errichtete Skulpturenensemble, das heute zum Weltkulturerbe der UNESCO gehört, führt eine neue Auffassung der monumentalen Skulptur ein. Dabei geht es nicht nur um einen neuen Maßstab, die bloße Vergrößerung einer Form, wie die *Endlose Säule*, sondern um eine Installation, die ihren Sinn aus dem Dialog, der sich zwischen ihren einzelnen Elementen ergibt, und ihrer Einfügung in eine Umgebung bezieht, in diesem Fall ein in die Natur eingebettetes, baumbestandenes Grundstück nicht weit vom Geburtsort Brâncuşis. Der Künstler, der als Schöpfer der modernen, von jeglichem figurativen Bezug

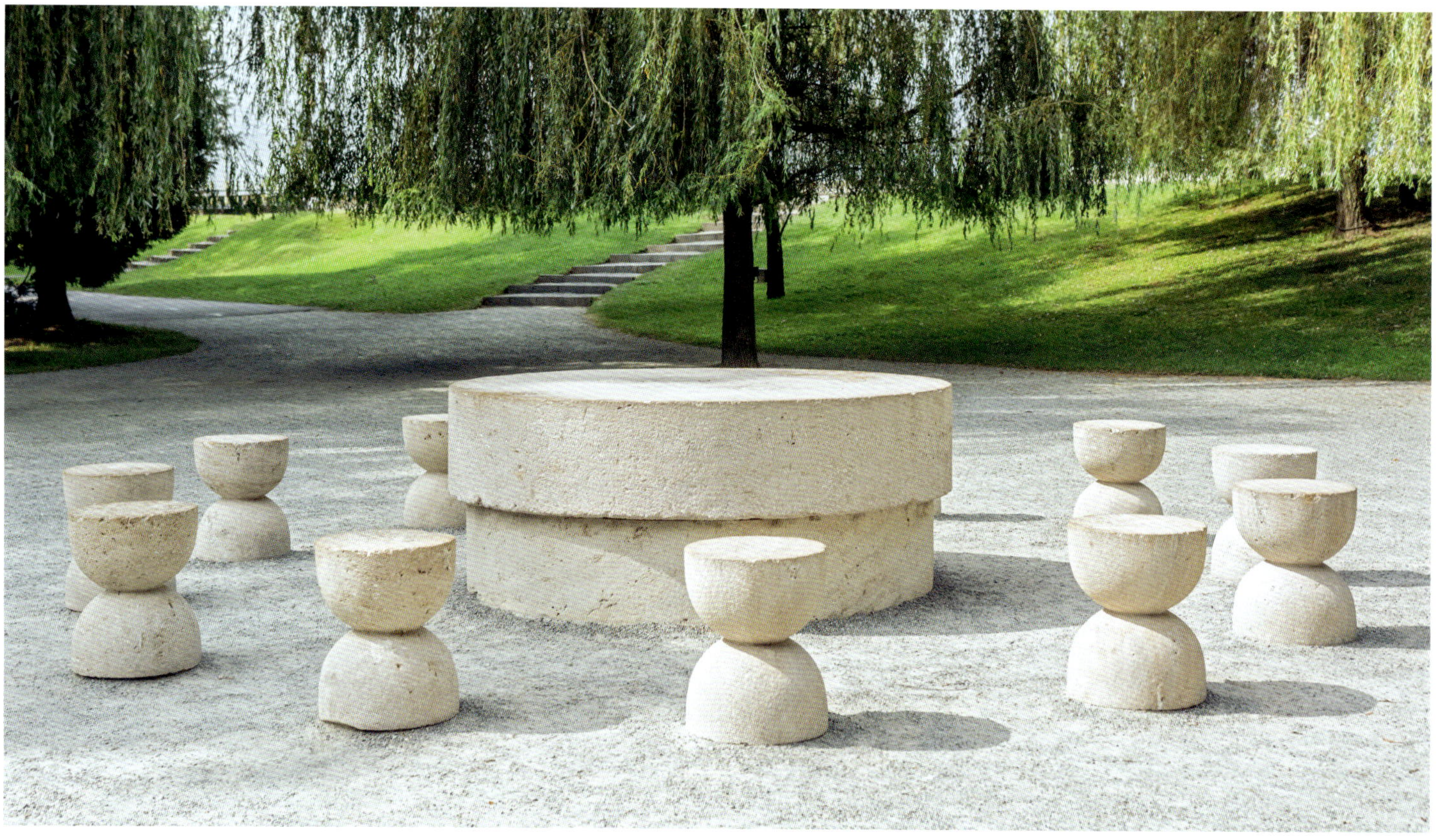

THE TREE OF VALBELLA
ANTHROPOMETRY OF A SCULPTURAL ENSEMBLE

In 1937–38, Constantin Brâncuşi created a unique 'sculptural ensemble' in Târgu Jiu, Romania, that left its mark on the history of modern sculpture and outdoor installations. The monumental installation was composed of three large sculptural structures in bronze and stone: *The Table of Silence*, *The Gate of the Kiss*, and the *Endless Column*, almost thirty metres tall. The last two works were a sort of apotheosis of essential, recurring forms in the artist's oeuvre.

Created in memory of the World War I dead, the ensemble is today a UNESCO World Heritage Site and introduces a new vision of monumental sculpture. It is not merely a matter of a different scale, of a simple enlarging of a shape like the *Endless Column*, but rather an installation that finds its meaning in the dialogue among its different elements and in its integration into an outdoor environment—in this case, a lawn in a public garden scattered with trees and surrounded by nature, situated near the village where Brâncuşi was born. The artist is considered the inventor of modern sculpture freed from all figurative references, endowed with metaphysical aspirations, and seeking, through complex abstraction, to reveal the essence of things rather than their outward appearance. In this installation, he brought one of his earliest dreams to life.

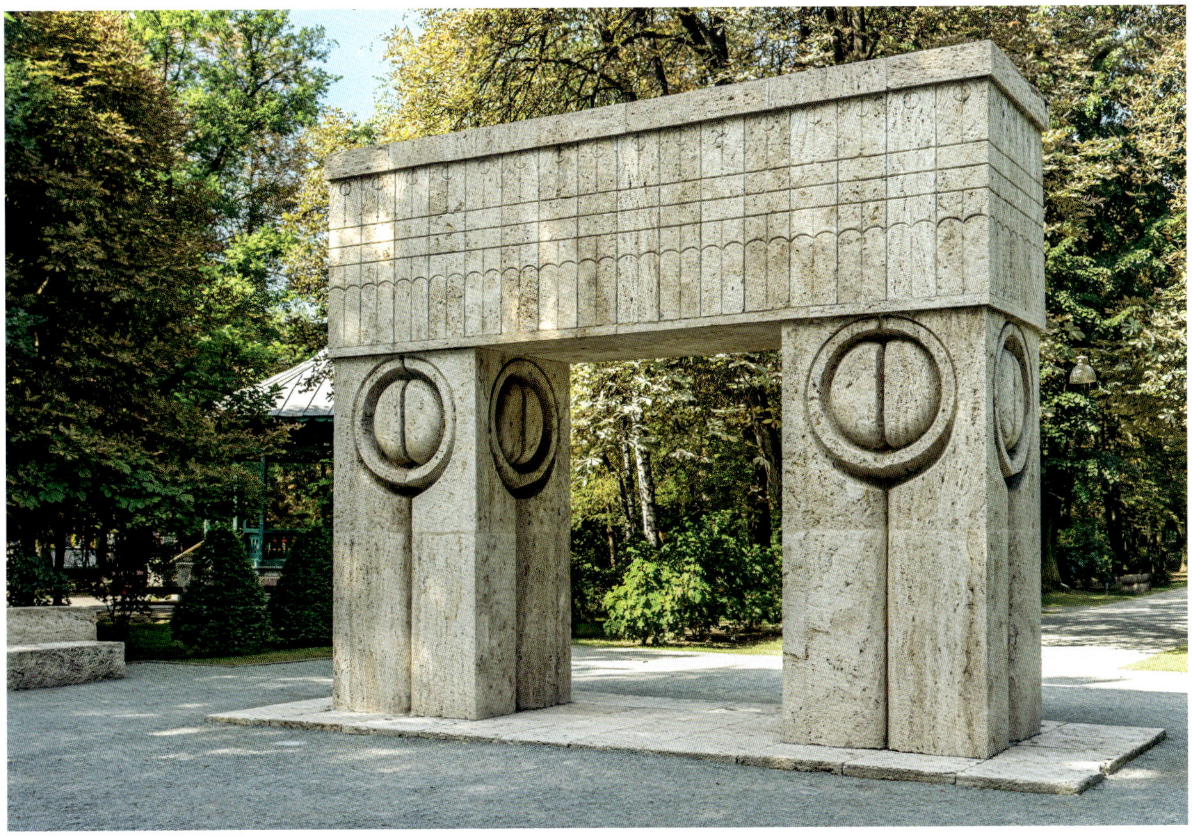

Links / Left: Constantin Brâncuşi, *La Table du silence*, ~ 1938, Târgu Jiu (Rumänien / Romania) / Auf dieser Seite / On this page: Constantin Brâncuşi, *La Porte du Baiser*, 1938, Târgu Jiu (Rumänien / Romania)

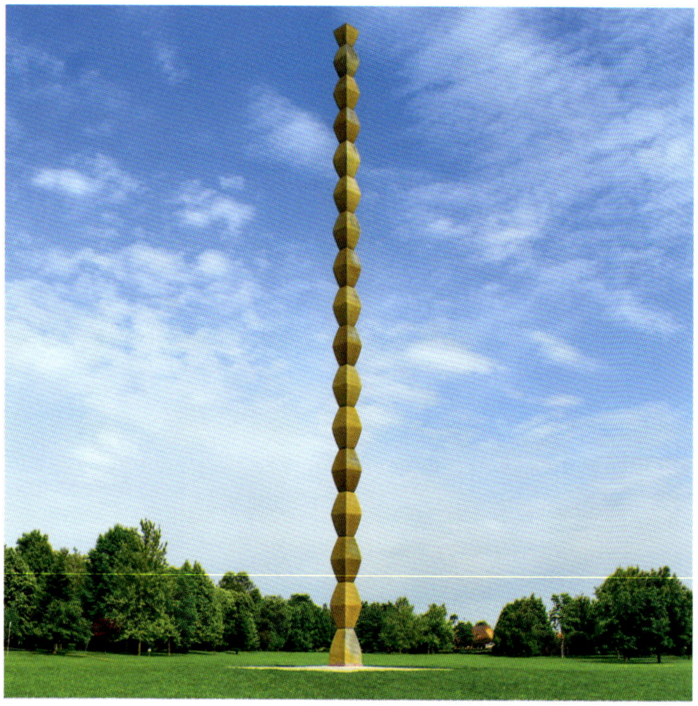

Constantin **Brâncuşi**, ***La Colonne sans fin***, **1938, Târgu Jiu (Rumänien / Romania)**

befreiten Skulptur mit metaphysischem Anspruch gilt und in der komplexen Abstraktion das Wesen der Dinge und nicht ihre äußerliche Erscheinung zeigen will, hat hier einen alten Traum realisiert.

Seit 1926 wollte Brâncuşi eine endlose Säule in einer grünen Umgebung verwirklichen, wie im Central Park in New York, der grünen Lunge der größten Stadt der Welt. Kunst in die Natur einfügen, der Versuch, eine Symbiose zwischen einem plastischen Werk und natürlichen Elementen hervorzubringen. So wie die ersten von Menschen errichteten Skulpturen, senkrecht aufgestellte, dem Himmel zugewandte Steine, wie die Menhire der Jungsteinzeit. *The Tree of Valbella* von Mirko Baselgia stellt ein weiteres „Skulpturenensemble" dar, dessen vertikale Elemente auch die Grundlagen der Geschichte der Skulptur und ihre Essenz ins Gedächtnis rufen. Alle Segmente dieser Installation erklingen auch im Verhältnis zueinander und erzählen in ihrem Zusammenklang eine Geschichte. Dieses Werk gehört zu einer Kategorie von Artefakten, die so komplex und multipel sind, dass nur der Begriff „Ensemble" ihre Pluralität vermitteln kann. Alles hat mit der Geschichte – oder besser gesagt dem Fällen – eines über hundert Jahre alten Baums begonnen, der im Garten von Thomas Abeggs Ferienhaus in Valbella stand. Tatsächlich ähnelt Mirko Baselgias Werk einem künstlerischen Palimpsest, das man Schicht für Schicht ermessen muss, ein bisschen, als würde man die Kapitel eines Romans durchblättern. Der Baum hatte zahlreiche Zweige: Das Kunstwerk oder besser gesagt, das Ensemble, birgt eine Verästelung von Gesten und Zeichen. „Die tibetanische Medizin besitzt Medikamente mit mehr als 20 Inhaltsstoffen, die dann in einer kleinen Kapsel zusammengepresst werden, um ihre Wirkung auf den Körper zu entfalten", sagt Mirko Baselgia. „Wenn ein Kunstsammler eine Arbeit kauft und fortan mit dieser lebt, dann sollte ihn diese Arbeit nicht nur die ersten fünf Minuten herausfordern, sondern über einen längeren Zeitraum hinweg sein Interesse wecken." Die endlosen Maserungen des Holzes finden sich in der Bronze wieder, wurden zu den gewundenen Linien einer endlosen Skulptur, die sich wie ein hermetisches Gedicht liest. „Calme bloc ici-bas chû d'un désastre obscur" – „Ruhiger Block, aus dunklem Unheil her verirrt": Stéphane Mallarmés Gedicht kommt angesichts dieses skulpturalen Ensembles von außergewöhnlicher Kunstfertigkeit und seltener Komplexität in den Sinn. Es umfasst mehr als 180 Bronze-Elemente, die in vierjähriger Arbeit entworfen und geschaffen wurden, unter Einbeziehung dutzender Menschen an verschiedenen Orten in der Schweiz und in Italien. Als der kritische Ästhet und anspruchsvolle Kunstsammler Thomas Abegg seinen 124 Jahre alten Baum fällen musste, sprach er darüber mit Mirko Baselgia, und sie entschieden, diesen Tod in eine Geburt zu verwandeln. Die Kunst ist das Leben, und ein originales Kunstwerk entsteht aus dem Ursprung. Mirko, der Künstler und Philosoph, liest Rumi, den Sufi-Mystiker, für den der Tod eine neue Geburt bedeutet. Es ist folglich kein Mausoleum des vergangenen Baums, dieses vier Tonnen schwere Skulpturenensemble, sondern seine neue Verkörperung. In seinem neuen Leben, in dem Bronze an die Stelle von Holz tritt, erstreckt sich *The Tree of Valbella* in vier Skulptur-Ästen oder -Segmenten: ein Paravent, eine Quelle, Bänke, Tore und ein Schlussstein – denn die Kunst ist immer ein Durchgang zu etwas anderem, und das Aufstellen eines Kunstwerks bedeutet stets, dem eigenen Garten einen Stein hinzuzufügen. In den vier Jahren

As early as 1926, Brâncuşi wanted to erect an endless column in a green environment, in this case New York's Central Park, the 'green lung' of what was then the biggest city in the world. He wished to integrate culture into nature, to attempt symbiosis between an artistic creation and natural elements, like the first sculptures put up by human beings, stones placed vertically, reaching to the sky like Neolithic menhirs.

Mirko Baselgia's *Tree of Valbella* is another 'sculptural ensemble,' whose vertical elements also recall the foundations of the history of sculpture and of its very essence. All the parts of this installation relate to one another, telling a story by the way they are grouped. The artwork belongs to the category of artistic creations that are so complex and multifaceted that only the word 'ensemble' can convey their multiple dimensions. All begins with the story—or rather the felling—of a hundred-year-old tree in the garden of Thomas Abegg's holiday home in Valbella. Mirko Baselgia's creation in fact resembles an artistic palimpsest that must be studied layer by layer, almost as if one were leafing through the chapters of a novel. The tree had many branches: the artwork, or rather the ensemble, contains a branching network of gestures and symbols. 'In Tibetan medicine, there are drugs that contain more than 20 ingredients, which are then compressed into a small capsule to have their effect on the body,' Mirko Baselgia says. 'If an art collector buys a work and then lives with it, then the work should not only challenge him for the first five minutes, but also be an interesting companion for him in the long term.'

The never-ending veins of the wood are found in the bronze, transformed into the sinuous lines of an endless sculpture that is to be read like a hermetic poem. "Calme bloc ici-bas chû d'un désastre obscur"— one thinks of the poetry of Stéphane Mallarmé when viewing this sculptural ensemble of exceptional virtuosity and rare complexity, comprised of more than 180 bronze pieces conceived and executed during four years of work involving dozens of people in many locations in Switzerland and Italy.

When he was obliged to cut down his 124-year-old tree, Thomas Abegg, a sophisticated art lover and ambitious collector, contacted Mirko Baselgia, and together they decided to transform this death into a birth and envisioned the metamorphosis of the tree into a work of art. Art is life, and a new work of art creates a new beginning. Both an artist and a philosopher, Mirko is a reader of Rumi, the Sufi mystic for whom death is a new birth. It is not, then, a mausoleum for the dead tree that we see today in this four-ton sculptural group, but its reincarnation. In its new life, in which bronze has been substituted for wood, the *Tree of Valbella* is composed of four 'branches', or sculptural segments: a screen, a fountain, benches, and a stone doorway—because art is always a pathway to something else, and installing a work is always adding a stone to one's garden.

The four-year process of work and artistic investigation that ended in the creation of the *Tree of Valbella* was the result of intense dialogue between Thomas Abegg and Mirko Baselgia. The collector evolved into a producer, not only financing the work but also engaging in regular conversations with the artist about the concept and development of the project. The history of art is punctuated with masterpieces commissioned for private homes that arose from the dialogue between artist and collector: Donatello's *David*, commissioned by Cosimo de' Medici in 1430; the sculptural furniture for Jacques Doucet's office that he asked the young designers Pierre Legrain and Rose Adler to create in Neuilly in 1925–27; all the way to Yves Saint-Laurent, who invited his friend Claude Lalanne to sculpt his dreams of Bavarian castles into mirrors with plant motifs for his Paris apartment in the Rue de Babylone – a monumental commission that the artist would take ten years to complete.

Baselgia's sculptural palimpsest is the result of an artistic approach resembling a kind of anthropometry. The artist dealt with the tree along the lines of the Renaissance anatomists—anatomy being a fundamental artistic discipline at that time—to implement a deep and rigorous analysis of the tree to its very core. Mirko transforms himself into a kind of coroner, cutting up the sections of the tree to reveal its

Identitätskarte des *Baums von Valbella*

Entstehungsjahr: 2014-2019

Maße:
Paravent: 2 × 4 Elemente von 330 × 102 × 5,5 cm
Quelle: H 110 cm, Durchmesser 88 cm
Liegende Reliefs: 55 × 354 × 88 cm
Tore: 2 Elemente von 220 × 36 × 5,5 cm
Schlussstein: 110 x 88 x 22 cm

Schreiner:
ca. 1440 Arbeitsstunden

Holzverbrauch von 1 Fichte:
Paravent:
Bretter und Abfallmaterial:
55 / 11 mm = 18 ml
22 ml
44 / 5,5 mm = 11 ml
14 ml
100 - 120 / 11 × 8,75 × 5,5 mm = 36 ml
42 ml (Windgötter)
22 / 11 mm = 88 ml
106 ml
19,25 / 1 1mm = 32 ml
38 ml
16,5 / 11 mm = 25 ml
30 ml
13,75 / 11 mm = 17 ml
20 ml
11 / 11 mm = 244 ml
295 ml
8,25 / 11 mm = 35 ml
42 ml
Insgesamt: 506 ml 609 ml

Tore:
Bretter:
8 Teile: 330 mm breit
3,5 - 4 m
7 Teile: 220 mm breit
3,5 - 4 m
6 Teile: 110 mm breit
3,5 - 4 m
4 Teile: 180 - 280 mm breit
3,5 - 4 m

Maschinen und Werkzeuge:
Feststehende Schneidemaschine: Schneiden der Tafeln
Feststehende Hobelmaschine: Hobeln der Streifen
Feststehende Kreissäge: Fräsen der Streifen
Tischzugsäge Precisio: Alle Winkelschnitte
Feststehende Bürstmaschine: Alle Streifen
Furnierpresse: Leimen der Tafeln
Plattensäge: Schneiden der Tore und der Transportboxen
Hand-Bürstmaschine
Meißel
Schleifpapier
Laubsäge: Für die Windgötter und die Tore
Waffenbürste für die Windgötter
Weißleim

Gießerei:
ca. 2100 Arbeitsstunden, geleistet von 16 Menschen
Menge Bronze: 4000 kg

Anzahl der Bronze-Elemente:
170-190 montierte Elemente (unterschiedlicher Größe)
Anzahl der Gießformen:
170-190 hergestellte Gießformen (unterschiedlicher Größe)

Gewicht:
4000 kg

Herkunft der Bronze:
Italien

Material der Gießformen:
Silikonkautschuk und Acrylharz

Produktionsorte:
In der Schweiz:
Fällen des Baums in Valbella
Zersägen des dicken Stamms in Bergün
Zersägen des dünnen Stamms in Churwalden
Trocknen der Tafeln in Churwalden
Herstellung des Paravents, der Windgötter und der liegenden Reliefs in Seewis
Herstellung der Tore in Malans
Bürsten der Streifen und Bretter in Churwalden und Lenzerheide
Herstellung der Vorlagen für die Windgötter in Chur
Druck der Karten in Chur
In Neapel:
Fräsen der beiden mittleren Tafeln

Fotografen:
Im Studio: Heinz Kunz
In der Schreinerei und in Valbella:
Bernd Grundmann
Des lebenden Baums in Valbella:
Stefan Altenburger
In Neapel: Amedeo Benestante und Dario de Simone

Identity Card of the *Tree of Valbella*

Years of creation: 2014–2019

Size:
Screen: 2 x 4 elements of
330 x 102 x 5.5 cm
Spring: H 110 cm, diameter 88 cm
Horizontal reliefs: 55 x 354 x 88 cm
Doors: 2 elements of 220 x 36 x 5.5 cm
Final stone: 110 x 88 x 22 cm

Carpenter:
approx. 1440 hours of work

Wood consumption of 1 spruce tree:
Screen:
Wooden list, with waste material:
55 / 11mm = 18 ml
22 ml
44 / 5.5 mm = 11 ml
14 ml
100 - 120 / 11 x 8.75 x 5.5mm = 36 ml
42 ml (wind gods)
22 / 11mm = 88 ml
106 ml
19.25 / 11mm = 32 ml
38 ml
16.5 / 11 mm = 25 ml
30 ml
13.75 / 11mm = 17 ml
20 ml
11 / 11mm = 244 ml
295 ml
8.25 / 11mm = 35 ml
42 ml
Total: 506 ml 609 ml

Doors:
boards:
8 pieces: 330 mm wide
3.5 - 4 mO
7 pieces: 220 mm wide
3.5 - 4 m
6 pieces: 110 mm wide
3.5 - 4 m
4 pieces: 180 - 280 mm wide
3.5 - 4 m

Machinery and tools:
Stationary cutter: to cut the boards
Stationary slicer machine: to plane the strips
Stationary table circular saw: to mill the strips
Festool Precisio: all angle cuts
Stationary brushing machine: all the strips
Veneer press: to glue the boards
Panel saw: for cutting the doors and the transport boxes
Hand brushing machine
Chisel
sandpaper
Scroll saw: for the wind gods and doors
Weapon brush for the wind gods
White glue

Foundry:
approx. 2100 hours of work with 16 people
Quantity of bronze: 4000 kg

Number of bronze pieces:
170-190 pieces assembled (different dimensions)
Number of moulds: 170-190 moulds made (different dimensions)

Weight:
4000 kilos

Provenance of the bronze:
Italy

Material of the moulds:
silicon rubber and acrylic resin

Production Locations:
In Switzerland:
Felling of the tree in Valbella
Sawing the wood of the thick trunk in Bergün
Sawing the wood of the thin trunk in Churwalden
Dry of the boards in Churwalden
Producing of the screen, wind gods, and the horizontal reliefs in Seewis
Producing of the doors in Malans
Brushing of the strips and boards in Churwalden and Lenzerheide
Producing of the wind gods' templates in Chur
Printing of the maps in Chur
In Naples:
Mill-cut of the 2 boards in the middle

Photographers:
In the studio: Heinz Kunz
At the carpentry shop and in Valbella: Bernd Grundmann
Living tree in Valbella: Stefan Altenburger
In Naples: Amedeo Benestante and Dario de Simone

Recherche und Arbeit hat sich der Prozess, aus dem *The Tree of Valbella* hervorgegangen ist, ausgehend von und in einem regen Dialog zwischen Thomas Abegg und Mirko Baselgia vollzogen. Der Sammler hat sich hier zum Produzenten gewandelt, nicht nur, weil er die Arbeit finanziert, sondern vor allem, indem er sich regelmäßig mit dem Künstler über das Konzept und die Entwicklung des Werks ausgetauscht und es ständig mit einem ersten Blick betrachtet hat. Die Kunstgeschichte ist reich an Meisterwerken, die von Privatleuten in Auftrag gegeben wurden und aus einem Dialog zwischen Künstler und Sammler hervorgegangen sind: Donatellos *David*, den Cosimo de Medici 1430 in Auftrag gibt; die Möbel-Skulpturen in Jacques Doucets Arbeitszimmer, die er von den jungen Designern Pierre Legrain und Rose Adler 1925-27 in Neuilly realisieren lässt; bis hin zu Yves Saint-Laurent, der seine Freundin Claude Lalanne beauftragte, seine Träume von bayerischen Schlössern in Form von pflanzlich inspirierten Spiegeln in seinem Appartement in der Rue de Babylone zu verwirklichen – ein Auftrag titanischen Umfangs, für dessen Vollendung die Künstlerin zehn Jahre brauchte.

Dieses skulpturale Palimpsest enthüllt eine künstlerische Vorgehensweise, die sich einer Form der Anthropometrie annähert. Der Künstler hat mit dem Baum in der Nachfolge der Anatomen der Renaissance gearbeitet – damals eine grundlegende künstlerische Praxis – und eine rigorose und tiefgehende Analyse des Baumes bis in seine Eingeweide vorgenommen. Mirko hat sich in eine Art Gerichtsmediziner verwandelt und den Baum zerteilt, um seine Geschichte und seine Wahrheiten zu offenbaren. Es ist der Körper des Baumes, den Mirko in diesem facettenreichen Werk feiert und mit dem er arbeitet. Der natürliche und der phantasierte Körper: Da ist die biologische Geschichte des Baumes, die uns der zum Naturforscher erwandelten Künstler bietet, und da ist die künstlerische Geschichte, der Wandel des Baumes, der zum Werk geworden ist, in dem kulturelle Bezüge anklingen, die so polymorph sind, wie es die natürliche Maserung des Baumes war – von der Symbolik der Morphologie der Winde im hellenistischen Griechenland bis zur asiatischen Zen-Philosophie. Hieraus ergibt sich, wie eine Ergänzung des Werks – oder sein wesentlicher Bestandteil –, eine Art anthropometrisches Profil des Baums aus dem Garten in Valbella, in seinen Ursprüngen und seiner Verwandlung in ein Kunstwerk.

Mirko Baselgia hat auch an den *Steingarten* des Soami gedacht, als er diese Arbeit konzipierte, die heute als sein Meisterstück gelten kann – im Sinne, dass *The Tree of Valbella* das komplexeste und anspruchsvollste Werk ist, das er bisher geschaffen hat. Der Besuch des Daisen-in-Tempels in Kyoto hat ihn in der Tat tief geprägt. *The Tree of Valbella* ist ebenfalls eine künstlerische Komposition, die sowohl zum Betrachten wie zur Meditation einlädt: „Die Geschichte beginnt und endet bei dem Baum im Garten und kehrt verwandelt dorthin zurück", erklärt Mirko Baselgia. „Die Jahresringe des Baumes erzählen uns von der Zeit, als es weder den Besitzer des Gartens noch das Haus gab. Zu jener Zeit gab es praktisch keinen Tourismus in dieser Gegend, in der Friedrich Nietzsche gerade das Lenzerheide-Fragment fertig gestellt hatte und ihn seine langen Spaziergänge vielleicht ganz in die Nähe dieses Baumes führten. Das gesamte Ensemble und die zugehörigen Skulpturen wurden aus dem Fleisch des Baumes handwerklich geschaffen und in Bronze gegossen." Das Fleisch des Baumes wurde zum Sujet der Kunst. „Ein Bild des Lebens", beschreibt Mirko Baselgia sein Werk, dessen Schönheit und spirituelle Kraft magnetisch wirken und uns einladen, uns für die Betrachtung Zeit zu nehmen. „Ein Kunstwerk sollte alle ansprechen und nicht nur diejenigen, die eingeweiht sind", erklärt Baselgia. „Ich glaube, wenn man sich vor einem vollendeten Werk befindet, dann erschließt sich dieses auf die eine oder andere Weise, egal ob man Kunstgeschichte studiert hat oder zufällig darauf gestoßen ist, und egal ob man 5 oder 88 Jahre alt ist. Was diese Arbeit betrifft, so versuchte ich vor allem, den Baum zum Sprechen zu bringen – über das Leben, den Tod, die vielen Formen, die das Leben annehmen kann, und die Strukturen, die uns mit unserem Umfeld verbinden." Aber wir haben alle schon zu viel geredet. Nun sollen unsere Augen dem *Tree of Valbella* lauschen.

history and its truths. It's the body of the tree that Mirko celebrates and interacts with in this multifaceted work—the actual body and the dreamed-of body. There is the biological history of the tree, revealed to us by the artist-turned-naturalist, and there is the artistic history, the reincarnation of the tree turned into a work of art with cultural resonances as polymorphic as the tree's natural veins—from the symbolism of the Hellenistic Greek morphology of the winds to the Zen philosophy of Japan. The result, like a complement to the work—or perhaps an integral part of it—is the production of a veritable anthropometric record of the tree in the garden of Valbella, in terms of both its origins and its metamorphosis into a work of art.

Mirko Baselgia also recalled Sōami's *Rock Garden* in his conception of what now constitutes his masterpiece—in the sense that the *Tree of Valbella* is the most complex and ambitious work he has created up to now. His visit to the Daisen-in temple in Kyoto made a profound impression on him. The *Tree of Valbella* is, in the same vein, one of those artistic compositions that provide as much to think about as to look at. 'The story begins and ends with the tree in the garden and returns there transformed', summarizes Mirko Baselgia. 'The annual rings of the tree tell us of the time when neither the owner of the garden nor the house stood there—at that time there was practically no tourism in this area where Friedrich Nietzsche had just finished the Lenzerheide-Fragment, and his long walks might have taken him very close to our tree. The entire ensemble and the sculptures it contains were handcrafted from the flesh of the tree and cast in bronze'. The 'flesh' of the tree has become the subject of the artwork. 'A picture of life', as Mirko Baselgia sums it up to describe his work, whose beauty and spiritual strength act as magnets, inviting us to take the time to observe it carefully.

'A work should be able to reach anyone, not just someone who is initiated', Baselgia explains. 'I believe that if you are in front of the finished work, the work will open up in one way or another, whether you have studied art history or just pass it randomly, whether you are 5 years or 88 years old. In this work, I am particularly interested in making the tree speak—about life, death, the many forms that life can take on, and the patterns that connect us to everything surrounding us.' But we've all already spoken too much. Let's use our eyes now to listen to the *Tree of Valbella*.

EIN MAUSOLEUM ALS ABBILD DES LEBENS IM GESPRÄCH MIT MIRKO BASELGIA

JÉRÔME NEUTRES

1 / Wie nahm dieses außergewöhnliche Projekt seinen Anfang? Hast du Thomas Abegg einen ersten Vorschlag unterbreitet? Welchen? Wie hast du das Projekt entwickelt?

MB: Thomas Abegg hatte bereits einige meiner Arbeiten für sein Haus in den Bündner Bergen, in Valbella, gekauft. Dann wollte er, dass ich in seinem Garten eine ortsspezifische Intervention vornehme. Und so initiierten wir das Projekt. Zuerst präsentierte ich ihm eine Idee, die in einem engeren Bezug zur Architektur des Orts stand. Später stellte sich heraus, dass Thomas einen 124 Jahre alten Baum fällen musste, und mir wurde sofort klar, dass dies der entscheidende Wendepunkt für das Projekt und der Kern meiner künftigen Arbeit war. Wir verabschiedeten uns allmählich von dem ganzen Hausprojekt und legten den Schwerpunkt auf ein Skulpturenensemble. Das Projekt entwickelte sich im konstanten Dialog mit Thomas, und dank dieses Austauschs erhielt es seine komplexe, konzentrierte Form.

2 / Dein einzigartiges Werk ist schwer zu beschreiben, da es einer Erzählung mit verschiedenen Kapiteln gleicht und eine Geschichte in sich birgt: Kannst du bitte die wichtigsten Kapitel der Geschichte, die du uns erzählst, zusammenfassen?

MB: Die Geschichte beginnt und endet mit einem Baum im Garten des Auftraggebers, der in veränderter Form dorthin zurückkehrt. Die Jahresringe geben uns Aufschluss über die Zeit, als weder der Besitzer des Gartens noch das Haus existierten – zu der Zeit gab es nahezu keinen Tourismus, und Friedrich Nietzsche hatte gerade sein Lenzerheide-Fragment abgeschlossen. Seine langen Spaziergänge könnten ihn in unmittelbare Nähe unseres Baums geführt haben. Das gesamte Ensemble wurde zusammen mit den Skulpturen aus dem Baum gefertigt und in Bronze gegossen.

3 / Deine Arbeit gleicht einem Prozess mit verschiedenen Schritten, einer langen Reise durch diverse Materialien. Dieser Prozess ähnelt visuell einem Palimpsest, da die erzählerische Installation mehrere Arbeitsebenen umfasst. Hast du einen bestimmten Zweck verfolgt? Ging es dir darum, dich der großen Herausforderung zu stellen, das bisher komplexeste Kunstwerk zu realisieren? Beschreibe mir einige der Ebenen dieses Prozesses...

MB: Die tibetanische Medizin besitzt Medikamente, die mehr als 20 Inhaltsstoffe enthalten und dann in einer kleinen Kapsel zusammengepresst werden, um ihre Wirkung auf den Körper zu entfalten. Wenn ein Kunstsammler eine Arbeit kauft und fortan mit dieser lebt, dann sollte ihn diese Arbeit nicht nur die ersten fünf Minuten herausfordern, sondern über einen längeren Zeitraum hinweg sein Interesse wecken. Die Arbeit ist nicht so komplex – sie basiert auf einem Baum, besser gesagt, auf dem Holz eines Baums, das nachfolgend in Bronze gegossen wurde. Es gibt eine Quelle, einen Paravent, zwei liegende Reliefs, zwei Tore und einen Schlussstein.

4 / Was ist der rote Faden dieses Prozesses? Nach was hast du gesucht?

MB: Es handelt sich um eine Hommage an einen gefällten Baum – ein Mausoleum und ein Abbild des Lebens. Normalerweise wird das Holz eines Baums wie des „unsrigen" nicht für anspruchsvolle Arbeiten verwendet. Meist dient es als Feuerholz oder wird zu Leimholzplatten verarbeitet. Die günstigen Arbeitsprozesse in der Holzindustrie sind heutzutage so weit fortgeschritten, dass es nicht länger um den

A MAUSOLEUM AS A PICTURE OF LIFE CONVERSATION WITH MIRKO BASELGIA

1 / How did this never seen project started? Did you come to Thomas Abegg with a first idea? Which one? How did you develop the project?

MB: Thomas Abegg had already bought some of my works for his house of the Grisons mountains, in Valbella. Then he wished to get from me a specific intervention in the garden and that is how we started the project. First, I gave him an idea that was more related to the existing architecture of the site. Later it became clear that Thomas wanted to cut an old tree that was 124 years old, and I knew immediately that this was the decisive turnaround for the project and the key of my upcoming work. We gradually dissolved the entire project from the house and focused on an ensemble of sculptures. The project evolved into a constant dialogue with Thomas and the exchange led the project ever further to the complex and concentrated form that it has today.

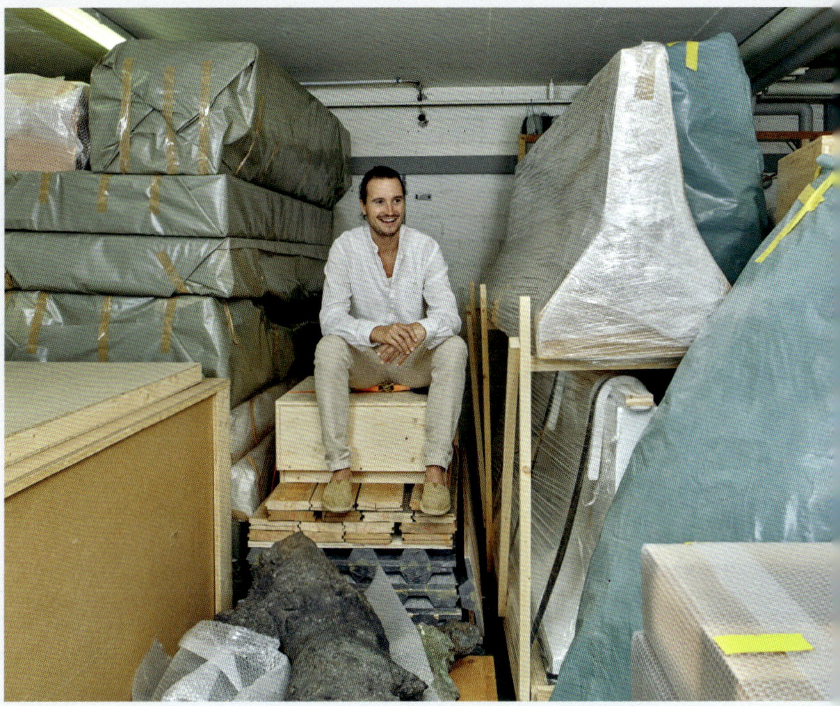

Mirko Baselgia in seinem Lager in Tiefencastel / Mirko Baselgia in his storage in Tiefencastel

2 / Your unique work is hard to describe as it is like a novel with different chapters and a true story: could you summarise the main chapters of the story your work is telling us?

MB: The story begins and ends with the tree in the garden of the commissioner and returns there transformed. The annual rings tell us of the time when neither the owner of the garden nor the house stood there – at that time there was practically no tourism and Friedrich Nietzsche had just finished the Lenzerheide-Fragment and his long walks might have taken him very close to our tree. The entire ensemble and the sculptures it contains were hand-crafted from the flesh of the tree and cast in bronze.

3 / Your work is in fact a process, with various steps, a long-time journey through various materials; this process looks visually as a palimpsest, meaning there are many levels of work in this installation story. Was it a specific purpose? A virtuous challenge of creating the most complex artwork ever? Tell me some of the levels of the process...

MB: In Tibetan medicine, there are medicines that contain more than 20 ingredients and can then be compressed into a small capsule to have an effect on the body. If an art collector buys a work and then lives with it, then the work should not only challenge him for the first five minutes, but also be an interesting companion for him in the long term. The work is not so complex, it consists of a tree. Better said, of the wood of a tree that was subsequently cast in bronze. There is a spring, a screen, two horizontal reliefs, two doors and a final stone.

individuellen Baum geht, sondern um abstrakte Zahlen in einer Statistik oder auf einer Karte. Dieser einzelne Baum – das Subjekt hier wird zum Symbol für alle Bäume. Jeder Baum hat seine eigene Geschichte. Dieser spezifische Baum erzählt uns die Geschichte seines Orts und seines Lebens an diesem Ort. Darüber hinaus ist es wichtig für mich, dieses Leben nicht zu abstrahieren, sondern seinen spezifischen Wert zu erfassen. Dadurch kann etwas auf universeller Ebene sichtbar gemacht werden.

5 / Welche Künstlerinnen und Künstler haben deine künstlerische Entwicklung beeinflusst?

MB: Mir ist bewusst, dass wir auf den Schultern von Riesen sitzen, wie man so schön sagt. Für meine Arbeit in Valbella war es eine eindringliche Erfahrung, nach Japan zu reisen und den Daisen-in Tempel in Kyōto zu besuchen, dessen steinerner Garten mich nachhaltig inspirierte. Wenn ich richtig informiert bin, wird der Garten Sōami zugeschrieben. Allgemein geprägt wurde ich durch Irving Stones Romanbiografie über Michelangelo Buonarroti, die mir meine Großmutter im Alter von elf Jahren gab, und die mich dazu anregte, Künstler zu werden. Nachdem ich das Buch über Michelangelo verschlungen und sofort versucht hatte, Bildhauer zu werden, legte sie mir Walter Bauers Buch über Vincent van Gogh nahe, und dann die Alberto Giacometti-Biografie von James Lord. Mir war klar, welchen Weg ich einschlagen würde. Ich fühlte mich zur Kunst berufen und suchte nach einer eigenen künstlerischen Sprache. Während meiner Reise traf ich zahlreiche interessante Künstlerinnen und Künstler, die mich sicherlich beeinflusst haben, auch wenn ich mich nicht auf eine bestimmte Person berufen kann. Meine Familie, meine Freunde, mein Umfeld und meine fortlaufende Auseinandersetzung mit mir selbst und mit der Welt durch die verschiedenen Medien haben einen weitaus größeren Einfluss auf mich und meine Kunst.

6 / Der Dialog mit Thomas Abegg ist das entscheidende Element, um den Prozess deiner Arbeit zu verstehen. Ist es das erste Mal, dass du einen solchen Dialog mit einem Sammler geführt hast, um eine Arbeit zu realisieren? Agierte Thomas Abegg in diesem Fall mehr als Produzent denn als Sammler?

MB: Während meiner Studienzeit hatte ich öfters die Möglichkeit, mit anderen Künstlerinnen und Künstler dialogische Arbeiten zu entwickeln und konnte darüber hinaus Bühnenbilder für verschiedene kleine Theatergruppen entwerfen. Im Rahmen dieses Projekts unternahm ich jedoch das erste Mal so eine lange Reise mit einem Kunstsammler. Thomas war ein leidenschaftlicher, offener, geduldiger und, zum Glück, meistens sturer Auftraggeber, der sich nicht mit der erstbesten Lösung zufriedengab und mich als Künstler dazu herausforderte, noch mehr aus dem Projekt herauszuholen.

7 / Warum hast du die Gießerei in Neapel gewählt? Hast du dort neue Ideen gefunden?

MB: Mich verbindet eine lange Freundschaft mit der Familie Del Giudice. Wir arbeiten seit fast zehn Jahren zusammen. Ich wusste, dass ich die Arbeit dort ausführen wollte. Sie sind ausgezeichnete und leidenschaftliche Handwerker – eine Kombination, die ich wirklich schätze.

8 / Du scheinst verschlüsselte Arbeiten zu mögen, die voller Geheimnisse und Rätsel stecken und die nur diejenigen, die eingeweiht wurden, verstehen können. Welche Rolle spielt für dich ein Kunstwerk? Insbesondere dieses?

MB: Mir geht es nicht darum, eine Arbeit zu verschlüsseln oder zu verrätseln. Ein Kunstwerk sollte alle ansprechen und nicht nur diejenigen, die eingeweiht sind. Ich glaube, wenn man sich vor einem vollendeten Werk befindet, dann erschließt sich dieses auf die eine oder andere Weise, egal ob man Kunstgeschichte studiert hat oder zufällig darauf gestoßen ist, und egal ob man 5 oder 88 Jahre alt ist. Was diese Arbeit betrifft, so versuchte ich vor allem, den Baum zum Sprechen zu bringen – über das Leben, den Tod, die vielen Formen, die das Leben annehmen kann, und die Strukturen, die uns mit unserem Umfeld verbinden.

4 / What is the vertebral column of this process? What did you search for?

MB: It is a tribute to the felled tree, a mausoleum and a picture of life. Usually the wood from a tree like 'our' is not used for high quality work. In most cases it turns into firewood or is processed into glued panels. The economic processes in the timber industry are today so advanced that it is no longer about the individual tree but about an abstract figure in a statistic or on a map. This single tree—the subject here becomes the symbol for all trees. Every tree has a story to tell. This specific tree tells us the story of its place and its life in this place. It is also important to me not to fall into this form of abstract life, but to lend it as much as possible to its specific value. This can make something universally visible.

5 / Who are the artists who influenced you in your developments?

MB: I am aware that, as we say, we are sitting on the shoulders of giants. For the work in Valbella, a trip to Japan and the visit to the Daisen-in temple in Kyoto was a profound experience, where the rock garden had a lasting inspiration. If I'm properly informed, the garden is attributed to Soami. As a general influence in my work, when I was eleven years old my grandmother gave me the novel biography of Irving Stone about Michelangelo Buonarroti and led me to the decision to become an artist. After devouring the book about Michelangelo and immediately trying to be a sculptor, she recommended the book by Walter Bauer on the life of Vincent Van Gogh and then the biography of Alberto Giacometti by James Lord. It was clear to me where my path would go. I felt called to art. After that, I was artistically looking for a language of my own until I graduated from high school. On my journey, I met many exciting artists who might have had an influence on me, but I feel difficult to call on someone. My family, my friends, my environment and my current occupation with myself and with the world through the various media have a far greater impact on me and my art.

6 / The dialogue with Thomas Abegg is a key to understand the process of your work. Is it the first time you have such a dialogue with a collector to create a work? Don't you think we could consider in that case Thomas Abegg as a sort of art producer, more than a collector?

MB: There were many possibilities for a dialogic work with other artists during my studies and in the time when I was allowed to design stage sets for different small theatre groups. But it is the first time I have embarked on such a long journey with an art collector. Thomas was a passionate, agile, patient and fortunately sometimes stubborn patron, who was not satisfied with the first solution and has challenged me as an artist to go one step further.

7 / Why did you choose a Naples foundry? Did you find there new ideas of development?

MB: A long friendship connects me to the Del Giudice family. We've been working together for almost 10 years; it was clear to me that I wanted to do the work there. They are great craftsmen and passionate, a combination that I really appreciate.

8 / You seem to like the coded works, with their secrets and mysteries that one can understand only if he is initiated. What is for you the role of an artwork? Of this one in particular?

MB: For me it's not about coding a work or making it cryptic. A work should be able to reach anyone and not just someone who is initiated. I believe that if you are in front of the finished work, the work will open up in one way or another, whether you have studied art history or just pass it randomly, whether you are 5 years or 88 years old. In this work, I am particularly interested in making the tree speak about life, death, the many forms that life can take on and the patterns that connect us to everything surrounding us.

9 / Looking at your personal library in your studio, I can see how important is the philosophy history for you. When did you start studying the philosophers' texts? I know also you have been

9 / Wenn man deine persönliche Bibliothek in deinem Atelier in Augenschein nimmt, fällt auf, wie wichtig die Philosophiegeschichte für dich ist. Wann hast du begonnen, die Texte der Philosophen zu lesen? Du hast auch einige Arbeiten als Illustration oder Hommage an Bourdieu oder Platon realisiert. Kannst du diese beschreiben?

MB: Als ich die 7. Klasse besuchte, fühlte ich mich unterfordert. Ein junger Aushilfslehrer erkannte dies und gab mir *Sofies Welt: Roman über die Geschichte der Philosophie* von Jostein Gaarder – so begann das Abenteuer der Philosophie für mich. Die Arbeiten, die du erwähnst, sind keine Illustrationen einer Theorie oder eine Hommage an die Philosophen. Sie sind vielmehr das Ergebnis einer Suche nach dem kleinsten gemeinsamen Nenner. Im Fall von Bourdieu ging ich der Frage nach, auf welche Weise die Klassengesellschaft Materialien und Formen im öffentlichen Raum zum Ausdruck bringt. Was für ein Bild entsteht, wenn eine Revolution, die die Auflösung der traditionellen Strukturen anstrebt, auf einen kleinen Ausstellungsraum begrenzt wird, sodass die Situation für die Betrachter konkret greifbar wird. Im Fall von Platon ging es um die Erkenntnis, dass das Fundament meiner christlichen Erziehung auf dem Wertesystem einer spezifischen westlichen Philosophenschule basiert. Meiner Meinung nach wohnt Platons Geradengleichung und Parabeln im Allgemeinen eine verführerische Komponente inne. Sie vermittelten mir das Gefühl, ein Instrument zur Verfügung zu haben, mit dem man sich von unten nach oben bewegen konnte, um zur Erkenntnis oder sogar Erleuchtung zu gelangen. Etwas Wichtiges fehlt jedoch, das Nietzsche ins Spiel bringt, eine menschliche Eigenschaft, die unseren Körper geformt hat und die wir heutzutage viel zu wenig praktizieren – das Gehen – oder die Bewegung. Nietzsche war ein leidenschaftlicher Spaziergänger. Er hinterließ eine Anmerkung, wohin er in der Lenzerheide überall hinging oder hingehen wollte. Seinem Vorbild folgend sammelte ich Äste. Das Gehen und Denken sind Verbündete. Der Pilgerstab symbolisiert die essenziell notwendige Bewegung im Raum und die mentale Migration, die erforderlich ist, um einen Einblick zu gewinnen. Der aus Keramik gefertigte Pilgerstab ist jedoch keine adäquate Stütze. Würde man ihn zum Wandern verwenden, würde er beim ersten Auftreffen auf einer harten Oberfläche zerbrechen. Damit wandte ich mich von Platon ab, und fand mein Glück mit Epikur.

10 / Kannst du etwas über dein grundlegendes Verhältnis zur Natur in deinem Leben und in deiner Arbeit sagen? Folgst du einer ökologischen Vision?

MB: Mich spricht insbesondere die Vorstellung von Ökologie im Sinne von Ernst Haeckel oder im Zusammenhang mit einer Verwendung im wissenschaftlichen Sinn an. Ein Film von Franz Reichle (einer meiner Professoren an der Zürcher Hochschule der Künste) regte mich dazu an, mich eingehender mit den Vorstellungen von zwei chilenischen Biologen und ihrem Umfeld auseinanderzusetzen. Francisco Varela und Humberto Maturana waren von der Biosophie beeinflusst und betrieben bewusst Philosophie mittels der Praxis des Biologen. Die Auseinandersetzung mit der Ökologie geht mir nicht weit genug, da sie nicht explizit die Philosophie einschließt. Obwohl mir der Begriff Künstler-Philosoph nicht zusagt, ist die philosophische Dimension für meine künstlerische Arbeit von großer Bedeutung.

creating some works as an illustration or tribute to Bourdieu or Plato, can you explain it?

MB: When I was in seventh grade, I felt under-challenged and a young substitute teacher recognized this and gave me *Sophie's World: A Novel About the History of Philosophy* by Jostein Gaarder—that's how the adventure of philosophy started for me. The works you mention are not illustrations of a theory or tribute to the philosophers for me—they are the result of a search for a least common denominator. In the example of Bourdieu, I wondered how the class society expresses materials and forms in public space. Which picture appears when a revolution that strives for the dissolution of the traditional structures is shown as reduced as possible in a small exhibition space, so that the situation becomes sensually tangible for the recipient? In the case of Plato, it was rather the realization that the foundation of my Christian education is based on the value system of a specific Occidental philosophy school. For me, Plato's line equation and the parables in general have a seductive component. They make me believe that I have an instrument with which we can move from bottom to top to realization or even to enlightenment. I believe that something important is missing, something that Nietzsche brings into the game. A human quality that has shaped our body and we practice far too little today— walking—or movement. Nietzsche was a passionate walker. He left a note where he went or wanted to go in Lenzerheide. In his footsteps I collected the branches. Walking and thinking are allies. The pilgrim's staff symbolizes the necessary movement in the room and the mental migration that is necessary to gain insight. The pilgrim rod made of ceramic is not a good prop, if you would use it for hiking, it would break after the first touch down on a hard surface. With that I move away from Plato and I found my luck with Epicurus.

10 / Can you speak about your special and fundamental relationship with nature in your life and work? Would you say you follow an ecological vision?

MB: When I think of the concept of ecology in the sense of Ernst Haeckel or in connection with the use in a scientific sense, I feel more addressed. A film by Franz Reichle (one of my professors at the University of Arts in Zurich) inspired me to deal more intensively with the ideas of two Chilean biologists and their environment. Francisco Varela and Humberto Maturana had written their room with 'biosophers'—which is so pertinent because they consciously practice philosophy through the practice of the biologist. For me, the approach of ecology may not go far enough because it does not explicitly include philosophy. Though the term Artist-Philosopher is not attractive, the philosophical dimension is definitely very important for me in my work.

JEDER BAUM IM WALD

LAURA GIUDICI

Im Wald fühlt sich Mirko Baselgia zu Hause. Die Bäume vermitteln ihm ein Gefühl von Sicherheit. Dasselbe beruhigende Gefühl empfindet er, wenn er an einem Familientreffen teilnimmt oder schöne Momente mit Freunden oder der Dorfgemeinschaft erlebt. Es steht daher außer Frage, dass er die jahrhundertealte Fichte, die den Ausgangspunkt für *The Tree of Valbella* bildet, als ein Individuum mit eigener Identität und Geschichte betrachtet. Bäume faszinieren ihn nicht nur aufgrund ihrer Struktur und Funktion, sondern auch aufgrund ihrer außergewöhnlichen Anpassungsfähigkeit und der Überlebensstrategien, die sie entwickeln können. In Anlehnung an verschiedene neuere wissenschaftliche Studien[1] erkennt Baselgia die Sensitivität und die Intelligenz von Bäumen und Pflanzen sowie die grundlegende Rolle an, die ihnen im Leben aller lebenden Organismen auf der Erde zukommt. Daher erscheint es aus dieser Perspektive folgerichtig, einem alten Bau, der gefällt werden musste, mit einem beeindruckenden skulpturalen Ensemble Tribut zu zollen, und den Baum mit unserem Leben zu verknüpfen. Anders ausgedrückt, der Baum und die daraus hervorgehende Arbeit dienen als Symbol für die unverzichtbare Rolle der Pflanzen in unserer Existenz sowie für das Leben selbst. Die verschiedenen Bronzeelemente, aus denen *The Tree of Valbella* besteht, sind aus dem in Bronze gegossenen Holz der Fichte gefertigt. Holz ist eines von Baselgias bevorzugten Materialien, mit dem er eine Vielzahl von Arbeiten realisiert hat. Es ist aber auch, wie in diesem Fall, das Subjekt einiger seiner Werke. Das Holz begleitet ihn seit seiner Geburt: vier Generationen wurde das Schreinerhandwerk bis zu seinem Vater weitergegeben, und darüber hinaus war sein Patenonkel, als wenn das schon nicht reichen würde, ein Förster. Der Geruch von Holz durchdringt seine Kindheitserinnerungen, die Arbeiten wie *Structura digl gôt* (2016) – *Struktur des Waldes* in Romanisch –, zugrunde liegen. Diese Installation wurde aus dem Sägemehl von sieben Bäumen aus Graubünden realisiert, das über dem Boden verteilt und in einem geometrischen Muster in sieben verschiedenen Farben angeordnet wurde. Die Besucherinnen und Besucher waren aufgefordert, über die Oberfläche zu gehen. Diese partizipative Erfahrung involvierte nicht nur die Augen, sondern auch den Geruchs-, Tast- und Hörsinn – wie ein Spaziergang durch den Wald.

Baselgias Verhältnis zum Holz ist zuallererst persönlich und emotional, so wie sein Interesse für die Baumrinde. Bei hölzernen Pflanzen besteht die Rinde aus lebendiger und abgestorbener Rinde und erfüllt unter anderem eine Schutzfunktion, die der menschlichen Haut vergleichbar ist. Die Haut in ihren vielfältigen Erscheinungsformen ist ein immer wiederkehrendes Thema in Baselgias Arbeiten, ein Interesse, das eng mit seiner Biografie verbunden ist. Seit seiner Geburt leidet Baselgia unter einer vererbten Hautkrankheit, der *Ichthyosis vulgaris*, die eine trockene, schuppige Haut an einer oder mehreren Körperstellen verursacht. Während sich die Auseinandersetzung mit der Haut im Allgemeinen darauf konzentriert, was einen Organismus von seinem äußeren Umfeld abgrenzt und schützt, versucht Baselgia den möglichen biographischen Ursprüngen dieser Krankheit auf den Grund zu gehen und zugleich die Reflexion über die eigene Identität zu vertiefen. Was sagt unser Körper über uns und unser Leben aus? Baselgia stellt sich diese Frage nicht nur in Bezug auf die eigene Person, sondern weitet sie auf Bäume, Muschelgehäuse oder Schildkröten aus. *La pel digl gôt* (2015) – *Die Haut des Waldes* in Romanisch – und *Landscape of growing*

EVERY SINGLE TREE IN THE VAST FOREST

In the forest, Mirko Baselgia feels at home. The trees give him a sense of security, the same comforting feeling of attending a family reunion, sharing a pleasant moment with friends or with his village community. For him the century old spruce that served as a starting point for *The Tree of Valbella* is an individual, with its own identity and history. Trees fascinate him not only for their structure and function, but also for their extraordinary adaptability and targeted survival strategies they are able to develop. In line with several recent scientific studies[1], Baselgia recognizes the sensitivity and intelligence of trees and plants in general, as well as the fundamental role they play in the life of all living organisms. From this perspective, paying homage through an impressive sculptural ensemble to an old tree that had to be felled appears obvious, as does the link with our own life. In other words, this tree and the resulting work become a symbol of the indispensable role of plants in our existence and for life on Earth in general.

The Tree of Valbella contains central themes and concerns in Baselgia's artistic practice, such as his affection for wood, the recurring themes of skin and growth, his desire to make structures visible and to reflect on the ecological principle that we are all interconnected. The aim of the present essay is to focus on these aspects, creating bridges between the sculptural ensemble and other works by the artist that are formally and conceptually close to it.

The various bronze elements that make up *The Tree of Valbella* were made from casts of the spruce wood elements. Wood is one of the artist's favorite materials, with which he has created numerous works, but, as in this case, it is also the real subject of some of his creations. Wood has been part of his life since he was born: for four generations, down to his father, the craft of carpentry has been handed down in his family. Moreover, his godfather was a silviculturist. The smell of wood permeates his childhood memories. In the wake of these memories came the *Structura digl gôt* (2016)—*Structure of the forest* in Romansh—, an installation realized with sawdust from seven trees, native from Graubünden, that has been laid on the floor in a geometrical pattern of seven different colors. The viewers are invited to walk on the surface of the work and this participative experience involves not just the eyes, but also the senses of smell, touch, and hearing - just like a walk in the woods.

Baselgia's relationship with wood is above all very intimate and emotional, as is his interest in the bark. In woody plants, the bark is the sum of live and dead bark, and, among other things, has a protective function comparable to that of human skin. Skin, in its various forms, is one of the recurrent themes in Baselgia's work, and the origin of this interest lies in the artist's biography. Since birth, he has had a hereditary skin disease called vulgar ichthyosis, which causes dry, scaly skin in one or more areas of the body. While reflections on the skin generally focus on what delimits and protects an organism from the external environment, in his specific case they are an opportunity to identify the possible biographical origins of this disease and at the same time deepen his reflections about his own identity. What does our body tell about ourselves and our life? Baselgia not only asks this question in relation to one's own being, but extends it to trees, shells or turtles. *La pel digl gôt* (2015)—*The skin of the forest* in Romansh—and *Landscape of growing II* (2017) are examples of reliefs that reproduce barks. The first, made of glazed ceramic with pigments, shows the surface of a spruce, an emblematic tree of Graubünden, the same species of *The Tree of Valbella*. The second, in bronze, reproduces the bark of a type of fast-growing tree he found in Beijing. The artist

II (2017) sind Skulpturen, die Rinde reproduzieren. Die erste besteht aus glasierter Keramik mit Pigmenten und präsentiert sich mit der Oberfläche einer Fichte, dem typischen graubündnerischen Baum und dieselbe Spezies wie in *The Tree of Valbella*. Die zweite Arbeit, aus Bronze, gibt die Rinde eines schnell wachsenden Baums wieder, den Baselgia in Peking entdeckte. Er stellte fest, dass die Bäume dort so schnell wachsen, dass ihre Rinde aufreißt und sich eine Art Landschaft auf ihrer Oberfläche formiert. *Landscape of growing II* setzt sich unter anderem mit den Erscheinungsformen und Überlebensstrategien der Natur im widrigen Umfeld einer Megastadt auseinander. Die Skulpturen behandeln nicht nur Themen, die sich auf die Haut beziehen, sondern auch auf das Wachstumsprinzip. Kann Wachstum – auch im figürlichen Sinn – anhand einer Skulptur zum Ausdruck gebracht werden? Dieselbe Frage liegt auch *Determination* (2013) zugrunde, die Marmor-Reproduktion einer 5,5 cm langen Gastropodenschale, die Baselgia auf 180 cm, seine Körpergröße, vergrößerte. Die kunstvolle geometrische Form dieses spiralig aufgewickelten Gehäuses faszinierte Baselgia, der darin eine visuell verdichtete Vorstellung von Leben und Wachstum erkennt. Das Gehäuse wächst zusammen mit der Molluske, die in ihrem Inneren lebt. Die Wachstumslinien sind auf ihrer Oberfläche sichtbar, während ihre Form und Struktur Aufschluss über ihre Biografie geben. Die Skulpturenserie *Tartaruga* (*Schildkröte*, 2018) setzt sich ebenfalls auf anschauliche Weise mit dem Ablauf der Zeit auseinander. Der Schildkrötenpanzer wird zum materiellen Ausdruck ihrer Biografie. Die Hornschilde, die den Panzer überziehen, weisen eine Reihe von konzentrischen Rillen auf, die in etwa einem Lebensjahr des Tieres entsprechen. Baselgia geht es nicht nur darum, die Rinde und die Jahresringe der Valbella-Fichte hervorzuheben und den Baum als ein Individuum mit einer eigenen Geschichte darzustellen, sondern auch den Zeitablauf sowie die Naturgesetze, die dem Wachstum der unterschiedlichsten Organismen zugrunde liegen, auf eine visuelle Ebene zu überführen.

Zahlreiche von Baselgias Arbeiten entstanden aus dem Bestreben heraus, Strukturen sichtbar zu machen, unabhängig davon, ob es sich um die Grundstrukturen eines einzigen Organismus, ein bestimmtes System oder Strukturen handelt, die die Interaktion zwischen verschiedenen Organismen, zwischen verschiedenen Organismen und einem bestimmten Umfeld oder zwischen verschiedenen Umfeldern und Realitäten auf unserem Planeten regeln. Das Erfassen, Analysieren und Offenlegen dieser Strukturen bieten Baselgia die Möglichkeit, ihre Komplexität zu beleuchten, sich diese Strukturen anzueignen und teilweise neu zu bestimmen, um alternative Strukturen bereitzustellen und die Aufmerksamkeit auf unsere wesentliche Fähigkeit zu lenken, unser Leben und unsere Gesellschaft neu zu gestalten. Baselgia ist überzeugt davon, dass die Kunst das Potenzial besitzt, das eigene Leben zu formen und, vielleicht auch, andere Menschen dazu anzuregen, ihr Leben zu gestalten. Baselgias Interesse für die Naturwissenschaften und die Philosophie fördert diese Reflexionen nachhaltig. In

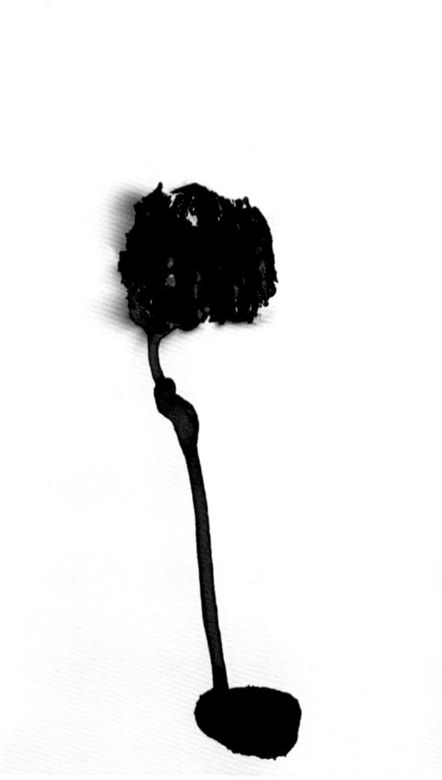

Auf dieser Seite / On this page: Mirko Baselgia, *Autolyse – Coprinus Comatus*, 2019, Coprinus comatus Tinte auf handgeschöpftem Papier der Papiermühle Basel mit Nussholzrahmen / Coprinus comatus ink on handmade paper from Papiermühle Basel with walnut wood frame, 54 x 33 cm / Rechts / right: Mirko Baselgia, *Endoderm (marmot burrows)*, 2012-2013, Bronze, Grösse / size 1:1 - 22 x 154 x 77 cm

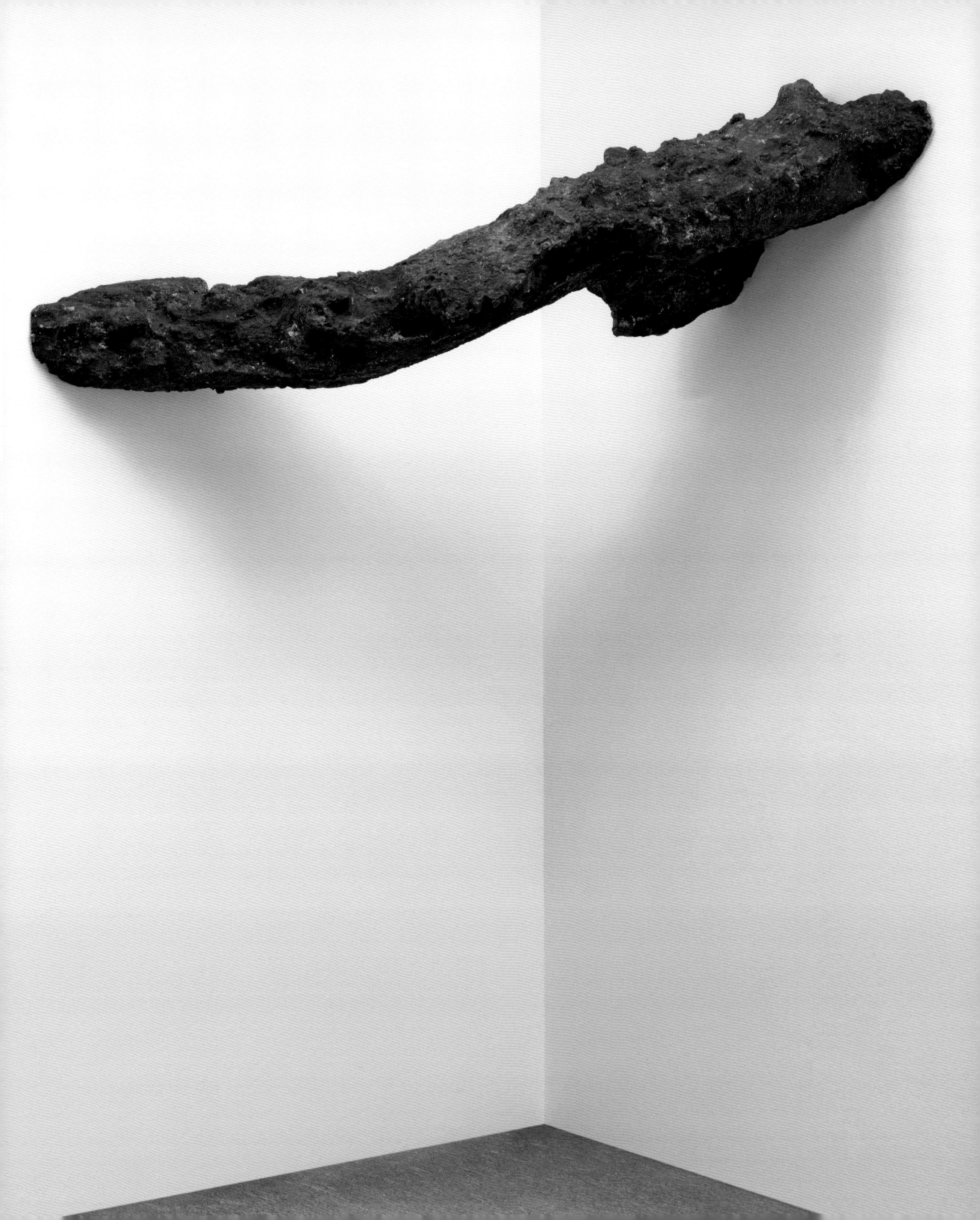

Links / Lef : Mirko Baselgia, *Rascha*, 2015, Fichtenharz (Lantsch/Lenz) auf handgewebtem Leinwand aus Tessanda Val Müstair auf Fichtenholzkeilrahmen gespannt / spruce resin (Lantsch/Lenz) on handwoven linen from Tessanda Val Müstair strechted over spruce wood frame, 44 x 33 cm
Rechts / Right : Mirko Baselgia, *Landscape of growing II*, 2017, Bronze mit dunkler Patina / Bronze with dark patina, 77.5 x 56 x 5 cm, edition of 3 + 1 AP

p. 101
Mirko Baselgia, *Structura digl gôt*, 2016, Ausstellungsansicht / Exhibition view *Prix Mobilière 2016*, artgenève, Ahorn, Lärche, Eiche, Nussbaum, Zirbelkiefer, Buche, Fichte Sägemehl / Maple, larch, oak, walnut, stone pine, beech, spruce wood sawdust, 330 x 550 cm

diesem Zusammenhang haben auch die Recherchen von Humberto R. Maturana und Francisco J. Varela einen großen Einfluss auf sein Leben und seine Arbeit. In ihrem Buch *Autopoiesis and Cognition: The Realization of the Living* (1980), in dem sie lebende Systeme als autonome, selbstreferenzielle und sich selbstaufbauende geschlossene Systeme beschreiben – sie sprechen von *autopoietischen Systemen* –, legen sie es nahe, lebende Systeme nicht hinsichtlich ihrer Funktion oder ihres Zwecks, ihrer Organismus-Umfeld-Beziehungen oder ihrer kausalen Interaktionen mit einer Außenwelt zu beschreiben. Maturana und Varela traten hingegen für eine theoretische Biologie, die topologisch ist, und eine Topologie ein, in der die Elemente und ihre Verhältnisse ein geschlossenes System bilden, oder noch radikaler, eines, das aus der „Perspektive" des Systems selbst vollkommen selbstreferenziell ist und kein „außen" besitzt. Wenn diese Reflexionen auf einen der Grundsätze der biologischen Komplexität Bezug nehmen, das Prinzip der „Organisation", dann beginnt sich herauszukristallisieren, wie sich das eigene Leben formen lässt. Gemäß diesem Prinzip sind lebende Systeme geschlossene Systeme hinsichtlich ihrer inneren Organisation. Sie sind jedoch nach außen offene Systeme, die mit der Außenwelt Materie, Energie und Informationen austauschen. Jeder Organismus ist zwangsläufig mit seinem Umfeld verbunden, und diese Verbindung ist so notwendig, dass es unmöglich ist, sich die Existenz eines von seinem Umfeld isolierten oder isolierbaren Organismus vorzustellen. Die persönliche und individuelle Interaktion mit dem Umfeld bietet Baselgia die Möglichkeit, sein eigenes Leben zu gestalten. Da er von seinem Umfeld animiert wird, egal ob es ein natürliches oder menschliches ist, erkennt er in dem Verhältnis, das uns mit diesem verbindet, den Keim, der Veränderungen hervorbringt. In diesem Sinn verspürt er zunehmend den Wunsch, dass seine Arbeiten und das Material, aus dem diese bestehen, diese Werte so weit wie möglich zum Vorschein bringen, und dass sie insbesondere seine direkte Verbindung und seinen konstanten Dialog mit dem natürlichen Umfeld bezeugen, und darüber hinaus als Inspirationsquelle für unser persönliches Verhältnis zu unserem Umfeld dienen.

Die Bilderserie *Rascha* (2015) steht exemplarisch für dieses Bemühen. Baselgia geht es hier darum, die Vorstellung eines Ökosystems auf die Kunstwerke zu übertragen, indem er zur Realisierung dieser Bilder nur Materialien verwendet, die aus seiner Region stammen. Handgewebte Leinwände von der lokalen Handweberei Tessanda im Val Müstair werden auf die Keilrahmen gespannt, die Baselgia aus dem in diesem Gebiet gesammelten Fichtenholz anfertigt. Von demselben Baum rührt auch das Harz her, das er in mehreren Schichten über seine Leinwände verteilt, nachdem er es verflüssigt hat. Die Leinwand fungiert demnach nicht nur als reiner Bildträger, sondern wird dank ihres repräsentativen Charakters selbst zum Kunstwerk. Ihre Materialität wird hervorgehoben

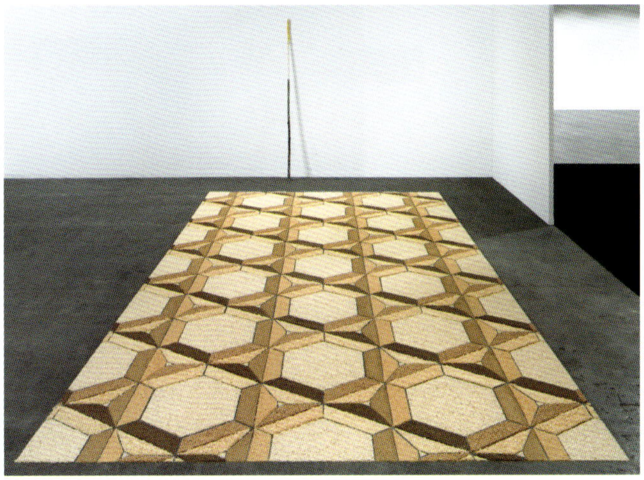

noticed that trees there grow so fast that their bark rips open and creates a sort of landscape on their surface. *Landscape of growing II* addresses the manifestations and survival strategies of nature in the hostile environment of a megacity. These reliefs not only deal with issues related to skin, but also with the principle of growth. Can growth—also in a figurative sense—be made visible in a sculpture? This same question is also at the origin of *Determination* (2013), a marble reproduction of a 5.5 centimeters long gastropod shell that Baselgia enlarged up to 180 centimeters, to match his own height. The elaborate geometry of this spirally coiled shell fascinated the artist, who sees in it a wonderful visual reduction of the idea of life and growth. The shell actually grows together with the mollusk that lives inside, and the growth lines visible on its surface together with its shape and structure tell us its biography. The series of sculptures *Tartaruga* (2018) also highlights a visible manifestation of the passage of time, showing the shells of turtles as, among other things, the material expression of their biography. The scales covering the shell have in fact a series of concentric striations, each roughly corresponding to a year of the animal's life. Baselgia's decision to highlight the bark and annual rings of the Valbella spruce in various ways is not only a consequence of his desire to present the tree as an individual with its own history, but also part of his recurring concern for the visual transcription of the passage of time, as well as the natural laws that underlie the growth of the most diverse organisms.

Many of Mirko Baselgia's works arise from his desire to make structures visible, whether they are the constituent structures of a single organism, of a particular system or structures that regulate the interaction between several organisms, between different organisms and a particular environment or between different environments and realities present on our planet. Identifying, analyzing and revealing these structures is an opportunity for the artist to perceive their complexity, make them his own and, at times, redefine them, to propose alternative structures and draw attention to the fundamental faculty that we have to shape and restructure our lives and ultimately society. Baselgia firmly believes in the potential of using the tools of art to shape one's own life and, perhaps provide inspiration for other people to shape their own. The artist's interest in the natural sciences and philosophy definitely fuels these reflections. The research of Humberto R. Maturana and Francisco J. Varela have a particular influence on his life and work; in their book *Autopoiesis: The Organisation of the Living* (1980), where they define living systems as autonomous, self-referring and self-constructing closed systems—in short, *autopoietic systems* in their terms—, they suggest the abandonment of the characterizations of living systems in terms of function or purpose, or of organism—environment relations, or of causal interactions with an external world. In fact, Maturana and Varela proposed a theoretical biology which is topological, and a topology in which elements and their relations constitute a closed system, or more radically still, one from which the 'point of view' of the system itself, is entirely self-referential and has no 'outside'. If these reflections are related to one of the fundamentals of biological complexity, the principle of 'organization', the way to shape one's life begins to emerge. According to this principle, living systems are closed systems with respect to their internal organization, but they are systems open to the outside, with which they exchange matter, energy, information. Every organism is necessarily connected with the environment, and this connection is so vital that it becomes impossible to even conceive the existence of an organism isolated, or isolable, from its environment. It is precisely in this intimate and individual interaction with the environment that Baselgia sees the opportunity to shape his own life. In so far as he feeds on his environment, whether natural or human, in the quality of the relationship that unites us with it, he sees the seed of change. In this sense, he increasingly feels

und erforscht, um ein alternatives und persönliches Bildkonzept vorzubringen. Zugleich kann die Arbeit, die mit Materialien aus Baselgias Region ausgeführt wurde, als eine abstrakte Landschaft eines spezifischen Ökosystems betrachtet werden. Die Werkserie *Albula* (2018), die der Werkserie *Rascha* folgt, setzt sich ebenfalls damit auseinander, die Vorstellung eines Ökosystems zum Ausdruck zu bringen. Baselgia arbeitet derzeit an einer neuen Serie, die denselben Grundsätzen folgt. Er experimentiert mit verschiedenen Materialien, um noch einen Schritt weiterzugehen und seine eigenen Leinwände herzustellen. Die Werkserie der Holzreliefs, *Midada da structura* (2012 ff.), geht ebenfalls auf die enge Interaktion zwischen Baselgia und seinem natürlichen Umfeld zurück. Es handelt sich um verschiedene Reproduktionen einer Honigwabe, die einem Experiment unterzogen wurde. Baselgia setzte eine Wachsplatte mit einem von der islamischen Kunst inspirierten sechseckigen Muster anstelle der Platte mit dem traditionellen sechseckigen Muster in den Bienenstock ein, um herauszufinden, inwieweit dies die Arbeit der Bienen beeinflussen würde. Die daraus resultierende, teilweise durch das ungewöhnliche Muster geformte Bienenwabe wurde anschließend vergrößert und mit einer computergesteuerten Maschine in Arvenholz gefräst. Die Verflechtung von künstlichen und natürlichen Strukturen ist somit das visuelle Ergebnis der Interaktion zwischen menschlicher und tierischer Welt, eine Art persönlicher Zusammenarbeit zwischen dem Künstler und den Bienen. Verschiedene Werkserien auf Papier (2018 ff.) basieren auf einer analogen Zusammenarbeit mit dem *Coprinus comatus*, bekannt als „Schopf-Tintling" oder „Tintenpilz" aufgrund der ungewöhnlichen Art, seine Sporen zu verbreiten. So löst diese Pilzart ihren eigenen Hut auf, um die Sporen zu verbreiten. Während des Auflösungsprozesses – *Autolyse* – werden der Hut und die Lamellen zu einer schwarzen, dickflüssigen Tinte. Autodestruktion, die die nächste Generation hervorbringt, erhält so eine unerwartete positive Bedeutung. Baselgia, den dieses besondere Phänomen faszinierte, sammelte Tintlinge auf den Wiesen, um ihre Tinte nach einem alten Rezept zu extrahieren. In der ersten Werkserie führte er mit der Tinte des Pilzes und dem Bleistift einige Zeichnungen aus, die den Pilz in seinem natürlichen Ambiente wiedergeben. Für die zweite Werkserie verwendete er jedoch den gesamten Pilz. Er ordnete mehrere Coprinus-Pilze direkt auf dem Papier an. Anschließend hob er den Tisch an einer Ecke hoch, sodass die Tinte das Blatt hinabfließen konnte. So hinterließ die Zersetzung der Pilze abstrakte Tintenkleckse auf der Oberfläche. Baselgia machte sich die natürliche Schwerkraft und den Prozess der Autolyse zunutze, um seine Zeichnungen zu gestalten.

Neben dem Prozess der Autolyse faszinierte Baselgia noch ein weiterer mit dem *Coprinus comatus* verbundener Aspekt. Da seine Tinte seit dem 18. Jahrhundert zum Briefeschreiben verwendet wurde und sich seine Sporen folglich dort verbreiteten, wohin der Brief versandt wurde, sieht Baselgia in der weltweiten Verbreitung dieses Pilzes eine Metapher für die Dynamik der globalen Vernetzung unserer Gesellschaft. Der *Coprinus comatus* verweist darauf, dass die Samen, die wir säen, weitaus größere Entfernungen zurücklegen können, als wir annehmen, und dort Früchte tragen, wo wir es niemals erwarten würden. Jede individuelle Handlung zählt, genauso wie jeder Baum seine Daseinsberechtigung im Wald hat. Selbst die Fichte im Garten in Valbella hat ihre Daseinsberechtigung. *The Tree of Valbella* ist somit eine Ode an seine bescheidene, aber notwendige Existenz, und, wenn man noch weiter geht, eine Aufforderung, sich des Werts jedes einzelnen Lebens und jeder einzelnen Handlung bewusst zu werden.

1 Siehe beispielsweise: Stefano Mancuso, *The Revolutionary Genius of Plants: A New Understanding of Plant Intelligence and Behavior*, New York: Atria Books, 2018; Emanuele Coccia, *Die Wurzeln der Welt: eine Philosophie der Pflanzen*, München: Carl Hanser, 2018; Emanuele Coccia, *Métamorphoses*, Paris: Rivages, 2020.

the desire that his works and the materials that make them up reflect these values as much as possible and, above all, that they bear witness to his direct link and his constant dialogue with the natural environment so they may also be a source of inspiration for our personal relationship with our surroundings.

The series of paintings *Rascha* (2015) is one of the most evident examples of this intent. Here, Baselgia's aim is to transpose the concept of *ecosystem* in artworks by using only materials coming from the same region to create the paintings. Handwoven canvases from the local Tessanda Val Müstair are stretched on frames constructed by the artist with spruce wood he found in his region. The same tree also offered him the resin he spread on the canvases in many layers after having given it a liquid consistency. The canvas is not a mere support for an image, but it is a representation, an artwork in itself. Its materiality is highlighted and investigated with the desire to propose an alternative and personal idea of painting. At the same time, the work, realized with materials coming from the same region, can also be seen as an abstract landscape of a specific ecosystem. Following the series *Rascha*, the series *Albula* (2018) also deals with the idea of materializing the concept of *ecosystem*, and the artist is currently working on new series based on the same principles, as well as experimenting with different materials in order to go a step further and create his own canvases. The series of wooden reliefs *Midada da structura* (2012-ongoing) is also the result of a close interaction between Baselgia and his natural environment. These are different reproductions of a honeycomb that has undergone an experiment. The artist inserted a wax base in a beehive; this base has an Islamic-inspired hexagonal pattern instead of the traditional hexagonal design, to see if it would influence the bees' work. The resulting honeycomb, which has actually been partly shaped by the unusual pattern, has been enlarged and sculpted in Swiss stone pine wood with a digital machine. This intertwining of artificial and natural structures is the visual sign of the interaction between human and animal world, a sort of personal collaboration between the artist and the bees. For the realization of different series of works on paper called (2018-ongoing), Baselgia had a similar collaboration with the Coprinus comatus, common fungi also known as "shaggy manes" or "inky caps" because of the unusual method they use to distribute their spores; this type of fungi digests its own cap, which contributes to the dissemination of the spores. As auto-digestion—*Autolyse*—takes place, the cap and gills change into a black, thick ink. Self-destruction acquires an unexpected positive meaning, allowing the growth of the next generation. Intrigued by this peculiar phenomenon, the artist went looking for these fungi in meadows and collected them to extract their ink following an old recipe. For the first series of works, he just used the fungi's ink and pencil to realize some drawings representing the mushrooms in their natural environment, but, for the second series, he decided to use the whole mushrooms. He placed them directly on the paper and gave the table a slope by lifting one edge so that the ink could run down the sheet. The mushrooms' disintegration left abstract inkblots on the surface and Baselgia used the natural forces of gravity and the process of autolysis to shape his drawings.

Beyond the process of autolysis there is another fact related to the Coprinus comatus that fascinated the artist. As its ink has been used for writing letters since the 18th century and its spores were therefore spread wherever the mail was sent, he sees in the planetary expansion of this mushroom a metaphor for the dynamics of global interconnection characteristic of our society. The *Coprinus comatus* reminds us that the seeds we plant can go much further than we thought and bear fruit where we never expected. Every individual action matters, just as every single tree has its own purpose in the vast forest. Even the spruce tree in the garden of Valbella had its own reason for being and *The Tree of Valbella* is an ode to its humble but proud existence and, in extension, an encouragement to become aware of the value of every single life and every single action.

1 See for example: Stefano Mancuso, *The Revolutionary Genius of Plants: A New Understanding of Plant Intelligence and Behavior*, New York: Atria Books, 2018; Emanuele Coccia, *The Life of Plants. A Metaphysics of Mixture*, Oxford: Polity Press, 2018; Emanuele Coccia, *Métamorphoses*, Paris: Rivages, 2020.

ANHANG / APPENDIX

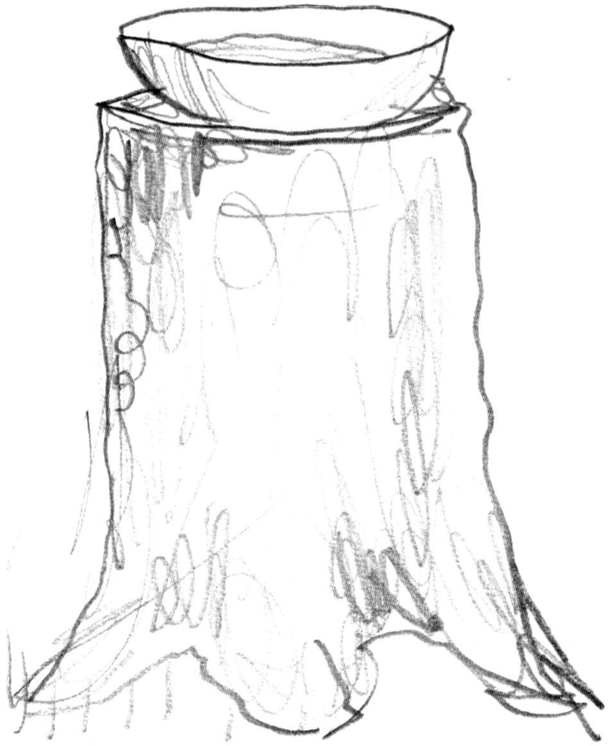

Mirko Baselgia, Studie für die Quelle des skulpturalen Ensembles / Study for the spring of the sculptural ensemble *The Tree of Valbella*, 2016, Bleistift auf Papier / Pencil on paper, 18 x 27 cm

Die dendrochronologische Untersuchung

MATHIAS SEIFERT

HOLGER GARTNER

Die Radienmessung Nr. 3 umfasst mit 124 Werten alle Jahrringe vom Mark bis zur Waldkante (letzter gebildeter Jahrring unter der Rinde). An den Radien Nr. 1 und 2 fehlt der innerste Teil, bei diesen beiden Proben konnten die Jahrringbreiten von insgesamt 100 bzw. 99 Jahrringen gemessen werden. Alle drei Messungen konnten untereinander einwandfrei korreliert werden.
Aus den drei Radienmessungen wurde durch Mittelung der Werte die Einzelholzkurve 89245 errechnet. Die Einzelholzkurve 89245 konnte aufgrund des übereinstimmenden Jahrringverlaufes auf mehreren Lokalsequenzen, optisch und rechnerisch am besten auf den Mitteln 3892 SG/ MELS/WEISSTANNEN-MATELLS (1825-2012 n.Chr.) und 3896 SG/ MELS/ WEISSTANNEN-OBERSIEZ/ EIGERHUETTLI (1816-2012 n.Chr.), sicher auf das Endjahr 2015, das auch dem Fälljahr entspricht, datiert werden. Aufgrund der vollständigen Ausbildung des letzten Jahrringes mit Früh- und Spätholz wird die Fällung im Winterhalbjahr 2015/16 erfolgt sein. Das Mark (innerster Teil des Stammes), also der Wuchsbeginn, kann dem Jahr 1892 zugewiesen.

Der Wuchsverlauf bis in die 1970er Jahre zeigt keine Auffälligkeiten. Mit Ausnahme des Jahres 1897 liegen die Breitenwerte immer über 1 mm. Das Jahr 1975 fällt durch den gegenüber den vorherigen und folgenden Jahren deutlich geringeren Zuwachs auf. Ab 1976 ist die starke der Breitenzunahme nicht zu übersehen. Sie könnte damit zusammenhängen, dass durch Auflichtungen in der Umgebung des Standortes für den Baum bessere Wuchsbedingungen geschaffen worden waren, möglicherweise bedingt durch die baulichen Eingriffe in den 1970er Jahren.

Auffällig sind die wellenförmigen Verläufe der Jahrringe vor allem im jüngeren Teil des Stammes. Deren Ursache sind mir nicht bekannt. Zur Beantwortung dieser Frage und auch zu weiteren Aussagen bzgl. der Wuchsgeschichte des Baumes leite ich die zu Grunde liegenden Daten an Holger Gärtner weiter.

Mathias Seifert: Dendrochronologischer Bericht vom 31.05.2019. Dendrolabor Archäologischer Dienst Graubünden/Schweiz.

Ich kann mich bezüglich der Wuchsgeschichte des Baumes den Ausführungen von Herrn Seifert nur anschliessen. Der Baum zeigt ein relativ gleichmässiges Wachstum bis ca. Mitte der 1950er Jahre, dann erfolgt ein leichter Zuwachsrückgang bis 1975. („Gleichmässig" bezieht sich auf die durchschnittliche Jahrringbreite über die Jahrzehnte, nicht auf die jährlichen Schwankungen.)
Ab 1976 beginnt ein deutlicher Anstieg im Zuwachs. Diesen Zuwachs zeigt auch die Mittelkurve 3892 SG/MELS/WEISSTANNEN-MATELLS (1825-2012 n.Chr.), wenn auch nicht so stark.
Die Zuwachssteigerung ist damit sicherlich grundlegend klimatisch beeinflusst, mit grosser Wahrscheinlichkeit haben aber die von Herrn Seifert aufgeführten Massnahmen / Veränderungen im Umfeld des Standortes einen sehr grossen Einfluss auf das Wachstum.
Die Unregelmässigkeiten / Ausbuchtungen der Jahrringe werden als Haselwuchs bezeichnet.
Sie sind genetischen Ursprungs, jedoch wohl auch durch Umweltfaktoren beeinflusst (z.B. starkem Wind), dies ist allerdings eher Spekulation.
Bei Fichten ist Haselwuchs hoch gefragt und für den Instrumentenbau besonders gut geeignet, denn es verleiht dem Holz ein sehr ausgewogenes und reiches Klangspektrum.

Online-Publikation zu Haselwuchs:
https://issuu.com/museumsverein_klostertal/docs/publikation_haselfichte

Email vom 21. Oktober 2019 von Dr. Holger Gärtner
Forest Dynamics / Dendrosciences. Swiss Federal Research Institute WSL, 8903 Birmensdorf, Schweiz

The dendrochronological examination

Radius measurement no. 3 includes 124 values for all growth rings from the pith to the waney-bark (the last growth ring formed under the bark). The innermost part of radii 1 and 2 is missing, with these two samples, the annual ring widths of 100 and/or 99 annual rings were measured. All three measurements could be perfectly correlated with one another. Single tree-ring curve 89245 was calculated from the three radius measurements by averaging the values. Single tree-ring curve 89245 could be visualised and best computationally determined based on the correlating tree-ring progression of several local sequences on sample 3892 SG/MELS/ WEISSTANNEN-MATELLS (1825-2012 AD) and 3896 SG/MELS/ WEISSTANNEN-OBERSIEZ/ EIGERHUETTLI (1816-2012 AD) and they may be reliably dated to 2015, which also corresponds to the felling year. Due to the complete formation of the last tree-ring with early and late wood, felling would have taken place in the winter six-month period of 2015/16. The pith (innermost part of the trunk), i.e. the start of growth, may be dated to 1892.

The growth process up to the 1970s showed no abnormality. With the exception of 1897, width values were always over 1 mm. 1975 stood out because of significantly lower growth compared to previous and following years. From 1976 on, robustness of the increase in width may not be ignored. This could be related to the fact that better growing conditions were created for the tree through clearing the area in the tree's vicinity, possibly due to building work in the 1970s.

The undulating patterns of the tree-rings are particularly noticeable in the younger part of the trunk. The cause is unclear to me. To answer this question, and also additional assertions regarding the growth history of the tree, I will forward the underlying data to Holger Gärtner.

Mathias Seifert: Dendrochronological report dated 31 May 2019. Dendrolabor Archaeological Service Graubünden/Switzerland.

I can only concord with Mr. Seifert's conclusive remarks regarding the history of the tree's growth. The tree shows relatively uniform growth up to approx. the mid-1950s when there was a slight decrease in growth until 1975 ("uniform" refers to the average annual ring width over the decades, not to the annual variation). From 1976 onwards, a significant increase in growth may be observed. Mean curve 3892 SG/ MELS/WEISSTANNEN-MATELLS (1825-2012 AD) also shows this increase, albeit not as markedly.
The increase in growth is therefore certainly fundamentally influenced by climate, but there is a high degree of probability that the conditions/changes in the vicinity of the location listed by Mr. Seifert have had a very significant influence on growth.
These irregularities and bulges in the annual growth rings are known as hazel growth.
They are of genetic origin but are also probably influenced by environmental factors (e.g. strong wind), but this is speculation.
Hazel growth is in high demand for spruce and it is particularly well suited for making musical instruments, as it gives the wood a very balanced and rich sound spectrum.

On-line publication on hazel growth:
https://issuu.com/museumsverein_klostertal/docs/publikation_haselfichte

E-mail dated 21 October 2019 from Dr. Holger Gärtner
Forest Dynamics/Dendrosciences. Swiss Federal Research Institute WSL, 8903 Birmensdorf, Switzerland

Mirko Baselgia

1982 Geboren in Lantsch/Lenz, Schweiz
Lebt und arbeitet in den Schweizer Bergen

AUSBILDUNG

2010 M.A. in Bildender Kunst, Zürcher Hochschule der Künste, Schweiz
2008 B.A. in Bildender Kunst, Zürcher Hochschule der Künste, Schweiz

EINZELAUSSTELLUNGEN

2019 *Les étoiles ne sont pas seules*, Galerie Heinzer Reszler, Lausanne, Schweiz
2018 *Habitat*, Galerie Urs Meile Luzern, Schweiz
Pardis (Curzoin), Abbatiale de Bellelay, Bellelay, Schweiz
2017 *Transmutaziun*, Kunst in der Krypta No5, Grossmünster Zürich, Zürich, Schweiz
Membrana, Galerie Heinzer Reszler, Lausanne, Schweiz
Cuntradas, Galerie Heinzer Reszler, artgenève, Genf, Schweiz
2016 *Antupada I + II*, Kloster Schönthal, Langenbruck, Schweiz
Lontan e manevel – ma fee mishkleh, Maarad li yawm wahed in Zusammenarbeit mit der Schweizerischen Botschaft im Libanon, Beirut, Libanon
2015 *Val-bella*, Galerie Pesko, Lenzerheide, Schweiz
Igl tor muribund, Markus Vonlanthen, Chur, Schweiz
SOZEIN TA PHAINOMENA, Galerie Heinzer Reszler, Lausanne, Schweiz
2014 *"The pattern which connects"*, Kunstmuseum Olten, Olten, Schweiz
Aleph – er bugliaint, Choisi – One at a time, Lugano, Schweiz
2013 *Primavera*, Manor Kunstpreis, Bündner Kunstmuseum, Chur, Schweiz
Midada da structura, Galerie Edition Z, Chur, Schweiz
2011 *Spatio-Temporal Pattern*, Herrmann Germann Contemporary, Zürich, Schweiz
2010 *Meisterstück*, Museum für Gestaltung (Garten), Zürich, Schweiz

GRUPPENAUSSTELLUNGEN (Auswahl)

2020 *Morcote 2020 – Habitat*, Public Art Biennial, Morcote, Schweiz
Hortus Conclusus, Museo Villa dei Cedri, Bellinzona, Schweiz
Mit Beethoven unter einem D-A-CH, ArtDialog Bonn, Bonn, Deutschland
2019 *Jahresausstellung der Bündner Kunstschaffenden*, Kunstmuseum Chur, Chur, Schweiz
Paradise, Lost; 6. Skulpturen-Biennale Weiertal 2019, Weiertal, Schweiz
Bêtes de Scène, Villa Datris Fundation, L'Isle-sur-la-Sorgue, Frankreich
2018 *Jahresausstellung der Bündner Kunstschaffenden*, Kunstmuseum Chur, Chur, Schweiz
Verre en scène, MUDAC, Lausanne, Schweiz
Beehave – Die Biene als künstlerischer und gesellschaftlicher Impulsgeber, Kunsthaus Baselland, Muttenz/Basel, Schweiz
Formen der Natur: Pure Nature Art, Museum Villa Rot, Burgrieden-Rot, Deutschland
2017 *Jahresausstellung der Bündner Kunstschaffenden*, Kunstmuseum Chur, Chur, Schweiz
Extended Ground, Galerie Urs Meile, Luzern, Schweiz
Triennale 2017 – Art Contemporain Valais, Martigny, Schweiz
Nach der Natur – Material, Form, Struktur, Museum Sinclair-Haus – Altana Kulturstiftung, Bad Homburg, Deutschland
Bex & Arts – Triennale de sculpture contemporaine en plein air, Bex, Schweiz
METAMORFOSI. Uno sguardo alla scultura contemporanea, Museo d'arte Mendrisio, Mendrisio, Schweiz
CLIMAX, Galerie Heinzer Reszler, Lausanne, Schweiz
2016 *Archiv – 80 Jahre Bündner Kunst*, Bündner Kunstmuseum, Chur, Schweiz
Kunst + Nachhaltigkeit Vol 5 – Prix Mobilière 2016, Mobiliar, Bern, Schweiz
Nominierter für den Prix Mobilière 2016, artgenève, Genf, Schweiz
2015 *Charaktere – Das Bündner Kunstmuseum zu Gast*, Kunsthaus Zug, Zug, Schweiz
Imagination of Nature – Der Traum von gebändigter Wildnis, Gebert Stiftung für Kultur – Alte Fabrik, Rapperswil, Schweiz
2014 *Junge Bündner Künstler*, Stalla Madulain, Madulain, Schweiz
2013 *Jahresausstellung der Bündner Künstlerinnen und Künstler*, Bündner Kunstmuseum Chur, Chur, Schweiz
Banana Split, Sonnenstube, Lugano, Schweiz
Vordemberge-Gildewart-Stipendium, Kunstmuseum Liechtenstein, Vaduz, Liechtenstein
2012 *Jahresausstellung der Bündner Künstlerinnen und Künstler*, Bündner Kunstmuseum Chur, Chur, Schweiz
Unter 30 VIII – Junge Schweizer Kunst, Kunsthaus Glarus, Glarus, Schweiz
Kiefer Hablitzel Stipendium, Swiss Art Awards, Basel, Schweiz

AUSZEICHNUNGEN UND STIPENDIEN

2013 Manor Kunstpreis Chur
2012 Kiefer-Hablitzel-Stipendium
2005 Förderpreis der Willy Reber Stiftung
2004 Förderpreis des Kantons Graubünden

KÜNSTLERRESIDENZEN

2017 Artist in Residence, Galerie Urs Meile, Peking, China
2016 Kunstsommer, Kloster Schönthal, Schweiz
2014 Stiftung Eduard Bick, Sant'Abbondio, Schweiz

PRIVATE UND ÖFFENTLICHE SAMMLUNGEN

Helvetia Kunstsammlung, Basel, Schweiz
Muzeum Susch, Schweiz
Kunstsammlung Roche, Schweiz
Sammlung Credit Suisse, Zürich, Schweiz
Raiffeisen Bank, Chur, Schweiz
Bündner Kunstsammlung, Chur, Schweiz
MUDAC, Lausanne, Schweiz
Burger Collection, Hongkong, China
Kunstmuseum Olten, Schweiz
Bündner Kunstmuseum, Chur, Schweiz
Sammlung Ricola, Laufen, Schweiz
Graubündner Kantonalbank, Chur, Schweiz
Altana Kulturstiftung, Bad Homburg, Deutschland
Stiftung Kloster Schönthal, Langenbruck, Schweiz
Artphilein de Pietri Foundation, Vaduz, Liechtenstein
Hahnloser Stiftung, Winterthur, Schweiz
Bordier & Cie, Genf, Schweiz
Schweizerische Nationalbank, Bern/Zürich, Schweiz
Zürcher Kantonalbank, Zürich, Schweiz

Mirko Baselgia

1982 Born in Lantsch/Lenz, Switzerland
Lives and works in the Swiss Mountains

EDUCATION

2010 MA in Fine Arts, Zurich University of the Arts, Switzerland
2008 BA in Fine Arts, Zurich University of the Arts, Switzerland

SOLO EXHIBITIONS

2019 *Les étoiles ne sont pas seules*, Galerie Heinzer Reszler, Lausanne, Switzerland
2018 *Habitat*, Galerie Urs Meile Lucerne, Switzerland
Pardis (Curzoin), Abbatiale de Bellelay, Bellelay, Switzerland
2017 *Transmutaziun*, Kunst in der Krypta No5, Grossmünster Zürich, Zurich, Switzerland
Membrana, Galerie Heinzer Reszler, Lausanne, Switzerland
Cuntradas, Galerie Heinzer Reszler, artgenève, Geneva, Switzerland
2016 *Antupada I + II*, Kloster Schönthal, Langenbruck, Switzerland
Lontan e manevel - ma fee mishkleh, Maarad li yawm wahed in collaboration with the Embassy of Switzerland in Lebanon, Beirut, Lebanon
2015 *Val-bella*, Galerie Pesko, Lenzerheide, Switzerland
Igl tor muribund, Markus Vonlanthen, Chur, Switzerland
SOZEIN TA PHAINOMENA, Galerie Heinzer Reszler, Lausanne, Switzerland
2014 *"The pattern which connects."*, Kunstmuseum Olten, Olten, Switzerland
Aleph - er bugliaint, Choisi - One at a time, Lugano, Switzerland
2013 *Primavera*, Manor Kunstpreis, Bündner Kunstmuseum, Chur, Switzerland
Midada da structura, Galerie Edition Z, Chur, Switzerland
2011 *Spatio-Temporal Pattern*, Herrmann Germann Contemporary, Zurich, Switzerland
2010 *Meisterstück*, Museum für Gestaltung (Garden), Zurich, Switzerland

GROUP EXHIBITIONS (selection)

2020 *Morcote 2020 - Habitat*, Public Art Biennial, Morcote, Switzerland
Hortus Conclusus, Museo Villa dei Cedri, Bellinzona, Switzerland
Mit Beethoven unter einem D-A-CH, ArtDialog Bonn, Bonn, Germany
2019 *Jahresausstellung der Bündner Kunstschaffenden*, Kunstmuseum Chur, Chur, Switzerland
Paradise, Lost; 6. Skulpturen-Biennale Weiertal 2019, Weiertal, Switzerland
Bêtes de Scène, Villa Datris Fundation, L'Isle-sur-la-Sorgue, France
2018 *Jahresausstellung der Bündner Kunstschaffenden*, Kunstmuseum Chur, Chur, Switzerland
Verre en scène, MUDAC, Lausanne, Switzerland
Beehave - Die Biene als künstlerischer und gesellschaftlicher Impulsgeber, Kunsthaus Baselland, Muttenz/Basel, Switzerland
Formen der Natur: Pure Nature Art, Museum Villa Rot, Burgrieden-Rot, Germany
2017 *Jahresausstellung der Bündner Kunstschaffenden*, Kunstmuseum Chur, Chur, Switzerland
Extended Ground, Galerie Urs Meile, Lucerne, Switzerland
Triennale 2017 - Art Contemporain Valais, Martigny, Switzerland
Nach der Natur - Material, Form, Struktur, Museum Sinclair-Haus - Altana Kulturstiftung, Bad Homburg, Germany
Bex & Arts - Triennale de sculpture contemporaine en plein air, Bex, Switzerland
METAMORFOSI. Uno sguardo alla scultura contemporanea, Museo d'arte Mendrisio, Mendrisio, Switzerland
CLIMAX, Galerie Heinzer Reszler, Lausanne, Switzerland
2016 *Archiv - 80 Jahre Bündner Kunst*, Bündner Kunstmuseum, Chur, Switzerland
Kunst + Nachhaltigkeit Vol 5 - Prix Mobilière 2016, Mobiliar, Berne, Switzerland
Nominations for the Prix Mobilière 2016, artgenève, Geneva, Switzerland
2015 *Charaktere - Das Bündner Kunstmuseum zu Gast*, Kunsthaus Zug, Zug, Switzerland
Imagination of Nature - Der Traum von gebändigter Wildnis, Gebert Stiftung für Kultur - Alte Fabrik, Rapperswil, Switzerland
2014 *Junge Bündner Künstler*, Stalla Madulain, Madulain, Switzerland
2013 *Jahresausstellung der Bündner Künstlerinnen und Künstler*, Bündner Kunstmuseum Chur, Chur, Switzerland
Banana Split, Sonnenstube, Lugano, Switzerland
Vordemberge-Gildewart-Stipendium, Kunstmuseum Liechtenstein, Vaduz, Liechtenstein
2012 *Jahresausstellung der Bündner Künstlerinnen und Künstler*, Bündner Kunstmuseum Chur, Chur, Switzerland
Unter 30 VIII - Junge Schweizer Kunst, Kunsthaus Glarus, Glarus, Switzerland
Kiefer Hablitzel Grant, Swiss Art Awards, Basel, Switzerland

AWARDS & GRANTS

2013 Manor Art Price Chur
2012 Kiefer Hablitzel Grant
2005 Willi Reber Foundation Promotion Award
2004 Promotion Award of Canton Graubünden

RESIDENCIES

2017 Artist in Residence, Galerie Urs Meile, Beijing, China
2016 Kunstsommer, Kloster Schönthal, Switzerland
2014 Fondazione Eduard Bick, Sant'Abbondio, Switzerland

PRIVATE AND PUBLIC COLLECTIONS

Helvetia Art Collection, Basel, Switzerland
Muzeum Susch, Switzerland
Roche Art Collection, Basel, Switzerland
Credit Suisse Collection, Zurich, Switzerland
Raiffeisen Bank, Chur, Switzerland
Bündner Kunstsammlung, Chur, Switzerland
MUDAC, Lausanne, Switzerland
Burger Collection, Hong Kong, China
Kunstmuseum Olten, Switzerland
Bündner Kunstmuseum, Chur, Switzerland
Ricola Collection, Laufen, Switzerland
Graubündner Kantonalbank, Chur, Switzerland
Altana Kulturstiftung, Bad Homburg, Germany
Stiftung Kloster Schönthal, Langenbruck, Switzerland
Artphilein de Pietri Foundation, Vaduz, Liechtenstein
Hahnloser Stiftung, Winterthur, Switzerland
Bordier & Cie, Geneva, Switzerland
Swiss National Bank, Berne/Zurich, Switzerland
Zürcher Kantonalbank, Zurich, Switzerland

Biographien der Autoren / Authors' biographies

Jérôme Neutres (Tassin FR, 1970)

Der Publizist und Kunstexperte Jérôme Neutres promovierte in Paris in Semiologie von Text und Bild, inszenierte weltweit rund 40 Ausstellungen und veröffentlichte zahlreiche Texte über Kunst. Nach einer Karriere als Kulturattaché der französischen Botschaften in Spanien, Indien sowie den Vereinigten Staaten, wurde er Direktor der Réunion des Musées Nationaux - Grand Palais für zehn Jahre, sowie Präsident des Musée du Luxembourg in Paris. Heute konzentriert sich Neutres auf seine Forschungen und Ausstellungen. Er ist auch Kunstberater und Mitglied des Beirats von Apricum Circle.

Ph.D. in Semiology of the text and the image from the University of Paris, he has been curating some fourty exhibitions in museums all over the world, and has published numerous texts on art. After a carreer of cultural diplomat in the French embassies in Spain, India and the USA, he was director at the Réunion des musées nationaux-Grand palais for ten years, and president of the Musée du Luxembourg in Paris. He focuses today his activities on research and art curation, and serves as Art Consultant and Advisory Board member of Apricum Circle.

Laura Giudici (Bellinzona CH, 1984)

Laura Giudici absolvierte ihr Magister- und Promotionsstudium in Kunstgeschichte an der Universität Freiburg, Schweiz. Nach einem Praktikum bei Pro Helvetia (2009-2010) war sie als Dokumentarin bei Blondeau Fine Art Services in Genf (2010-2012) tätig. Von 2012 bis 2016 war sie wissenschaftliche Mitarbeiterin und Dozentin an der Universität Freiburg. Seit 2017 ist sie als Beraterin für Recherche sowie Inhalte und Vermittlung beim Studio Mirko Baselgia verantwortlich. Darüber hinaus schreibt sie regelmäßig Beiträge für die Schweizer Kunstzeitschrift *Kunstbulletin* und arbeitet als freie Kuratorin und Dozentin.

Laura Giudici holds a MA and a PhD. in art history from the University of Fribourg, Switzerland. After an internship at Pro Helvetia (2009-2010), she has occupied the position of documentalist at Blondeau Fine Art Services in Geneva (2010-2012). From 2012 to 2016, she has been research assistant and lecturer at the University of Fribourg. Since 2017, she has been consultant and responsible for research, content and its mediation at Studio Mirko Baselgia. Additionally, she is a regular contributor to the Swiss art review *Kunstbulletin*, an independent curator and lecturer.

Christoph Eggenberger (Basel CH, 1945)

1971 Promotion in Kunstgeschichte.
1973-1975 Denkmalpflege des Kantons St. Gallen.
1975 bis 2000 Leiter der Abteilung Visuelle Künste bei der Schweizer Kulturstiftung Pro Helvetia. Seit 1985 Privatdozent, später Titularprofessor an der Universität Zürich für Kunstgeschichte des Mittelalters. 2001 bis 2010 Leiter der Handschriftenabteilung der Zentralbibliothek Zürich. Lehr- und Publikationstätigkeit in den Gebieten der Kunst der Spätantike, des Mittelalters, der frühen Neuzeit – mit besonderer Berücksichtigung der Buchmalerei - und der Gegenwart.

1971 PhD in art history.
1973-1975 Preservation of historical monuments Canton of St Gallen.
1975 to 2000 Head of the visual arts department at the Swiss cultural foundation Pro Helvetia.
Since 1985, private lecturer, later adjunct professor at the University of Zurich for Medieval art history.
2001 to 2010 Head of the manuscript department of the Zentralbibliothek Zürich. Teaching and publishing activities in the areas of art from late antiquity, the Middle Ages and the early modern era – with special study field in illuminated manuscripts – and the modern era.

Danksagung / Acknowledgements

Zunächst möchten wir **Thomas Abegg** für die Verwirklichung dieses Projekts danken.
First of all, we would like to thank Thomas Abegg for making this project possible.

Wir möchten allen Kunsthandwerkern, Galeristen und ihren Teams, die dieses Projekt und diese Publikation ermöglicht haben, unseren Dank aussprechen: /
We would like to express our gratitude to all the craftsmen, gallery directors and their teams who made this project and this publication possible:

Daniel Margreth, Schreiner / Carpenter
Mit seiner Frau Doris und seinem Sohn Linard Margreth /
With his wife Doris and his son Linard Margreth

Florinett Holz AG, Bergün
Rico und / and Andrea Florinett, Eigentümer / Owners
Curdin Gregori, Forstwart / Feller

Fonderia Nolana Del Giudice, Nola
Pasquale, Antonietta, Antonio, Luca, Marcello und Giuseppe Del Giudice mit ihrem ganzen Team /
Pasquale, Antonietta, Antonio, Luca, Marcello and Giuseppe Del Giudice with their whole team

Galerie Urs Meile, Beijing-Lucerne
Urs Meile, Co-Direktor / Co-director
Karin Seiz, Co-Direktorin / Co-director

Galerie Heinzer-Reszler, Lausanne
Antoine Reszler, Direktor und Partner / Director and Partner
Jean-Baptiste Heinzer, Partner

Wir sind all jenen dankbar, die in verschiedenen Formen zum Projekt und zu dieser Publikation beigetragen haben: /
We would like to express our gratitude to all those who, in various ways, have contributed to the realization of the project and this publication:
Stefan Altenburger; Amedeo Benestante; Javier Figueroa; Adrian Flütsch; Catherine Giudici; Bernd Grundmann; Heinz Kunz; Dario de Simone

Unser herzlicher Dank gilt schließlich den Teams von **Apricum Circle**, **Silvana Editoriale** und **Studio Mirko Baselgia** für ihre großartige Arbeit. /
Finally, our warmest thanks go to the teams of Apricum Circle, Silvana Editoriale and Studio Mirko Baselgia for their great work.

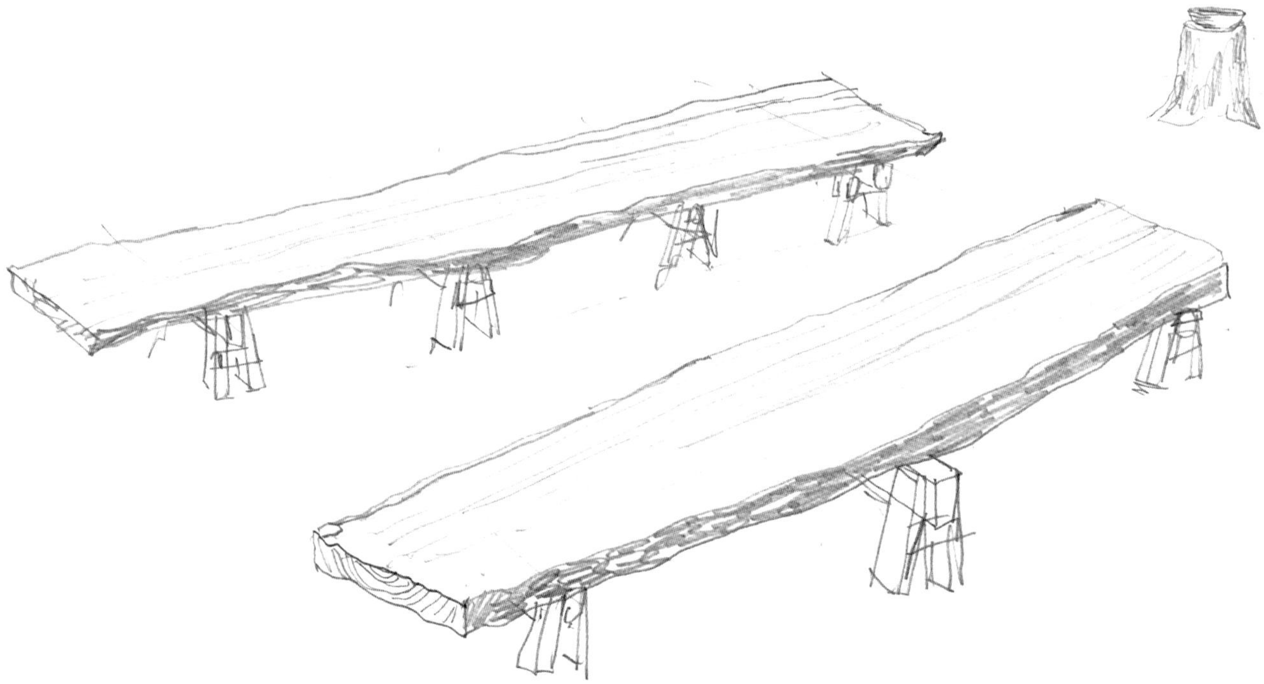

Mirko Baselgia, Studie für die Quelle und die liegenden Reliefs des skulpturalen Ensembles / Study for the spring and the horizontal reliefs of the sculptural ensemble *The Tree of Valbella*, 2016, Bleistift auf Papier / Pencil on paper, 27 x 18 cm

Verzeichnis / Contents

Umschlag / Cover
Installationsansicht des skulpturalen Ensembles /
Installation view of the sculptural ensemble *The Tree of Valbella* für / for
artgèneve / sculptures 2019, Promenade de la Treille, Genf / Geneva

Silvana Editoriale

Verlagsleiter / Direction
Dario Cimorelli

Art Director
Giacomo Merli

Redaktionskoordinator / Editorial Coordinator
Sergio Di Stefano

Redaktion / Copy Editor
Lorena Ansani (Englisch / English)
Cristina Pradella (Deutsch / German)

Übersetzungen / Translations
Contextus: We translate Art
(Kathrin Fuchs, Alison Kennedy, Richard Kutner, Julia Rader)

Layout
Daniela Meda

Produktionskoordination / Production Coordinator
Antonio Micelli

Redaktionsassistentin / Editorial Assistant
Giulia Mercanti

Foto / Photo Editor
Alessandra Olivari, Silvia Sala

Pressestelle / Press Office
Lidia Masolini, press@silvanaeditoriale.it

Silvana Editoriale S.p.A.
via dei Lavoratori, 78
20092 Cinisello Balsamo, Milano
tel. 02 453 951 01
fax 02 453 951 51
www.silvanaeditoriale.it

Reproduktionen, Druck und Einbindung
wurden in Italien ausgeführt /
Reproductions, printing and binding in Italy
Gedruckt von / Printed by Grafiche Aurora S.r.l., Verona
im / in November 2020

APRICUM
CIRCLE

Apricum Circle ist eine unternehmerische Dialog-Plattform und ein unabhängiges Family Office in Zürich.
Apricum Circle steht für eine kulturell interessierte und philanthropisch engagierte Community, die Inspiration vermittelt, Horizonte erweitert und Perspektiven schafft.

In diesem Kontext publiziert Apricum Circle gemeinsam mit dem Verlag Silvana Editoriale regelmässig Bücher rund um Kunst, Kultur und Lebensart.

Apricum Circle is an entrepreneurial dialogue platform and independent family office in Zurich. Apricum Circle stands for a culturally interested and philanthropically engaged community that provides inspiration, broadens horizons and creates perspectives.

In support of this spirit Apricum Circle publishes a series of books in cooperation with the publishing house Silvana Editoriale, primarily focusing on art, culture and lifestyle.

Bildnachweise / Image Credits

Stefan Altenburger (SS. / pp. 2, 4-10, 22, 30-31, 77-78, 81, 98-100, 103)
Amedeo Benestante
Radu Bercan/Shutterstock.com
Ron Ellis/Shutterstock.com
Adrian Flütsch
Bernd Grundmann
Heinz Kunz
Peter G. Lawson/Shutterstock.com
Pixeljoy/Shutterstock.com
Dario de Simone
Special View/Shutterstock.com
Studio Mirko Baselgia

FSC
www.fsc.org
MIX
Paper from responsible sources
FSC® C110860